Fresh Jersey

Stories from an Altered State

Mike Kelly

Camino Books, Inc.
Philadelphia

Manufactured in the United States of America

All of the columns appearing in this collection were originally published in *The Record*. This book is published by arrangement with *The Record*.

1 2 3 4 5   03 02 01 00

Library of Congress Cataloging-in-Publication Data

Kelly, Mike, 1953-
    Fresh Jersey : stories from an altered state / Mike Kelly.
        p. cm.
    ISBN 0-940159-59-7 (trade paper : alk. paper)
        1. New Jersey—Social life and customs—20th century—Anecdotes. 2. New Jersey—Biography—Anecdotes. 3. New Jersey—Social conditions—20th century—Anecdotes. 4. National characteristics, American—Anecdotes. 5. Nineteen nineties—Anecdotes. I. Title.

F140.K48 2000
974.9—dc21   00-040316

Cover and interior design: Jerilyn Kauffman

This book is available at a special discount on bulk purchases for promotional, business, and educational use. For information write to:

Publisher
Camino Books, Inc.
P.O. Box 59026
Philadelphia, PA 19102

www.caminobooks.com

DEDICATION

This book is dedicated to my daughters,
Michelle & Anne
. . . who noticed early on that their father spends more time
staring at a blank computer screen than actually writing.

ACKNOWLEDGMENTS

The gentle, graceful touch of my wife, Judy, can be found in many of these columns. Sometimes she patiently listened as I read sentences as deadline approached. Always she challenged me to find the right path to walk. One of life's great gifts is to be loved by her.

At *The Record*, many colleagues brought a keen eye to my work and inspired me to reach higher. I am especially grateful to Vivian Waixel, Jeff Page, Jim Wright, Deirdre Sykes, Mike Semel, Leonard Reed, Carmine Galasso, Carol Ann Campbell, and David Hall.

Also at *The Record*, Lois DiTommaso and Marc Watrel of the newspaper's book division and Jennifer Borg, vice president and general counsel, nurtured this project through its early stages. At Camino Books, Edward Jutkowitz and Michelle Scolnick pushed the book over the finish line.

Finally, I want to express a special note of thanks to *The Record*'s chairman, Malcolm A. Borg, who grants me and others here broad freedom to do our jobs. In a world of impersonal newspaper chains, his family-owned newspaper remains a strong beacon for the best in American journalism.

CONTENTS

PART THREE - SIGNS

PART FOUR - WONDERS

INTRODUCTION

I came on a lark, lured by a college friend who mentioned something about a job. I ended up calling this place home.

New Jersey.

No kidding.

It was my first newspaper job, in Hackensack, the same river town that Billy Joel sang about so disdainfully. *Who needs a house out in Hackensack? Is that all you get for your money?*

That first summer, Main Street seemed so empty and the outlying suburbs so uneventful that I swore I'd be gone by Labor Day, off somewhere presumably exotic. But I stayed, first a year, then another, then a decade, then more.

My father was born here, in a Jersey City tenement, the son of a Depression-era plumber named John and a woman named Mary who left behind a tiny gold wedding band when she died with another son in childbirth — mother and baby buried in the same coffin. With the coming of World War II, my father joined the Marines and stayed. He returned home only as a visitor, finding his roots instead in places like Guadalcanal and Peleliu, Korea and Yokosuka, Saigon and Quantico. Here, I set down my own roots. I got married, fathered two daughters, bought a house on a street shaded by a cathedral canopy of oaks, struggled with a mortgage and the crabgrass. I later learned that my corner of New Jersey was the same one that Ozzie and Harriet called home in the 1950s, where Pat Boone settled in the 1960s, where several members of the cast of *Sesame Street* have lived since the 1970s, where Eddie Murphy moved in the 1980s, where Richard Nixon lived out his final days in the 1990s, where Hollywood came at the end of the century to find a setting for *The Sopranos*.

OK, I liked it too.

After all that youthful yearning as a writer for someplace that seemed more alluring, I actually grew fond of this small corner of America, even the fact that the view from the newspaper city room included a moth-balled World War II submarine, a jail, a cement factory, a Revolutionary-era graveyard, and a hamburger joint that had been converted into a bank. In New Jersey, we know all about diversity.

And then, I discovered something else about myself and this place: The America I longed to understand and explore could be found right here in this vest-pocket of a state that is no bigger than Israel, is the most densely populated in the Union, and has such a schizophrenic view of the world that it named rest stops on the New Jersey Turnpike after a poet (Joyce Kilmer) and a football coach (Vince Lombardi).

New Jersey may be a centerpiece of jokes on the late-night talk shows, but beneath the cliché-laden veneer I found a refreshing microcosm of the entire nation — of middle-class parents trying to live out suburban American Dreams, of rusting cities trying to rediscover their youth, of racial tension and racial miracles, of beach towns trying to mix boardwalks with sand dunes, of old truck farms trying to dodge new ribbons of encroaching highways, of quiet mountain hamlets trying to retain their pristine innocence, of new immigrants trying to understand a new land, of seniors beset by health care woes, of cops and cons trying to outfox each other, of political struggles over taxes and capital punishment and AIDS and schools and potholes. On this small canvas, I could find hopeful soccer moms and bitter downsized executives, oil traders and stock hustlers, gamblers flushed with a card player's swagger after a pilgrimage to an Atlantic City casino and millionaire horse farmers trying to save fox-hunting pastures from split-level housing developers. I might even find a wise guy or two, repeating one of those weird legends about the mob — like the one about Jimmy Hoffa being buried in the end zone at Giants Stadium. Or I might find a teacher, laboring valiantly in the blackboard trenches.

Maybe Paul Simon was right when he sang, *Counting the cars on the New Jersey Turnpike, they've all come to look for America.*

I begin each day with a journalist's notebook and the privilege of a columnist in search of people and their stories. Sometimes I walk away angry and disillusioned at the lonely river of pain that engulfs some people. Sometimes I walk away a better man, amazed at how the most ordinary among us can teach us the most extraordinary lessons.

In the last decade, I've produced more than 1,400 columns, the vast majority reported and written in one or two days, the last keystrokes punched, sometimes clumsily, into a computer as deadline looms and my desk becomes home to a stack of empty coffee cups and snippets of notes.

I have stood on a winter's sidewalk where a homeless veteran froze to death. I have looked into the humble eyes of a hero who leaped from a rolling train to push two toddlers off the tracks. I have visited an orphanage where AIDS-infected children go to die. I have watched the sun rise with a Hudson River fisherman. I have taken an elevator with mob boss John Gotti. I have sat in a silent hospital room as a mother cried about institutionalizing her deformed baby. I have walked the streets of a town that tried to ban cursing. I have browsed the shelves of a library that tried to ban a homeless man who wanted to begin his day by reading the *Wall Street Journal*. I have marveled at such characters as Fat Man, Slim Nick, Hubcap Joe, Elevator Sam, Frankie the barber, and a woman who won the lottery and then gave away her winnings to a church and a volunteer fire and ambulance department.

And yes, I even tried to find Jimmy Hoffa's grave in that Giants Stadium end zone. No kidding.

Welcome to the neighborhood.

PART ONE

FACES

Adventures of Slim

Forget baseball; dieting is the national pastime. Only in New Jersey do people bet on this.

Slim Nick slides into the booth of Ridgewood's Daily Treat restaurant. Just coffee, he says, a little sweetener. No pancakes.

The waitress doesn't even give Nick a menu. She knows. Nick is still doing that diet thing.

Over at the cash register, manager Gus Hensz laughs to himself and shakes his head. "Yeah, Nick," he says. "He used to eat like a mule. All he has is his coffee and disappears."

The disappearing man.

Eleven months ago, Nick Russo of Ridgewood was fed up. He was 360 pounds. His weekly restaurant tab was $400. His son dreamed Nick ate himself to death.

Enough, said Nick. No more restaurant meals until his weight dropped below 200. Anyone who caught him cheating would get a $25,000 bounty from Nick for a favorite charity.

Slim Nick can make this kind of offer. Besides his fat waist, he carried a fat millionaire's wallet.

And as you might expect, this kind of behavior made Nick a pop cultural comet. Got him on *Donahue*, in the *Star* tabloid, in *People* magazine. Slim Nick, diet guru, giving inspirational speeches, testing diet cookies and diet tea. There was even a T-shirt.

Now Slim Nick is 238. His waist is 47 inches, down from 60. And there is this unexpected cultural development: Women want him.

Slim Nick — Hunk.

So far, there have been six marriage proposals. A 32-year-old New Zealand woman craves Nick. So does a 42-year-old divorcée from Florida, an L.A. actress, and a Minnesota TV personality. Nick pulls their business cards from his wallet.

"I try to answer all the mail, whether they're 110 or 300 pounds."

For the record, Slim Nick, 55 and divorced, is still available.

One more thing — Slim Nick is cheating on his diet. Even if you're not interested in his body, there's still the chance for his bounty.

"It's a crazy world," says Nick.

He may be famous and women may want his body, but Slim Nick still has the urge to live dangerously. Order a steak. Dare fate.

"I was in Tahoe, in a hotel restaurant. My son wanted to take another ski run. He said give me 15 minutes and order. The meal came and it's sitting there, and it's now 45 minutes. I figure my son met some girl, and I started looking at this prime rib."

NOTE TO READER: Nick's eyes water as he describes this.

"I'm thinking. I'm in Tahoe. Everybody's gambling. Why don't I take a shot and eat it.

"I finished it off quick, and I get up to pay the check. A couple from Utah, who had seen my picture in *People*, spot me and say they're going to be watching me. Fifteen seconds earlier and I would have been out $25,000."

Nick also cheated in a diner outside Pittsburgh. "Beautiful stuffed peppers," says Nick. "I had to have one."

But he never got caught. Even the private detective who followed him for a month missed him. And a man from Virginia was so desperate that he claimed the $25,000 after seeing a picture of Nick smelling a plate of pasta. Every whiff is five calories, the guy said.

"No way," says Nick. "They have to catch me eating."

It's now almost the holiday season, time for big meals. But Nick is not afraid. He is approaching his one-year diet anniversary 38 pounds short of his 200-pound target. For incentive, he plans to increase the bounty to $50,000.

And when he whittles himself to 200 pounds, Regis and Kathie Lee say they'll take Nick to the Four Seasons. Then, maybe Nick will do a film, *Diet — The Movie.*

Slim Nick. Daredevil. Diet hero. Hunk. But movie star?

"On and on and on," says Slim Nick. "It's been non-stop."

Hubcap Joe's Bumpy Road to Success

Most of us pray for smooth roads, free of potholes. Not Joe DeMarco. Potholes are his friend – not to mention a way to make a living.

Hubcap Joe is miffed.

On the concrete river known as Route 80, where the billboards on 100-foot-high stilts seem like giant fly swatters as they peer down on the insect-swarm of traffic, Hubcap Joe was expecting a patch of potholes.

Why, just the other day, Hubcap Joe had driven his Buick Century — outfitted with a CB radio, a cellular phone, Motley Crue tapes, and a stuffed miniature bear on the dashboard with a plastic Dallas Cowboys helmet — over this section of washboard highway, relishing every sweet rut and bump, his brain in overdrive over the chrome-plated possibilities of hubcaps rattling loose and spinning off Camrys and Tauruses and — YES, PLEEEEEASE GOD — Volvos.

"I love Volvo caps," he explains later. "I have 10,000 hubcaps, but I have only three Volvos. That's why I like the hunt. I want what I don't have."

But what is this now?

"Ah," Joe says, a frown rutting his forehead at the smooth road, "they paved it. This is no good."

Or is it?

A piece of chrome glistens. Then another. And another. In all, 14 hubcaps — silvery mushrooms amid the gray-black grime — sit along a 50-yard stretch, reminders of the potholes that were filled just a few days before.

Hubcap Joe pulls over on the shoulder, flips on the specially installed orange flashers, slips on a pair of white gardening gloves, pulls at his orange reflective vest, then walks along the shoulder taking only the best of the lot — hubcaps for a Ford, a Geo, and a Camry.

"Not bad," he says, tossing them in the trunk.

Joseph DeMarco, aka Hubcap Joe, has perhaps one of the most arcane perches from which to watch the stream of modern life pass by. He collects the rounded refuse of America's car culture — then sells it back to us. He even has an e-mail address.

"Hubcap Joe goes cybergeek," DeMarco says, laughing at himself and reciting his code: hubcapjoes@aol.com

He is, by nature, something of an iconoclast. While a student at Bergen Catholic High School in the mid-1970s, DeMarco would collect hubcaps in his free time, sometimes leaving school in his sport coat and tie and wandering the roads on foot. He has scaled bridges, trekked across exit ramps, and sprinted across Route 17 in search of hubcaps. Once, he walked from his home in New Milford along Route 4 to New York City, filling a plastic trash bag with disks.

The childhood hobby eventually blossomed into a full-blown career — maybe an obsession. While most of the nation was basting turkeys on Thanksgiving Day, DeMarco and his brother Rick — who, like Joe, is unmarried — removed more than 5,000 hubcaps from the garage of the New Milford home where they grew up. The brothers stacked the hubcaps on the driveway and cleaned them with a power washer.

"Then," Rick says, smiling proudly, "we watched the Dallas Cowboys game."

Picking up hubcaps is not exactly the sort of career move that is lauded in the pages of *Smart Money*. But then, maybe the gray-suit crowd on Wall Street that spends its time searching for small-cap-value stocks never understood the sheer, pride-in-your-gut value of snatching a wire-spoked "cap" from the wilds of the Cross-Bronx Expressway and reselling it for $50.

"I can spot a hubcap, upside down, at 60 miles per hour," Joe DeMarco says, "and know what it is."

His business philosophy is simple. Suburbanites make a habit of commuting long distances, often traversing roads pockmarked with potholes. And often, those potholes are located on dangerous highways or in bad city neighborhoods. DeMarco is afraid of neither.

"I go back to the spots where my customers won't go," he says.

He is standing now on the shoulder of Route 17, not far from the Paramus sprawl, in a spot with a semi-permanent bump. He returns to it regularly when he needs a supply of hubcaps. He will take a visitor there, but only if the precise location is kept secret.

The roadside is littered with all manner of junk — crushed coffee cups, plastic soda bottles, even a toaster oven. On this day, however, the hubcap crop is sparse — only one cap from a Camry.

For DeMarco, the potholes, fissures, and bumps that are the enemies of motorists are his friends. He has found other rough spots on roads and highways, logging their locations and scouting them on Sunday mornings. And he mourns a bit when the road crews eventually discover the potholes and fill them in.

"They repaved this," DeMarco says, driving over a patch of fresh asphalt on Route 17. "That hurt me."

The words may seem odd, but DeMarco takes his work personally.

At his hubcap shop on Kinderkamack Road in Oradell, the walls are decorated with more than three dozen caps, from cars ranging from old Chevys and Oldsmobiles to Geos and Fords. In a back room, he stores new hubcaps. As business has boomed, DeMarco has turned to buying a portion of his hubcaps directly from the manufacturers. There just isn't enough time to search the roads and still meet customer demand.

One afternoon, a middle-aged woman walked in. DeMarco eyed her car as she pulled into the driveway, then looked away.

"I've never bought a hubcap before," the woman announced.

"Oh," DeMarco answered, "there's always a first time."

By a desk, Rick was smiling. He has heard this conversation dozens of times. A motorist has lost a hubcap and has come to this store, filled with silver-colored disks, in search of a replacement. It's a bit like entering a passport office for the first and only time in your life.

"I know what you need," DeMarco said. He then proceeded to tell the woman the precise year, make, and model of her car — a mid-1980s Lincoln Continental — and the precise type of hubcap she needed.

"How do you know this?" the woman asked, surprised.

"I know," DeMarco said. "I've been doing this a long time."

They are the words of a professional, and when you hear them from a man who collects hubcaps they seem surprising. But then, this is DeMarco's career, complete with the same business trappings the rest of us have.

While the rest of us have our work routines — morning coffee, a trip to the bulletin board, a gossipy chat with the boss — he observes something of a routine, too. Each Sunday — his main hubcap search day — he attends Mass at St. Helena's Church in the Bronx, then has breakfast at Ellie's Diner. From there, he spends an hour searching for hubcaps in his favorite domain — the Cross-Bronx Expressway.

It is midmorning on a Thursday, and DeMarco has decided to hunt again along the Cross-Bronx Expressway — a hunt that will be virtually fruitless. Before he gets to the Bronx, however, he wants to check out a hubcap he longs to get.

He is passing now through the tolls on the lower level of the George Washington Bridge. The January morning sun glistens off the pavement, still wet from a nighttime drizzle.

"I'm looking for this cap I spotted just the other day," DeMarco says, removing his sunglasses and leaning forward on the steering wheel and squinting in the glare.

"There!" he says, pointing. "See it?"

If ever there was the hubcap equivalent of a pearl that is too deep for a diver to reach, this is it. On the left side of the highway that leads onto the bridge sits a wire-spoked, shiny chrome hubcap from a Buick Park Avenue. It is impossible to snatch — unless, of course, you stop your car, risk an accident in the automotive rush, and jeopardize your own life by standing in the left lane of the bridge traffic to get the hubcap.

DeMarco considers the possibilities, and keeps driving.

"I can't get it," he says. "I can't stop here. I'm not crazy."

Lighting One Candle

Few of us can solve big problems. But sometimes we can make the world better for one person.

Ron telephoned in May. It had been years since they had spoken, two decades since they had last seen each other. He just wanted to say hello and ask for a photo from their opera days with *Madame Butterfly* or *La Bohème*.

Oh, one more thing.

Ron had AIDS.

Joan Sena-Grande remembers hanging up the phone in her Teaneck home that day, wanting to help. But how?

"It dawned on me — God, he must be needing money, but he can't bring himself to ask," she said. "What do I do?"

Like most of us, Joan knew of the many ways to raise money for the fight against AIDS, most of them grandiose. Thousands of victims need millions of dollars. Understandably, people think big. Big mail campaigns. Big concerts such as Sunday's "Music for Life" performance at Carnegie Hall.

But sometimes a helping hand is just that — one hand reaching out to one person with perhaps only enough money for one day. In these days of satellite-connected telethons, one person helping another may be something of a forgotten concept.

"If I could just help one person," Grande explained, "it's like lighting one candle."

And from one flame, maybe a fire can spread.

Joan Sena-Grande, who was born in the back room of a Brooklyn hair salon 57 years ago and went on to become a New York City Opera soprano before retiring to raise two sons, reached out the only way she knew how. She sang.

The concert hall was her living room. And even the last-minute news that plasterers could not fix a 2-by-2-foot hole in the ceiling from a leaky upstairs shower did not stop her. Tickets were $10 — or whatever you could give.

On a Sunday, as Carnegie Hall was preparing for its AIDS extravaganza, 34 people came to Grande's elegant Tudor home, some in jeans, some in suits. They sat on folding chairs and on couches, as Grande performed with pianist Amy Duran, Metropolitan Opera tenor Anthony Laciura, and Met violinist and concertmaster Elmira Darvarova. Afterward Darvarova rushed to Carnegie Hall with Joan's husband, John, the Met's music librarian, to play again.

The Carnegie Hall fest raised more than $1 million for AIDS victims. Joan Grande raised $435 for her friend Ron, now 50, a former Met and New York City Opera baritone who was too sick to attend. Two weeks earlier, he got $300 at a similar concert with an audience of 21. You can't put a value on his emotional boost.

"I'm shocked," he said the next day on the phone from his Manhattan apartment. "It's a bit overwhelming. I didn't even ask for this."

Grande's low-budget fund-raiser will never be enough to wipe out AIDS — or even help one victim over all the hurdles. But it's enough to send a message.

"I could have just written a check," said Grande, who still keeps a picture of herself and Ron on a wall of opera stars that includes a photo of her with Luciano Pavarotti. "But there was a message that had to be given out. I was annoyed at the people who profess to be human and Christian and concerned and yet are so judgmental. They're missing the boat. God is supposed to do the judging. We're supposed to do the loving. These people, whether they got AIDS from a homosexual relationship, from intravenous drugs, or at childbirth, they're victims."

Ron has some health insurance, but not enough for all his bills. His disease, which was diagnosed in 1987, has already taken the sight from his right eye and has left him too weak to sing opera anymore. His goal now is to collect photos of every singer he has performed with. He keeps them on a wall next to his bed in his apartment. Consolation, he says.

"Sometimes I feel lonely," he said. "But I don't feel forgotten."

Not as long as one candle burns.

The Riverman

In the shadows of a modern city, Ron Ingold lives in the past, trying to save a river from itself.

Ron Ingold does not have a phone, which tells you something about his connection to modern life. To find him these days, you must go to a tar paper fishing shack that hangs over mud flats at the bottom of the Palisades cliffs in Edgewater.

As the forsythia bloom each spring, he returns to this phone-free spot on the Hudson River from his phone-free apartment in Garfield, a lonely attempt to keep a flame of tradition alive in a world of machines and man-made schedules. His schedule is framed by the tides, his eye hard on the water to watch for the annual return of shad.

It is 10 a.m., a weekday, and the May sun shimmers on the Hudson, throwing off a blue-gray haze. Ingold, in rubber orange pants and brown rubber boots, bends over the gunwale of a gray, flat-bottomed boat that floats in the watery netherworld between New Jersey and New York. To the east, cars sweep along the West Side Highway like schools of silverfish. To the west, boxy high-rises atop the Palisades look down like giant cereal boxes. A gull sweeps low and squawks.

Ingold, who is 54 but whose weather-beaten face makes him seem 10 years older, has been doing this since he was a boy. He draws on a Pall Mall and pulls on the net.

"Fish," he says, turning to his friend Louis Lasher, who steers the boat into position. "We got some."

Ingold pulls a foot-long shad from the net and tosses it into a plastic garbage can. With the help of his 26-year-old son, Scott, he pulls another. And another. And another.

It's a fishing method that dates back to the 1600s — and, for Ingold's family, to the 1920s. "All my life, this is what I remember doing each spring," says Scott Ingold, who takes leave from a job at a North Jersey fish store to help his father. "I grew up here. I've done a lot of things in my 26 years. This is something I always come back to."

It is the hard, hand-over-hand work of planting 60-year-old hickory poles upright in the river in late March, then setting nets each day in April and May across the current — like window screens — to snare shad as they swim upriver to spawn. The process ends with removing the hickory poles and "bedding" them lengthwise in the muck along the riverbank to keep them waterlogged and rot-free.

"This," says Lasher, a 69-year-old retired contractor, "is the old way."

He points to the series of nine poles that he and the Ingolds have set this year a quarter-mile from shore. "I remember this when I was a kid. I think that's why I come back now. It's nice here."

It means living round-the-clock in Ingold's riverside shack for two months, sleeping on musty beds, sipping lukewarm coffee, and eating on the run. You set the nets just as the tide runs in; you pull them up just as the tide turns. You do this twice a day. In between, you mend nets or nap.

Author Joseph Mitchell immortalized Ron Ingold's father and other Edgewater fishermen in the *New Yorker* magazine and in his 1960 non-fiction book, *The Bottom of the Harbor*. Back then, there were a dozen shad fishermen south of the George Washington Bridge. Now there is just one — Ron Ingold. Several others operate up the river, near Piermont and Nyack.

Ingold smiles as he is reminded of this. This year's fishing expedition hardly compares to what he once mounted. His nine hickory poles hold only about 100 feet of net. In the 1980s, he would set two rows of 30 poles each — some 600 feet of net in each row.

"I come back here because it's tradition," he sighs. "It's heritage. You feel part of it."

He pauses.

"And there's no one else doing it anymore in this town."

Ingold is sitting now in a chair outside his fishing shack. Across the deck, skitter-scatter, are the implements of his trade — a rope, a knife, motor oil, worn gloves, boots, empty coffee cans, pieces of net, an old lifesaver from the Circle Line. On the water, a barge bobs in the current. To his left sit pieces of his makeshift dock, the wood taken from old railroad barges that once dotted the riverbank.

Ingold gazes toward the Hudson. "The river's so vast," he says. "Everything's so vast. It'll pass over you if you don't stop and take it in."

To hear him is to hear a bit of Huck Finn, older now perhaps, looking back — the river philosopher trying to remind us of this massive body of water that flows by our doors and goes mostly unnoticed, except in the radio traffic reports about traffic jams on "river crossings."

With a chuckle, Ingold says residents of the high-rise apartments atop the Palisades watch him through telescopes, then drive down to ask what he's doing. When he tells them he's a fisherman, he says they invariably ask why he would want to fish the Hudson. Then he shows them a bucket of shad.

"Their eyes open wide," he says. "They can't believe something so beautiful could come from the river."

Ingold, who keeps a small apartment in Garfield, spends his winters helping fishermen in New England. But like a magnet, he returns each March to Edgewater. "I come here each spring for the change," says Ingold. "When you work around Mother Nature, you learn to live with it. It's a change of pace. There's an old Indian saying, 'When the buds on the trees are as big as mouse ears, the shad are in the river.' And you know something, it's true."

Indeed, the shad now reflect something else — the pace of nature's battle against man and pollution.

In the early 1970s, the shad population dropped, largely because the river had become so polluted. But thanks to improved water-pollution controls on sewage-treatment plants and riverside factories, the water became cleaner and by the late 1970s the annual shad run was turning into a stampede of fish.

In recent years, the shad numbers seem to have dropped slightly again. But this time, pollution is not the culprit — not directly anyway.

Some environmentalists say the rising striped bass population feeds on the young shad. And one reason stripers are so plentiful is that commercial fishermen like Ingold are banned from catching and selling them because their meat is contaminated from industrial pollution that was stopped years ago but persists in the ecosystem.

"Too many PCBs in their meat," says Ingold, referring to the suspected carcinogen known as polychlorinated biphenyls that were dumped into the river for years by factories and found their way into the striped bass food chain.

Without commercial fishermen to thin their ranks, the striper population has multiplied and grown to levels that are dangerous to the shad. Ironically, shad have remained free of PCBs, largely because they use the Hudson mainly for a spawning pit stop and don't stay long.

"The stripers are bigger than shad and eat them," says Russ Allen, a senior fisheries biologist for the New Jersey Division of Fish, Game, and Wildlife.

In the Delaware River, says Allen, stripers are so plentiful that several shad fishermen have decided not to set their nets this year, even though shad are abundant. In the Hudson, he says, the shad schools are noticeably smaller, resulting in smaller catches.

For Ron Ingold, the battle between stripers and shad has a practical side effect. With stripers so plentiful, his nets snag more of them. But because of the ban on selling stripers, he must sort through his catch, keeping the shad and tossing the stripers back into the Hudson, still alive and fighting.

"He bit my thumb," said Ingold as he tossed back a 2-foot-long striper.

By the end of their work one morning, the Ingolds and Louis Lasher pulled in 250 pounds of shad, most of them the more sought-after females. At $1 a pound on the wholesale market, they won't get rich.

"We get by," says Ingold, pausing again as he looks out on the Hudson and takes a sip of coffee. "I still hope I'll be doing this in 20 years," he says softly. "It's good to come to the river each spring. It's in the blood."

◆ ◆ ◆

Epilogue

It seems Ron Ingold didn't toss all his striped bass back into the Hudson. In late 1998, he pleaded guilty to illegal fishing charges after federal authorities discovered he secretly sold contaminated stripers at the Fulton Fish Market in New York City, passing them off as shad and priced at $1.25 per pound. In late 1999, five Fulton fish wholesalers were charged with selling the stripers caught by Ingold to fashionable Manhattan restaurants where the fish was priced as high as $36 per entrée.

Sparky's Dream

In New Jersey, there are six great religions: Christianity, Judaism, Islam, Hinduism, Buddhism — and Sinatra. Here is a visit to one of the shrines.

Down the hall from the room with the cheese steaks on the griddle and the bowling trophies in the window, Sparky waits for his dream to come true in the place he calls his "Sinatra Den."

Sparky even put out a new bottle of Dewar's and cooked extra Pasta Lenticchie. He invited the usual crowd — Angelo, Uncle Louie, Cosmo, and Big Ears. And then, he ordered a cake with eight blue roses and this inscription in blue and red letters:

"Happy Birthday, Mister Sinatra. We Love You."

"After 75 years," says Sparky, "he deserves to be called 'Mister.'"

But Frank never showed.

Not that anybody expected him to. A few days before, Frank turned 75. But in the back room at Sparky's Piccolo Clam Bar in Hoboken, another birthday passed with another cake and no birthday boy.

"That's my dream," said Sparky, whose real name is Joe Spaccavento. "My dream is to meet Frank Sinatra."

Explaining why is something else. "He's an entertainer. He's the tops. He's . . . "

Sparky knows the next question as well as he knows "Night and Day." Why would Hoboken care about a man who has done his best to ignore his hometown?

"That personal stuff, that's different," Sparky says. "That's his life."

No matter. Here, on Hoboken's car-clogged streets, around the corner from LaJa's Tavern and the Hudson County Homing Pigeon Club, Sparky's restaurant is the place to pay homage to the man Hoboken once called "Skinny" and Hollywood still calls "The Chairman of the Board."

Outside, the cops don't mind if you double-park. Inside, you can still get an egg sandwich for $1.40. And in the back room, beyond a "Sinatra Drive" sign, Sparky serves up Sinatra in the "Sinatra Den."

All day, Sinatra sings from the stereo. And on the walls, Sinatra smiles from dozens of photographs. There is Sinatra with Tommy Dorsey, Sinatra with the Hoboken Four, with President Reagan. And — yes — there is Sinatra with Sparky.

Sparky points to a photo of Sinatra in the bleachers at a 1939 high school baseball game. Behind Sinatra is the mischievous face of a 10-year-old with black, wavy hair.

"This is me," says Sparky, now 61. "I never even said hello."

But this is no time to wonder why. It's 12:26 p.m., and 23 people are in the Den, telling stories about Sinatra concerts, Sinatra autographs, Sinatra sightings. On the stereo, Sinatra sings "Under My Skin."

And the phone rings.

"Maybe it's Frank," someone calls out.

It's not.

"You never know," says Angelo Palladino, 53, an electrician.

"Yeah," adds builder Frank Trombetta, 61, "they try to get him."

Cary Silken, 34, walks in. He has eight tickets to the night's Sinatra concert, but there are no takers. Everyone here has a ticket.

Miriam Aponte, a 38-year-old secretary, nibbles on a piece of Sinatra cake and announces: "I want to give him a kiss and a hug."

Tony Dibranco, 67, tells how his father, a tailor, sewed buttons on Sinatra's blazer before a concert long ago. And Hoboken Police Lt. Anthony Falco, 41, tells how he once lived in the "same house and same apartment" on Monroe Street that Sinatra was born in.

Sparky beams with pride at each story, then points to a Sinatra poster, signed "To Sparky, All the Best, Frank Sinatra."

"I just wish I could meet him," Sparky says. "That's the one wish I have."

"How about a daily double?" Falco says, laughing.

But Sparky cuts him off.

"Forget about it. Never."

Unknown Commuter

Not every death makes the news. As the world focused attention on a commuter train wreck, I found another commuter who had died in a far more solitary way.

It was a week of commuter death, with horrific scenes of railcars tossed about the winter landscape like crumpled soda cans, sobering reminders that a mundane, predictable trip to work is not always a safe journey.

Against that tragic backdrop, a few smaller tragedies slipped by unnoticed. This is one of them.

Her name was Carol Saad. She was a waitress, a mother, a wife. She lived in West New York. She died under the wheels of a truck in Manhattan. She was 33. She loved Emma Thompson films and spoke fluent Portuguese, Spanish, Italian, and French.

Her death at the beginning of the week was a lonely counterpoint to the headlines that accompanied the three deaths at week's end when two NJ Transit trains crashed in the Jersey City meadows. There was a brief story about Carol Saad in a New York newspaper, a four-paragraph obituary in another paper across the Hudson. That's it.

Nonetheless, the story of how Saad died underscores the same sense of vulnerability and happenstance as those on the railroad.

As dawn broke in Manhattan — a Monday — Saad was walking from the Port Authority Bus Terminal to a job as a waitress in a coffee shop in the Marriott Marquis hotel. Minutes earlier, she had stepped off a commuter bus that had taken her through the Lincoln Tunnel from West New York. She was killed instantly, police say, when she stepped off a curb at Eighth Avenue and 44th Street and was blindsided by a tractor-trailer.

It was 7:17 a.m. Her 9-year-old son hadn't even left the family's apartment yet for his morning classes at a Fairview Catholic school.

Anyone who has ever ventured into Manhattan on foot knows that it can be a perilous excursion. There are horn-honking taxis, snorting buses, angry cyclists — and the pedestrian temptations of ordinary pedestrians to shave seconds off the commuter trek by darting into traffic. Saad died, say police, because she tried to cut across the street without waiting for a traffic light to change.

The driver of the tractor-trailer that struck her told detectives that he never saw her or realized he had hit anyone as he rounded the corner. Police say the driver had to be flagged down by other pedestrians as he drove east on West 44th.

A police spokeswoman, Officer Sara Carpenter, said there were no plans to file charges against the truck driver. She labeled Saad's death an accident.

A week later at the Encore restaurant, where Saad had been a waitress for 10 years, her colleagues cried when they spoke of her. "She was always in a good mood," said Illiana Santiago. Fellow waiter Ruben Ramos added: "She loved to talk about vacations and traveling. And the theater. She was always interested in what you were doing."

Saad worked the breakfast and lunch shifts at the coffee shop. Her husband, Galal, an Egyptian emigré, was the maitre d' on the dinner shift at the hotel's upscale restaurant, "The View." Theirs was a two-paycheck marriage, with commuter schedules that catered to the centerpiece of the couple's life: their son, Christopher. "The thing I'm saddest about," said Ruben Ramos, "is she loved her son terribly."

In West New York on Monday, Saad's father, William Moreira, was helping to clean the family's apartment. He said Saad's husband plans to return to Egypt. Moreira, a former chef who grew up in Brazil, offered this testament for his daughter:

"She had brown eyes — like marble. And when she walked into a room, people used to look up and feel good."

Carol Saad was buried that Friday morning in a Fairview cemetery — two hours after the train wreck.

Mr. Blue-Chips

What can you say about a college basketball coach whose best friend is a bricklayer? Then again, Princeton's Pete Carril was no ordinary coach.

PRINCETON —
The man with the cigar was getting cosmic.

"You know about the rings of Saturn? Do you know what they are made of? DO YOU?"

He took a drag on the stogie, slowly releasing a cloud of smoke heavenward. His eyes brightened and his face slowly creased into a smile that let you know he had you.

"I know," said Pete Carril, pausing long enough to savor his small victory. "The rings are made of ice."

On this spring morning, when the tips of Princeton's oaks were sprinkled with red buds and the crew teams were dipping their oars in the frigid brown waters of Lake Carnegie, Pete Carril, basketball coach and philosopher, began the day in a coffee shop. He is officially retired, and yet in retirement he is more popular than ever. The day before he turned down an invitation from Jay Leno to appear on *The Tonight Show*, telling friends: "Why would I wanna fly to Los Angeles?"

As he sips coffee, Carril is discussing not just the nature of Saturn, but politics, sports, and other events of the universe. Einstein once did this in Princeton. But Carril will tell you he is no Einstein, unless you count basketball on the same level as physics, which many do in this brainy town because of the science-like mind that Carril brings to the game.

For 29 years, before he called it quits last week, Carril, 65, coached Princeton's men's basketball team, competing full-tilt in a sport that has become the domain of blow-dried men in Armani suits and Rolex watches, who dangle promises of sports cars and wallets thick with cash in front of teenagers who can jump higher than most ordinary Americans.

Carril never gave in to the money or the hype. In an age when sports has become as much narcissistic entertainment as it is competition, he is a throwback to a time when basketball "shoes" were called "sneakers."

"Armani suit?" he says, laughing. "Nah. You kidding me? Don't own one. Anyway, I stopped wearing ties to games long ago. I sweat too much."

On this day, Carril's pants are so wrinkled they look like he slept in them. His hair, white and wavy, is brushed back off his face, curling over the collar of his white golf shirt. He looks like he ought to be sitting on the rail at a racetrack, not pacing the same campus that F. Scott Fitzgerald once compared to Babylon.

Carril's father came from Spain and worked in the steel mills of Bethlehem, Pa. And while it's not uncommon for Carril to cavort with the monied stockbrokers and lawyers who dominate Princeton's alumni, he still remains true to his roots.

"Take this guy Ross Perot," says Carril, who switches easily from a discourse on the full-court press to a lecture on presidential politics. "What an idiot. I don't understand a country that goes for a guy like him. He wouldn't last five minutes in South Bethlehem."

In a way, Carril is a living, breathing lesson of the working-class values he passes to his players. Princeton may get the blue-chip science students, but it no longer attracts America's blue-chip athletes. Not that Carril's players are bad. But they were generally shorter and slower than those who go to Kentucky or UCLA or Syracuse or Arkansas.

For one thing, the Ivy League, which includes Princeton, bans athletic scholarships. All financial aid is based on how much help a student needs. What Carril dangles instead is a simple challenge: "If you come to Princeton, you're gonna work hard."

He was not just talking about basketball.

"Sports," says Carril, "has always been a reflection of society."

At Princeton, however, Carril has built a basketball society that is different from those at other schools. With rare exceptions, every member of his team graduates. "If you don't study here," says Carril, "you don't play. It's that simple."

He is sitting now in a chair in a corner of the Jadwin Gymnasium, vast and silent except for a few joggers on the track, which sits beyond the wooden basketball floor. Carril gazes across the 250,000-square-foot indoor space that is roughly the equivalent of eight football fields, then silently studies an elderly man, kneeling with a rag. The man slowly, methodically wipes a portion of the basketball floor. He has been working on the same spot for 30 minutes.

"See that guy," Carril says. "Now there's a complete man. He has been here for decades. And what he does now is take care of the small things in the gym. He is making sure there are no spots on the wood floor. And you know something? There won't be any spots. He takes the job in front of him that needs to be done and, no matter how small the task, he tries to do it perfectly. No cutting corners."

Carril stops. "That's what I try to do."

Pete Carril is from a time when coaches actually perspired and smoked cigars and talked history and politics with their players as well as jump shots and back-door passes. His values were forged in those years when the words "sneaker contract" were not part of the American sports vocabulary, when the nation allowed its student athletes to be kids, not performers, when athletes wore gray sweatshirts, not $300 nylon warmups adorned with logos.

"He didn't want to be a personality," says Bill Carmody, who will succeed Carril as Princeton's coach. "It seems a lot of people when they make it big they want to be a personality. Pete's not interested in that."

And yet Carril's individualism has made him just that — a personality.

His best friend is a bricklayer. He has never owned any other car except a Buick — for years a Buick Century, then switching to a LeSabre. He lives, he says, "exactly 1.7 miles from the gym."

"Precision," says bricklayer Tony "Red" Trani. "That's what makes him tick. Pete used to work for me in the summers. Drove me crazy. He was always trying to make the job better and better. The guy really respects perfection and he lives for it every day. He's a perfectionist."

Trani has dropped by the gym with a message for Carril that has nothing to do with basketball, but everything to do with the complex mind of Pete Carril.

"I've got that tape of *Phantom of the Opera* for you," says Trani.

Carril's eyes widen. "I like all types of music," he says.

Trani laughs. "Nah."

Carril turns. "Hey, how about that fellow Tchaikovsky? A genius. A GENIUS."

Carril will tell you that he sums up his life philosophy this way: "As a nation, we stopped looking for the intrinsic function of things. We looked at the stuff on the outside. People were judged on their appearance, not what's inside."

Last year, by his own account, Pete Carril looked into himself and decided it was time for him to leave Princeton basketball. "I was letting too many things slip," he says. "In the old days, I would never let any players make a mistake without correcting it. Now, I let four or five go by in a game."

He also found himself sitting down too much during games. "I usually stand up," he says. "I didn't like sitting down, but I was."

And so he made a decision.

"I looked into the mirror and saw it was time to go."

He says he may move from town.

"I don't want to be looked at as some old coach," he said.

But until he leaves, he will begin each morning in the coffee shop.

"Today, the big question was Saturn's rings," he says, laughing. "Tomorrow? We'll see."

The Reluctant Millionaire

What would you do if you won the lottery? Take a trip? Buy a mansion? Eleanor Boyer hit the jackpot — then gave it away. People think she's crazy.

If anyone deserved to be rich, surely Eleanor Boyer should be at the top of a list somewhere.

Around the Central Jersey community of Somerville, Boyer, 72 and retired, was known as a good soul, one of those anchors of the neighborhood who always seemed to be there with a quiet, random act of kindness such as a visit to a friend in the hospital.

She never married, had no children. Her town and her church were her family. As for trappings of wealth, Eleanor Boyer didn't demand much. She still drove a 1968 Chevrolet Malibu. She lived in the home she was born in.

But in a nation where drawing attention to yourself with a publicity stunt is an unfortunate thread in the cultural fabric, few people around Somerville were prepared for what Eleanor Boyer did when she won an $11.8 million lump sum in the Pick 6 state lottery.

She promised to give away the $8.5 million she will receive after taxes — every last cent, except for "maybe a little bit" for herself.

She made this announcement as quietly as she prays — which apparently is quite often. Eleanor Boyer's first stop each day is 8 a.m. Mass at her local Catholic church.

Now, consider for a moment, what Donald Trump might do if he decided to give away $11 million. Or George Steinbrenner. Or Madonna. Or one of those corporate CEOs who consider themselves successful if they can keep stock values high while they hand out pink slips to a thousand or so middle managers whose only sin was to stay too loyal for too long to one company.

In the look-at-me land of the pretentious, giving is rarely done quietly. If any number of American celebrities gave away $11 million, you could count on the gift being accompanied by some sort of "photo opportunity," where the TV cameras would whir and the strobe lights would flicker as the giver would pose with the needy. You could expect the requisite self-indulgent pining on how much it means to give rather than receive. And, finally, you could count on those chronicles of American narcissism, *People* magazine and *Hard Copy*, to package the story to a grateful public.

Eleanor Boyer had no publicity machine. She hired no agent, made no formal statement.

She just did it.

Boyer won the lottery after buying a single Pick 6 ticket. (In case you wondered, her winning numbers were 2, 14, 17, 25, 31, and 45.) But after winning, she didn't wait to call her broker or accountant.

Boyer contacted Somerville's Roman Catholic parish, the Church of the Immaculate Conception. Then, she reached out to the town's volunteer fire department and the rescue squad. Boyer said the church would get about half her winnings — with a large portion of it going to a parish-run home for unwed, pregnant women. The rest would be divided among the fire department, the rescue squad, and a few other town agencies.

And that was that.

As you might guess, a few people were impressed with this gesture. The man who sold Boyer the winning lottery ticket at Sam's Stationery, Rajesh Shah, hardly skipped a beat when I phoned and asked him to describe what she was like. "She's not a human being," said Shah. "She's an angel. She's a daughter of Jesus."

Shah says Boyer strolls in almost every day, and buys a newspaper and a lottery ticket. "She's not crazy for the money," he says. "We need a few more people like her."

Elsewhere, more than a few people in Somerville, a 2.4-square-mile community of 12,000 residents that is known as the home of the Cycling Hall of Fame, were scratching their heads to remember if they have ever met her. It turns out that Eleanor Boyer wasn't the type to draw attention to herself. "I don't think I even know the woman. I may have seen her in church but I don't know," said the town clerk, Ralph Sternadori. "But now everybody's commenting what a wonderful gesture this is. She strongly believes that we're only here for a certain period of time and that God gave us everything we need and we don't need more."

Such is the faith that seems to have carried Eleanor Boyer through life. And it may help explain why she is so unimpressed by what she did.

After accepting her winning check from a representative of the state lottery commission and informing her church of her impending $4 million donation, she instructed priests there not to single her out for praise at Mass. Rajesh Shah will tell you that she doesn't answer her phone now. At her church, one of the priests is more emphatic: "She's not doing any interviews."

After her appearance with the state lottery commission, Boyer's only explanation about her winning lottery ticket and the gift she made of it came as she walked into church on Sunday.

She was late. Her car had broken down. And when she approached the church, she was met by a wall of TV cameras and press photographers.

She stopped briefly, according to one account, and explained that her car was in the shop. But she added that there would be "no new car," nor was she planning a vacation. "My life is no different," she said. "I've given it up to God. I live in his presence and do his will, and I did that from the start."

As for the assembled media, who had come to town to find some sort of meaning in the old woman who tasted millions, then passed it on, Eleanor Boyer had one more thing to say.

"Now that's enough, all right? I want to pray a little bit."

Elevator Sam

Sometimes we get ever so close to something, only to find that a door shuts in our face. Sam DiPalma has made a career out of this — running an elevator in an athletic arena where he never gets to see a game, hear a concert, or catch a glimpse of the circus as it passes through town.

Elevator Sam is eavesdropping. "Hear that?"

Sam leans ever so slightly toward the faint roar and muffled thumping on the other side of the steel door. He is silent for a second or two, then smiles the smile of a man who can imagine something without actually seeing it.

"The Devils scored."

Another second passes. The elevator opens, and a man in a Devils hockey shirt walks on. "We scored," the man says, matter-of-factly.

"See?" says Elevator Sam. "I was right."

There are many ways to watch the world pass by. But the perch occupied most nights by Sam DiPalma surely ranks as one of the most frustrating.

DiPalma, 55, a cherub-cheeked grandfather with soft, wavy, gray hair who spends his days teaching math at Thomas Jefferson Middle School in Fair Lawn, moonlights at night by operating the VIP elevator at the Continental Arena in the Meadowlands.

In more than a decade of ups and downs, he has heard the muffled cheers for professional hockey and basketball games, for college basketball's Final Four, for concerts by the likes of Frank Sinatra and Bruce Springsteen, for all manner of ice-skating exhibitions, circuses, horse shows, wrestling matches, and track meets.

But he sees almost nothing.

Sam DiPalma's view is controlled by an elevator door that opens and closes like a slow-speed shutter on a camera. He has mastered the fine art of catching glimpses, of telling the story in snapshots.

His world is a 10-by-6-by-8-foot box that shuttles some 200 times each night between the five levels of the Continental Arena, inside a shaft of steel and cinder blocks. His air is controlled by a noisy fan. He gets his news when the elevator door opens.

And when it closes — well, here is where Sam DiPalma's perspective begins.

"I'm so close and so far away," DiPalma says, alone now and holding a sheaf of hockey statistics that he reads to pass the time. "I'm a little bit like a barber who people tell stories to. People talk to me in bits and pieces. I get a little piece here, a little piece there. And I try to put the pieces together to get an idea of how the game is going."

The door opens.

DiPalma takes a few steps out of the elevator. He is standing now in the arena's "halo" section, a circle of steel girders, flags, and speakers that is the arena's equivalent of a cathedral bell tower. For hockey games, scouts and journalists sit here, peering down like gargoyles on the ice and the ant-like players below.

But from his spot by the elevator, DiPalma cannot see the ice.

"I really can't leave the elevator and walk over to the edge where I can actually see things," he says. "I have to listen to the bell in the elevator in case someone wants to be picked up. But sometimes I step out and just listen . . . "

He pauses.

"Or I look."

Well, not actually.

From the elevator — or even a few steps beyond — the most that Sam DiPalma can see of the action inside the arena is a four-sided Sony "Jumbotron" that is the size of a four-wheel truck and hangs over the ice at halo-level. Each side of the Jumbotron is home to a television screen the size of a wall in an ordinary living room.

On this night, the Devils are playing the Hartford Whalers. And less than three minutes into the game, the Devils' Bobby Holik, a 6-foot-3, 220-pounder from the Czech Republic, slaps a goal into the net.

Inside his elevator, DiPalma has already heard the roar of the crowd. He is here now, on the halo, for the instant replay.

DiPalma glances at the Jumbotron screen, as a replay of Holik's goal is shown. It's a surreal moment, being inside the arena but not being able to see the events — watching instead a replay on a television screen. His view, such as it is, is the same as for any cable viewer at home.

"See," DiPalma says, pointing to the screen. "There's the goal."

BEEEEEEP.

The elevator signals that someone on a lower floor wants a ride.

"We have to go," DiPalma says. The elevator door closes and he rides to the first floor.

Sam DiPalma left Italy as a 14-year-old for America in March 1956. The timing is important. On its next transatlantic journey in July 1956, the ocean liner that had carried DiPalma to America, the *Andrea Doria*, sank 40 miles south of Nantucket island. Fifty-one people drowned.

His family settled in Hoboken. And after graduating from Jersey City State College and settling in Kearny with his wife and two sons, DiPalma landed a job teaching math in Fair Lawn in 1966. Both sons played soccer, and during the late 1970s DiPalma would take them to watch professional soccer games featuring the New York Cosmos at Giants Stadium.

"I used to see the ushers at the stadium standing there watching the game," DiPalma remembers. "I said, 'Gee, that is a nice job. Not only do you work and get paid, but you get to see the games.'"

DiPalma applied for a job and worked a year at Giants Stadium as an usher before transferring inside to the arena, starting July 2, 1981, the night it opened with a concert by Bruce Springsteen. ("It was my wedding anniversary," says DiPalma.)

Two years later, weakened by a thyroid condition, he gave up his usher's job to volunteer for elevator duty. He liked it so much he stayed.

The door opens.

"Hiya," DiPalma says, a wide smile lighting up his face.

The elevator is now at the arena's first floor. Standing before DiPalma, his hands gripped on a wheelchair with a disabled young man, is Frank Tricarico of Colts Neck.

"Hi, Sam," Tricarico says.

The moment repeats itself over and over again during the night as others enter the elevator, greeting DiPalma as if they are neighbors who happen to come across each other as they are walking out of their front doors to fetch the mail.

"What I like about Sam is that he's a regular guy," Tricarico says as he leaves the elevator, pushing the wheelchair. "And one more thing — he's a Devils fan, too."

Over the years DiPalma has given rides to such diverse travelers as opera tenor Luciano Pavarotti, Massachusetts Senator Ted Kennedy, and actor Tony Danza. On this night, he will give a ride to the pregnant wife of a Devils player who jokingly tells him he might have to deliver a baby on the elevator.

"Not yet," DiPalma says.

BEEEEEEEP.

DiPalma is called again to the halo. The door opens and here is the unofficial chaplain and spiritual conscience of the Devils, Monsignor Robert McCourt. DiPalma takes him to the first floor, and McCourt leaves.

As the door closes and DiPalma takes the elevator to another floor, McCourt smiles as he ponders the man he has come to know while traveling between floors of a sports arena.

"There are people-people and machine-people," McCourt says. "Some people like to be around machines all the time. Sam works all night in the elevator, but he's a people person. He's part of the game."

The door opens.

The game is almost over. DiPalma thinks about the scores of people he has talked with on this night, many of them several times as they ride the elevator between periods in the game.

"This relaxes me," he says. "I'm usually a quiet person. I don't talk a lot. But these people bring me out."

Home, Sweet Home

In New Jersey, people co-exist with all sorts of neighbors. This man's home was next to an oil tank farm.

He is surrounded by oil tanks, more than 200 of the giant white industrial stumps. In between, like exposed tree roots, run the pipelines. Overhead, high-voltage wires swing in the sulfurous air. And, a half-mile away, on the Arthur Kill, lies the twisted steel of the *Cibro Savannah* oil barge that blew up the other day.

Some call it Cancer Alley.

But John Kostiushko isn't worried about his neighborhood of Tremley Point in Linden, an eight-square-block island of 900 people, two churches, and one tavern in the middle of New Jersey's huff-and-puff industrial cauldron.

It's home.

And John Kostiushko, who is nearly 72 and has lived in Tremley Point since he was 2, wants all of us to know that he's happy with life. He wishes all these environmental types with their college degrees and their designer hiking boots would stop their be-bop fluttering every time a little bit of oil gets spilled.

"Hey, it's not poison," Kostiushko said. "It's oil."

And in John Kostiushko's neighborhood, oil is a staff of life, even on the day after the *Cibro Savannah* exploded in a petroleum fireball.

Oil refineries brought jobs, built parks, kept the taxes low in John Kostiushko's part of the world, which you get to by taking Route 1 past Fender's Bar and Grill, Cadillac Plastic, Dinettes Beautiful, a Harley-Davidson shop, and an auto workers union hall with a sign that says "Buy American for Full Employment."

John Kostiushko admits to having tumors on his bladder. But who's worrying? You get old, you get sick, he reasons.

And so what if there have been four major oil spills in the area since New Year's? The other day, John Kostiushko didn't even hear the *Cibro Savannah* go up. Neither did Mary Kostiushko, John's wife of 49 years. When the firetrucks and ambulances and TV crews screamed by with their equipment, John Kostiushko just sat on his living room couch.

"I've seen four tanks blow in my life," he said. "There used to be two inches of oil floating on the Kill. All of these creeks around here used to be covered with oil."

Kostiushko didn't have to spell it out, but his message was clear: Big deal. So there's an oil spill?

He is a proud working man with the callused hands to prove it. His father came from Poland and was a carpenter at the American Cyanamid plant next to the Citgo refinery where the barge exploded. Mary's father came from Czechoslovakia and pushed a wheelbarrow at a chemical plant. When they married, John also worked for Cyanamid and made $20 a week. He retired as a pipe fitter after 41 years.

When he stopped working, John and Mary didn't leave for Florida or a seniors community at the Jersey shore.

"I'm staying here," said Mary, who is 70, "until they carry me out in a coffin."

John nods. He forgives Exxon for bulldozing a baseball field and building the tanks. (Exxon built another field.) He also excuses Mobil for plowing under Corrine's Farm to put up its tanks. He griped when Northvale Oil told people that its tanks would be small — and then built them as big as Exxon's. And he wishes DuPont would say more about the chemicals it produces.

But. You can hear that word in everything John Kostiushko says. When he qualifies things, John Kostiushko is Everyman.

"But it used to be worse," he says. "When Cyanamid made wallboard, you would wake up every morning and everything would be covered with white stuff. It was like snow. We lived through it."

So, John Kostiushko is staying in Tremley Point, no matter how many oil spills or barge explosions or invisible pollutants invade his neighborhood.

It's home. He wants us to know that.

Pal Joey and God

New Jersey practically invented weird politicians. But few could top the exploits of Joe Lipari. God told him to run for office. Unfortunately a prison term intervened. Before that, I paid a visit.

Mayor Joe Lipari flops in the chair behind his desk at Passaic's City Hall. No, wait. Lipari is up and pacing. No, he's sitting again. He's up. He sits. He's up.

Got to have more coffee.

Yes, coffee. That's it. Lipari grabs a half-filled cup, struts to the office door, and calls his secretary.

"Can you get me some coffee? I've had five of these today and it's not right."

And it's not even noon yet.

The mayor sits again.

"What do you want?"

I mention God.

"Oh, no," he says. "Not that."

The mere mention of the Almighty causes the mayor to take a mighty leap from his seat. He heads for the door, then turns.

"I'm not going to talk about that. NOT THAT."

It's not that Joseph Lipari doesn't believe in his Maker. It's just that Joe Lipari is hearing conflicting voices these days.

From heaven, he hears: Thou shalt not resign. Yet, from some people in his city, he hears, "Yo, Joey, enough already. Go away."

Obviously, this is a strange predicament. And when you realize that Joe Lipari once owned a restaurant called "Something's Fishey," you can understand why he paces the floor and explodes occasionally.

As a believer, Lipari, 54 and now owner of a sausage factory, knows about the ultimate heavenly veto if you misbehave too much in places like Passaic. Yet, as a mayor, he also knows what the voters can do. Indeed, there are already enough names on petitions to order a special recall election in May. Lipari also knows he won the last election in 1989 with only 27 percent of the votes. And that was before the state and federal government started snooping around.

So it wasn't surprising when Joe Lipari announced his resignation, citing another set of voices.

"I am doing this on the advice of my physicians, who fear that my health has been seriously threatened by the stress I have been enduring. . . . It is not a question of choice. If it were, I would fulfill my term. I simply cannot continue."

Two days later, God called. Or as Lipari explained to one newspaper reporter: "I talked to God, who told me, 'Joey, finish your term.'"

And so, the mayor wrote a new letter that said, "Kindly disregard my letter of resignation."

Passaic's City Council responded by drawing up a resolution to hire a handwriting expert and an attorney to check whether the mayor talked to God and signed both letters. Or as Councilwoman Marge Semler explained: "Joey doesn't hear voices. Joey only hears his own voice. It's kinda twisted."

Semler, by the way, wants to be mayor. One Wednesday, Lipari was pacing his office like a man who was about to greet his loan shark.

The coffee arrives. Lipari takes a gulp, then reaches for a stack of bumper stickers that say "Joe, don't go." The bumper stickers also have a red heart on them, and Lipari says "a friend" printed them. But he knows the voices in Passaic. "They'll say I paid for them."

He calls City Clerk Sabatina Fiorellino and acting Business Administrator Henry G. McCafferty into his office. "I want them here to listen," Lipari says. And then he offers this about himself:

"I don't think anything. I have nothing to think."

He wants to talk about rebuilding his city. I mention the unresolved corruption investigations.

"Is this reverse psychology?" he asks. "I'm not going to talk about this issue. It's insanity."

"We got some big stuff happening," he says. "We got CNN coming in. Wait till they hear about that."

Joe Lipari leaves his seat again. He walks to another room, into what he says is a meeting with developers. As he closes a door, I hear him say, "Oh, my God."

I also hear him laugh.

Bill Bradley's Journey

I have followed Bill Bradley's political life since it began, in the heady days after he retired from the New York Knicks. Our first meeting, a month after he swished his last jump shot, was in a small library. Eighteen years later, as he was again changing careers, I found him again.

Bill Bradley glances up and down Manhattan's 48th Street, empty now except for two men who ask for his autograph, a lone car, and a puff of steam rising from a sewer. It is dawn, and the winter's thin, golden sunlight pours across Rockefeller Center like hot tea in an empty cup.

Bradley pulls the collar of his blue overcoat around his neck, hunches his shoulders. His brow furrows.

He has been up for almost two hours promoting his new book, first on radio, and, minutes before, on the *Today* show, where his blue suit jacket was so wrinkled that a producer asked that it be pressed before he went on the air. But now, there is a decision: How to get to the New York Hilton Hotel?

Seconds pass, then he blurts: "Let's go on foot."

Bradley strides off, without waiting for an answer, calling back: "The best way to get around is to walk."

It is one of those basic declarations that America has often heard from the eloquent, if sometimes elusive, Bill Bradley. The best way to get around is to walk.

The words resonate from his roots in Crystal City, Mo., a town where traffic was controlled by one stoplight and life revolved around the Ten Commandments. But hearing it now — at 52 years old — Bradley's basic-ness underscores something else.

Once again, Bradley is examining himself and what he wants to be. The man whose personal journey has taken him from Princeton's basketball court to the Olympics, from Oxford as a Rhodes Scholar to the Knicks and the NBA championship, from the U.S. Senate to his flirtations with a run for the presidency, is on a self-professed journey back to basics, especially in light of his decision to not seek a fourth Senate term.

It is a trek that, at times, seems deeply spiritual — indeed draped in Zen-like vocabulary, as he describes himself "anchored in nature, in God's grace, and in humanity's potential to grow."

But much like Bradley himself, this journey is hard to define. The man who begins and ends his memoir, *Time Present, Time Past*, by conceding that he has "always preferred moving to sitting still," is definitely on the move. But where?

"I don't know," says Bradley. He hints that he "might take a crack at the presidency," but he says he is far short of a decision on that.

Except for a proposal on campaign finance reform that would require a constitutional amendment, he has formulated no new policy proposals. Bradley is not in the campaign platform mode now — he admits this. He wants instead to listen to America. "I am leaving politics, but not public life," he says.

Something, he says, is missing in politics: an ability to blend people's personal stories into policy — how to cope, for example, with economic downsizing without just passing another jobs bill.

"There's a deeper level of things that people don't allow themselves to get into in politics," he says. "And that's what I've tried to do from time to time."

For Bradley, that deeper level is himself. What confounds him is how he fits into the current political landscape, how to blend his pragmatic side as a politician who can spend months formulating tax policy with the elusive, yet appealing, side that is drawn to understanding humanity and its core values.

He declined, for example, to attend one State of the Union address by President Clinton. "I have always felt like an extra there on a set," he says. "You stand up. You clap. You sit down. I don't enjoy it."

He would rather spend free time standing in the Port Authority Bus Terminal, listening to the off-the-cuff sentiments of commuters.

"You don't know what's going to happen," he says, smiling. "You are in the unknown. A lot of politicians don't like it, but I like it. There's a creative tension. You are stretched."

It takes Bradley only a few minutes to walk to the New York Hilton. He pushes through the revolving doors and walks into the lobby.

Bradley is still in good shape, not breathing hard from his fast walk across four city blocks, including a shortcut through a parking garage and two bolts of jaywalking across taxi-clogged traffic. He sheds his topcoat and drops his 6-foot-5 frame into a love seat, his legs sticking out like exposed girders on an unfinished skyscraper.

Bradley is here, conceding that he is following another voice in himself — his professed need to find out how things work. "Structure," he says, "I'm fascinated by it."

He shakes hands with a man who has written a new book about world corporations. After hearing of the book, Bradley asked to meet the author.

But within a few minutes of listening to the man's soliloquy about "market deregulation" and "economic globalization," Bradley is scratching his ear, rubbing his forehead, shuffling his feet under a coffee table. He seems bored and politely cuts the man off after 15 minutes, promising to talk again.

Moments later, the man gone, Bradley sips coffee. He seems apologetic.

"I do this," he says, "because there's always the chance I'll find THE nugget." He pauses, seeming to reflect on the words. "I love the unknown. But. . . ."

Bill Bradley seems troubled but in a way that makes him smile. This angst is nothing new, of course. His seemingly eternal quest for self-definition and what he will do with his life confounds his supporters and angers his critics who feel he is coddled too much by the media and Sixties-era liberal Democrats who see him as the complete politician — scholar, athlete, policy wonk.

"I've been this way since I was 21 years old," Bradley says of his search for definition and his need to talk about it. "What am I going to do? When I was getting ready to quit basketball, my wife finally said, 'I don't care what you do, but let's not talk about it anymore.'"

Bradley's internal journey, while very much at the heart of what makes him tick, nonetheless is also fodder for insults from critics.

Bradley and his wife, Ernestine Schlandt-Bradley, once drove to a bookstore near their home in suburban Washington, D.C., that alternates with their residence in Montclair. Ernestine, a professor of literature at Montclair State University, was looking for a computer manual. Bradley picked up a copy of a book on the battle of Gettysburg, and was standing in a cashier's line when a man walked up, grinning.

Bradley's long face contorts into a goofy smile, as he recounts the scene.

"Hey Bradddddd-leeeeeee, how ya doing?" the man said. Bradley started to say hello, but the man cut him off.

"Braddddd-leeeeee," the man chortled. "You're such a jerrrrrrrrk. But you're leeeeeaving, ha, ha, ha."

Bradley laughs as he recalls the man's words.

"I had my answer all ready," Bradley says. "I wanted to say, 'And you're such an ass.' But I didn't do it. I didn't know if he was joking or not."

He pauses.

"I unload occasionally. But I'm basically a nice guy."

A few years ago, Bradley might not have revealed such a personal side of himself — vulnerable, a tad vulgar, groping for words in the face of the unknown. That he finds humor in it now underscores a sense of newfound peace that seemed to elude him for several years, beginning with his near-defeat for reelection in 1990 by the then-unknown Christine Todd Whitman and a series of personal crises that included his wife's battle with breast cancer, the deaths of his parents, and the suicide of a close friend.

He is clearly looser these days — in part, he says, because of his announcement that he would leave the Senate after his term expires. But that is not the only factor behind his new mirth.

Emma Byrne, the former consumer affairs commissioner who joined Bradley's staff two years ago, notes that the change in Bradley began even as other Democrats seemed to sink into a funk under the weight of the Republican takeover of Congress. Bradley explains that the change began several years earlier, when he had decided to stop being what others wanted him to be and to listen to his own instincts.

This search for something deeper resulted in his series of candid speeches on race relations, says Bradley. It also caused him to be more critical of Clinton. "We don't talk much," Bradley says, his words clipped.

But all is not somber. Bradley rediscovered his sense of humor. Indeed, at one dinner gathering of Jersey politicos last summer, he caught an audience by surprise with his imitations of former governors Jim Florio and Brendan Byrne. Bradley concedes he loves to mimic people. His gravel-voiced rendition of former Boston Celtics announcer Johnny Most is near-perfect. *Bradley's holding Havlicek. Will ya look at it? What a crime! Holding his jersey. . . .*

And for a man whose calcified speaking style before large groups has been rated lower than Vice President Al Gore's, Bradley has a genuine knack for one-to-one storytelling.

◆ ◆ ◆

He is sitting in the passenger seat of a car now, as a driver hired by his book publisher negotiates traffic in Manhattan's Chelsea neighborhood. After the *Today* show and the meeting at the Hilton, the morning has been a jumble of radio interviews and quick stops in bookstores.

"We have lost the art of storytelling in politics," he says.

Far too many politicians, he adds, live such limited, sheltered lives that they rarely have time enough to hear the stories of ordinary citizens. "What most rely on is brief anecdotes," says Bradley. "And if you become president, you can never replenish yourself."

Bradley yearns to be a storyteller. "When I get out of the Senate," he says, "I want to attend those storytelling conventions."

When he speaks like this, Bradley comes off as something of a novelist, not a politician. For years, he says, he has kept notes of his travels and impressions in spiral notebooks and on scraps of paper.

"I don't keep a diary. I keep a journal," he says. "There's a difference. I'm constantly constructing movie shots, scenes, descriptions in my own mind. What's surprising to me is when something happens and nobody else sees it the way I do."

The notes grew. There were pieces of stories, impressions, descriptions. Then he started shaping his thoughts into a book, writing in longhand in a five-subject spiral binder. "I like the narrow-lined paper," says Bradley.

What resulted was his new memoir — and a yearning to hear more stories.

"I think there is a story to be told," he says. "And I think people are yearning for a story that they can locate themselves in and give themselves some idea of where they are, how they're connected to other people, and where they're going in their work life and, frankly, in their personal lives. And while you can't help people with their personal lives, you can certainly acknowledge their search for something beyond the material."

He tells a story he heard from a rabbi. It's about a woman — a tormented daughter of Holocaust survivors — who finds psychological comfort in playing a piano. But after falling on hard times — the woman lost her job through a corporate downsizing and her apartment rent was hiked — the woman felt she had to sell her piano to make ends meet. The rabbi stepped in and helped.

As Bradley finishes the story, his voice drops. He seems pained.

"Her life is sad," says Bradley of the woman, "until she touches the piano keys. It's her lifeline."

◆ ◆ ◆

It is midafternoon now. Bradley walks out of another radio studio, where he has told stories again of factory downsizing and friendships in the Senate. He lopes down a carpeted hallway, his voice silent, his brow knotted. The only sound is the thump-thumping of his black-laced shoes.

He walks into a sun-splashed room. A woman, who works as a publicist for another publishing company, is sitting on a couch with a book about a man who leaves Washington, D.C., and heads for the Alaskan wilderness and is never heard from again. His body is found by hunters. Bradley recognizes the title.

"Do you like it?" he asks.

"Yes," says the woman, looking up. She brightens as she recognizes Bradley, and hands him the book.

"Do you want it?" she asks. "Please take it. If you do, I promise to vote for you for president."

Bradley smiles, reaches for the book, and walks out, politely thanking the woman. Outside, by an elevator, he hands the book to an aide.

"People are always giving me things to read," he says. "I can never get to it."

Bradley is silent as he rides the elevator to the street level. As the door opens, he struts out, his coat collar high on his neck, shoulders hunched, his hands jammed into his pockets. He is moving fast now, cutting across traffic. He is alone.

The Doc on the Phone

In these days of managed care, some doctors still practice a hands-on style. I am grateful one of them treated my children.

He never discovered a vaccine, never performed a heart transplant, never went on the *Donahue* show to discuss the latest in celebrity medicine. But there ought to be a course in medical school about Dr. Vincent McAuliffe anyway.

McAuliffe was a children's doctor. And his gift to the medical world was a gesture as simple as it was unusual.

He answered his phone.

In these days of arms-length medicine, with electronic pagers and wait-for-the-beep answering machines, McAuliffe's style may have seemed out of sync with the times, probably not cost-effective.

No matter. Vincent McAuliffe, though born in Jersey City and a resident of Teaneck since 1948, was really just a country doctor in the shadow of New York City. No nonsense. Reliable.

Always there.

"Oh, yes, Dr. McAuliffe," a young mother said when she heard I knew him. "You can always get him."

Could there be any better way to describe a doctor today?

Vincent McAuliffe was there until one Saturday morning, when his heart gave out at his Teaneck home, and he died. He was 74. He never retired.

Even after he had reached his 70s, he still took only two weeks of vacation a year. In the last year, he announced he was cutting back. His idea of a cutback was to go to the office 4 1/2 days a week. And he still took phone calls.

But it wasn't just his availability that made him special. With Vincent McAuliffe, there was his manner.

In a way, he was a physician's equivalent of Walter Cronkite, calm in the most frantic of moments, patient with the most impatient of parents.

"He may have seemed calm, but underneath he was always worried about the children," said Jeanne McAuliffe, his wife for 44 years and mother of their eight sons. "Phone calls were as reassuring to him as the parents."

In the mornings, he took phone calls at a desk in the kitchen. Between calls, he drank coffee and scanned a newspaper.

"Nothing was ever too minor," said his nurse, Virginia Smith. "Parents always said they made it through the night knowing they could talk to him in the morning."

I know. I am one of those who called.

Our baby cried almost every night that week. What made things worse is that she was only 10 days old, the second of two daughters. The parenting books call this colic, and say she'll grow out of it.

But when? She hardly slept. She wasn't eating well. She didn't like her crib. And the dozen stuffed animals we bought didn't do the trick, either. She just wanted to be held by her mother. And even then, she cried or whimpered.

It was now 8 a.m., time for the "calling hour," as McAuliffe referred to his phone sessions. We had a two-page litany of questions and headaches that even six aspirins wouldn't tame. He picked up on the first ring.

"Ah, hello, Dr. McAuliffe here."

It didn't matter how minor the concern was. It didn't even matter if you called three days in succession. I know. We did that, too.

All that mattered at that moment was your child. And if you didn't call again to update him on how your sick child was, he phoned you.

I know. Vincent McAuliffe did that one morning during those long months of colic. He merely wanted to know how things were going, nothing more, just a status report. He signed off with some encouragement to hang in there.

His words always seemed to be like that — straightforward and grandfatherly.

But the prescription I remember most had nothing to do with sickness and everything to do with the way Vincent McAuliffe looked at life.

"Enjoy her," he often said as we left his office.

And we have.

The Marsh Warden

Living in a father's shadow is hard enough for most sons. But what if your father is a reviled political figure? Even after a half century, the wounds are still painful.

The father's house is remodeled now, its white colonial lines displaced by one of those Nineties bicoastal glass-and-stone, earth-tone blends that evoke L. L. Bean and Williams-Sonoma.

But the old ghosts of the Cold War still rumble sometimes into the rear meadow and the smaller farmhouse where the son still lives and wonders sometimes about the past.

Stiles Thomas, the son, is the marsh warden of Allendale, a volunteer job that requires him to keep watch over a 97-acre patch of reeds, wildflowers, and birds' nests known as the Celery Farm.

But in his memory, he monitors a marsh of another sort, too.

The father, J. Parnell Thomas, hunted Hollywood Communists as a congressman and kicked off the first of the McCarthy-era blacklists before a scandal over payroll kickbacks drove him from office. "It's the skeleton in the closet," says Stiles.

It's been 50 years since that angry time. But the son's voice still chokes when he talks about it. The son is 73.

"I loved my father deeply," says Stiles, "but our politics were very different."

Every son lives in the shadow of his father. But in the case of J. Parnell Thomas, who died in 1970, the shadow is long and stained indelibly by the hotblooded politics of the day and the public soapboxes that turned human beings into blustery caricatures. Even now, Stiles Thomas confesses he would rather avoid talking about the father his critics called "Mister Quisling" (after the legendary Nazi collaborator) and he called "Pop."

"Look," he says, "my hands are clammy just thinking about this."

In time, Stiles Thomas says he became his own man — even to the point of becoming an active letter-writing critic of the Vietnam War and a leading ecologist and director and treasurer of the state Audubon Society. And while he calls himself a Republican, he has nonetheless felt free to switch allegiances, voting for Jimmy Carter against Ronald Reagan and Bill Clinton against George Bush and Bob Dole.

By 1969, with his oldest daughter on the way to the Woodstock music festival with a vanload of friends, Stiles drove his Commie-hunting dad up Route 17 to Mount Peter to watch the throngs of hippies make their way northward. "He couldn't believe his eyes and got a real kick out of that," said Stiles. "By then, he had mellowed a bit."

But as much as the father and son remained close, they never talked about the central political drama that will forever ensure the father's small place on the national historical map. Stiles even grew to feel empathy for the blacklisted screenwriters and actors whose careers were derailed by his father. "These people were not a threat to our country," says Stiles. "It's as simple as that."

He never told his father, though.

"We just couldn't speak about it," said Stiles. "I still don't know why. He might have wished for me to talk about the hearings. I just couldn't. He was my father."

And father went to jail.

◆

Stiles Thomas is sitting in a wing chair now, as the afternoon breeze rolls through the maples out back and bends the wildflowers in the meadow that looks much the same as it did when his father was a Republican congressman from Bergen County and chairman of the House Un-American Activities Committee.

It was 1947. A few months after America launched the Marshall Plan to revive Europe's economy and Jackie Robinson broke the color line in baseball, John Parnell Thomas had crossed another line, trumpeting a piece of Cold War fear known as the "Federal Loyalty Act" and calling for hearings to expose "Communist infiltration of the motion-picture industry."

So began the series of anti-Communist investigations in Congress that framed the five-year period of American history known as the McCarthy Era. Such names as Joseph McCarthy, Roy Cohn, Richard Nixon, Alger Hiss, and Whittaker Chambers may have garnered bigger headlines. But the era began with J. Parnell Thomas gaveling to order a series of hearings into the "Hollywood Ten," a group of screenwriters that included Ring Lardner Jr. and Dalton Trumbo.

J. Parnell Thomas, who dropped his Irish-Catholic surname after his father died and held on to his mother's WASP-ish maiden name in part because he felt it would help him in Bergen's Republican-dominated politics, came to the hearings with dreams of bigger prizes. "He loved the limelight and felt this would launch him into higher office," remembers Stiles. "There was talk of him running for vice president."

Instead, J. Parnell Thomas went to prison after a secretary on his staff turned on him and exposed his practice of padding the office payroll with fictional employees and pocketing their salaries for his own use.

The father spent only eight months in the federal prison in Danbury, Conn., and was pardoned on Christmas Eve, 1950, by President Harry S Truman. But the stain of disgrace never disappeared.

"I just knew he would never recover from this," said Stiles.

As he unlocks this memory, his eyes walk across the room and meet those of his wife, Lillian, who dabs her eyes with a tissue. Just as a son confronts his father's shadows, so do the other members of a family.

Lillian, who grew up in Wyckoff and met her husband at Ramsey High School, finds it hard now to reconcile her memory of a father-in-law who seemed to enjoy a good laugh, and always seemed to be stoking his pipe, with the news clips that depicted him as something of an over-weight blowhard, addressing Hollywood screenwriters in a loud, pompous voice. In one of his hearings, J. Parnell Thomas banged his gavel so hard that he broke it — a fact that was cause for much laughter from Hollywood.

"He doesn't look like the man I knew," she says of the old news films. "And that's what bothers me. He doesn't look like the nice man I knew."

She is silent a moment, then continues:

"It's difficult when the person being vilified is someone you know and love."

Stiles and Lillian couldn't even bring themselves to tell their three daughters of their grandfather's prison sentence until two decades after the pardon and J. Parnell Thomas was about to die.

"We grew up thinking that going to prison was the worst thing that could happen to someone," said Stiles. "He's in jail. He's my father. It's humiliating. What more can I say?"

During the hearings in 1947, Stiles Thomas commuted each day by train to Manhattan and his job with an insurance firm. He remembers watching his fellow commuters reading the papers and talking about the hearings. He also remembers being afraid to venture an opinion or even acknowledge that he knew J. Parnell Thomas.

One day the criticism got to Stiles. A man in the office was deriding his father. Stiles, a former amateur boxer, punched the man.

But such an outburst was the exception. While all of America seemed to have an opinion about J. Parnell Thomas and whether he was right or wrong in his hunt for Communists, Stiles Thomas went out of his way not to speak about it, even with his father — even in later years.

"I have hardly no memories of those times," he says. "I went out of my way to avoid it, I guess. And my father never brought it up either."

In private, though, Stiles had his own feelings. He felt his father was wrong to hunt Communists. And he felt his father's payroll kickback scheme was wrong, too, even though the $8,000 that was pocketed was small change compared to modern-day political scandals. "My father lived beyond his means," said Stiles. "But what he did was wrong."

When the father went to prison, the son felt an ironic sense of freedom even though he visited his father regularly. "His going to jail," remembers Stiles, "was the best thing that ever happened to me."

Stiles quit his New York job that his father had helped him get and opened his own insurance business in Allendale. "I was my own man, my own boss," he says. "I was not J. Parnell Thomas' son anymore."

But he was his father's friend. After prison, J. Parnell Thomas drank heavily. His wife, Amelia, divorced him, but after several years and when Thomas curtailed his drinking, the two remarried. At the wedding, Stiles Thomas was his father's best man.

"The roles became exactly reversed," said Lillian. "Everything Stiles did, 'Pop' thought was right."

Before J. Parnell Thomas left Congress, he turned over the chairmanship of his committee to Richard Nixon, who used the post as a launching pad for higher office. And when J. Parnell Thomas died, Nixon, who then was president, penned a letter to Amelia Thomas. "It has always been my feeling," wrote Nixon in 1970, "that the difficulties which caused him so much anguish were in large part due to the fact that he was an absolutely fearless leader in the fight against subversive forces in this country."

On a recent afternoon, Stiles held the framed letter, silently reading it again.

"History will treat him more kindly," said Lillian.

"I don't know," says Stiles. "I don't know."

Unknown Soldier

For Memorial Day, 1991, I decided to chronicle the life and death of one of the handful of women who died in Vietnam. As I was writing and approaching deadline, my phone rang with news of the sudden death of another Vietnam veteran – my father. He was 67 and died after finishing a game of golf. I hung up the phone and finished this column in his honor.

Her grave is tucked by the fence at St. Andrew's Cemetery in River Vale on a gentle slope where elms shield the afternoon sun. Except for the flat concrete marker with the word "Vietnam," you might never know that Eleanor Alexander has a special corner in history.

Alexander, an Army captain and combat surgical nurse, was killed in Vietnam on November 30, 1967, when the transport plane she was in smashed into a mountain. She was one of eight female American soldiers to die in that war, the only one from New Jersey. She was 27.

She left behind a cedar chest with Fieldcrest towels and a wedding gown for a marriage she hoped she might have one day. She also left a shelf of books on the plight of Native Americans and a collection of snapshots in which she invariably had a confident look in her eyes.

Today, 23 years after her death, she leaves behind a memory void. In this year of acclaim for female soldiers, Eleanor Alexander is still an unknown soldier to most of us.

She volunteered for Vietnam, frustrated that her nursing skills were being wasted in a Manhattan hospital devoted to cosmetic surgery. "Rocky," her friends called her.

"There were young American men being wounded, and she was doing nose jobs," says her brother, Frank, 48, of South Orange, a vice president at Prudential Insurance. "She felt it was an improper use of her talent."

But outside her family and friends, little of Eleanor Alexander's story is known. In River Vale, there is an Alexander Court with 12 homes. There also is a sign on a bridge over the Pascack Brook with the names of Alexander and two local men who died in Vietnam. And near the goal posts at a football field, there is a brass plaque on a granite boulder that says you are standing on Eleanor Alexander Memorial Field.

But the boulder and the plaque didn't come until 1976, nine years after Alexander's death. And the dedication ceremony attracted all of a dozen people.

"I remember it well," said her sister-in-law, Susanne. "We could all fit into one picture."

Contrast that scene with the one in Oradell, when a crowd of 100 people watched Governor Florio dedicate elm trees in honor of Army Major Marie Rossi, who was killed during Operation Desert Storm, and you get an idea of how forgotten Eleanor Alexander has become. Street signs and plaques don't resurrect a memory.

"I'm sure thousands of eyes have passed over that plaque," says Frank Alexander, "and probably wondered who Eleanor was."

Or as River Vale's mayor, Walter V. Jones, puts it: "I don't think people realize the field is named after a woman."

"Not everybody is concerned. That's one of the things that bothers me," said Edward Carter, commander of the borough's American Legion Post, who sent packages to Alexander when she was in Vietnam and went to her funeral.

Carter visited Alexander's grave to plant an American flag. A few days later, Tony Lione of Emerson, a former Marine who was wounded in Vietnam, planted his own flag.

And in Fort Lee, photographer Denise DeFelice-Black, who served in Vietnam as an Army hospital administrator, keeps pictures of Eleanor Alexander in a wooden frame.

"I feel like I know her," said DeFelice-Black, pointing to a snapshot of Alexander in her uniform. "There's a connection. I feel by doing this, I can give her life."

On this Memorial Day in River Vale, there is another chance for life. Eleanor Alexander's name will be read during a ceremony to honor borough residents who died in America's wars. In this year of the female soldier, remember that Eleanor Alexander was one who led the way.

Homeless and Famous

In the early Nineties, as communities across America tried to cope with the burgeoning homeless problem, Morristown made national headlines. A local homeless man wanted to use the library – to read. The patrons thought he was too threatening. It soon became a court case.

Richard Kreimer's failure is his success. He is America's most famous homeless man. And soon, he will enter a top tax bracket, too, courtesy of a $150,000 settlement of a lawsuit he filed against Morristown.

Needless to say, his schedule is booked solid. Busy man, this homeless guy.

"Full-time job," Kreimer says.

Today, he is scheduled to ride in a limousine to a television talk show. He also is calling Geraldo.

And then, as soon as he can find the time, Richard Kreimer is scheduling a few days off. Listen to how he puts it:

"I desperately need a vacation. I don't have a day to myself. I need to get away."

Remember, this is a homeless man. Then again, it's always been this way with Richard Kreimer.

He sleeps under the stars.

He talks like a CEO.

"On the advice of my lawyer," he says, qualifying himself with all the aplomb of a banker facing indictment, "I do not plan to be homeless forever."

It's this sense of irony that follows Kreimer like a camera crew. He is able to remember phone numbers from a dozen journalists, yet he is unable to remember to wash his clothes. He is unafraid to file court suits, yet he is afraid to find an apartment.

And now he has money, a payoff from Morristown in exchange for dropping a civil rights suit.

He told me recently that he wants to become "a homeless Ralph Nader." He said he plans to visit former President Jimmy Carter and discuss "domestic issues." He said he "will address" the Democratic National Convention, then run for mayor of Morristown.

Yet, he has no plans for a home.

Or a job.

Or new clothes.

Or regular meals.

"The routine of my day is so ingrained that I'm not used to anything else," says Kreimer. "When you're homeless, you have other priorities. I live in a totally different world than you do. I just don't know if I have the desire to become part of the 9-to-5 world again."

As he talks, Kreimer stands in an alcove in the Morristown Library — the same place that once tried to ban him because he smelled bad but was blocked by a federal judge. I ask him to sit down; he says no.

"My back is hurting," he says. "It's from sleeping on the ground."

The people who know Richard Kreimer often say he suffers from something more than just a bad back, that something is wrong with him emotionally, that it's not normal to want to be homeless.

But what is wrong? Here the voices trail off and qualifiers emerge.

In 1985, a psychiatrist judged him to be schizophrenic. Yet this year, another psychiatrist said he was not schizophrenic at all.

And then there are other vague diagnoses from mental health officials — "socially dysfunctional," "incapable of functioning in anything but the most socially disorganized fashion," "no motivation to change."

The unfortunate truth is that Richard Kreimer is the sore that won't go away, the human reminder that America isn't equipped to solve homelessness. And yet, he is a paradox, a human reminder that homeless people often are not equipped to deal with what Kreimer calls "normal life."

And so, it's not money that Richard Kreimer needs. It's help.

But it's also Richard Kreimer's decision to make. He says he wants to volunteer for "lifestyle counseling" to help him return to our world. He just hasn't decided when or where to go for this counseling.

"I have the burden of everyone watching me," Kreimer says. "There's never been a person like me."

That's why the next sound he'll probably hear is Geraldo calling. It should be a counselor.

Days of Rage

I met Marilyn Flax only days after her husband was murdered. A decade later, the crime still haunts her.

The hardest part is still the anger. It's not that Marilyn Flax of Fair Lawn never gets hot under the collar or impatient or even a little furious. She commutes each morning on Route 4, where impatience and fury are a way of automotive life.

But this other anger — this rage, Flax calls it — is something else entirely. It arrives with little warning, then creeps through her emotional landscape, spewing from fissures so deep and painful, so despondent and crazed — well, Marilyn Flax can barely describe it except to say this:

"Raw emotion is scary."

Such is the legacy of a decade of watching your husband's murderer sit on death row in a state that can't decide what to do about the death penalty.

Marilyn Flax, 53-year-old grandmother and owner of an employment agency in Fort Lee, can barely explain the depth of her rage. To understand her emotional pain, she says, you need to be reminded of the emotional path she has walked.

You need to know that Marilyn Flax was living a quiet Fair Lawn life with her husband, Irving, until a January morning in 1989, when a drifter, murderer, and cocaine addict named John Martini kidnapped Irving, then shot him to death after Marilyn left a $25,000 ransom at a Route 4 diner.

You need to know that while she sat in a Hackensack courtroom two years later and watched as Martini was convicted and sentenced to death by lethal injection, Martini's defense lawyer singled out Marilyn Flax as being greedy. She had filed suit against the FBI and other law enforcement agencies that she felt had botched the attempt to catch Martini before he killed her husband.

You need to know that in 1996, Martini, then 65 and convicted of two more murders in Arizona, returned to a Hackensack courtroom, declaring that "jail is terrible" and that he wanted to suspend all appeals and go ahead with his execution.

You need to know that lawyers from the state Public Defender's Office went ahead with his appeals anyway.

You need to know that the state Supreme Court recently rejected a third and final appeal by the Public Defender's Office and that a Bergen County Superior Court judge in Hackensack signed a death warrant that sets September 22 as Martini's execution date. You need to know that Martini, now 68, would be the first person executed in New Jersey in 36 years. You need to know that as his execution date approached, Martini had a change of heart and filed an appeal.

And you need to know something else: Marilyn Flax says that even if you know all these factual tidbits about her legal and emotional journey, you still don't understand her whole story. For that, you need to hear from her.

You need to understand what it's like to have your photograph in the newspaper and suddenly feel this need to change your hair color because you are afraid that people will recognize you. You need to know that even when people say how much they admire you or how sorry they feel for you that such words sting with a pain that cuts to your soul. You need to know what it's like to commute to work each morning and pass the spot at Garden State Plaza mall where Martini dumped your husband's bloody body. You need to know what it's like to walk into a courtroom and have your husband's murderer stare back at you with eyes as cold as concrete in January. You need to know what it's like to telephone your friends and ask them to go to church or to the synagogue and pray that your husband's murderer is executed.

But Marilyn Flax tells herself that most people will never know these things — thankfully. Most people do not know what it's like to lose someone to murder. And for that reason, few will ever really know Marilyn Flax's rage.

"Most average people," she says, "do not feel that rage."

Nor do most average people understand what scars it leaves behind.

Let's begin with her memory.

Marilyn says she can't remember how long she was married to Irving Flax. This does not mean they were not in love. Flax calls Irving not only her husband, but her lover and best friend. To hear her speak of Irving is to hear someone long for a soulmate. She realizes that to tell people that she can't remember is to sound downright flighty. But her husband's kidnapping and murder left Marilyn Flax with gaps that she explains only as something akin to the post-traumatic stress syndrome of battle-scarred soldiers. At the same time, the kidnapping-murder left portions of her memory as frozen as a snapshot. She can, for example, still remember what she was making for dinner the night she heard that Irving was kidnapped.

"Steak and Caesar salad," Flax says.

For a year or so after the murder, Flax could not even let her eyes wander to the Forum Diner in Paramus as she passed by on Route 4. The popular diner was the spot where she handed over the ransom, thinking that it would buy her husband's safety.

But then, a few years later, Flax agreed to meet a client at the diner for lunch, making the appointment without hesitation and not even realizing it was the source of such painful memories.

"I wasn't aware until I got there," she says, again hoping that people who read such words won't feel she is irresponsible.

She persuaded herself to go inside — and then confronted a surprising reaction. "There was no feeling," she recalls. "It was devoid of emotion."

Flax cannot explain her lack of feeling that day, except to say that perhaps some small part of her emotional gyroscope was protecting her.

But then, she can't always protect herself.

"It amazes me how much anger comes back," she says. "It lays dormant. It probably goes to my subconscious."

She describes the process as being sick, then getting worse. "We've all had a 102 fever and know what it's like to feel sick," she says. "But all of a sudden, if your fever goes up to 106, you really feel the pain."

She can't predict when the fever of rage will rise, though.

Flax will tell you that her friends don't entirely understand — and sometimes she doesn't understand, either. When Fred Goldman became so angry during the O. J. Simpson trial at the murder of his son, Flax could understand. But such societal guideposts are rare.

She will tell you that she is a "believer in self-preservation" and that she made an important choice after her husband's murder. "I was very concerned that I could become this fragile, bitter woman who hated the world," she says. "Or I could be a survivor. I chose the latter."

But the rage still scares her. She hopes the rage will end with Martini's execution.

"I will always have pain," she says. "But that raw pain is what you can't deal with."

Priest to the Dying

In these days of TV spiritual- ity, Charles Hudson was a man who found his calling in the quiet loneliness of hospital rooms, counseling those near death and the ones they would leave behind. On a winter's day, his heart finally gave out.

There is an ironic poetry to the way Charles Hudson died.

He spent his life counseling people in their loneliest moments, as a Catholic priest who specialized in finding comfort for those suffering from terminal illnesses. It was a job — in metaphor and in real life — that often seemed a hard treadmill.

On a Tuesday in January, Hudson's abundant, vibrant heart gave out while he was on an exercise treadmill. He was 61. He was home alone.

The night before, Hudson, a Catholic priest for 34 years, had gone to sleep, energized by the day's events, say friends. In a song-filled ceremony, he had been given Drew University's Martin Luther King Jr. Humanitarian Award for his belief in "the importance of equality and equal love for everyone."

Hudson, Jersey City–born, was not known as a proponent of civil rights — at least, not the kind usually linked to the legacy of Martin Luther King Jr. But his work with dying patients, first at Holy Name Hospital in Teaneck and later as the founder of a hospice, was something of a human rights movement of its own.

"He knew the wounds," said Margaret Coloney, his friend and co-founder of the Center for Hope Hospice in Union. "It was something he was meant to do."

Coloney was a surgical nurse in the mid-1970s and Hudson had just left Teaneck for a chaplaincy at St. Elizabeth Hospital in Elizabeth, when the two noticed a gap in treatment. Doctors were attending to patients' medical needs just fine, but the trauma of dying often seemed lost in the medical shuffle. From that was born a hospital counseling center. A few years later came the Center for Hope Hospice, which now has five buildings, 100 employees, and more than 300 volunteers.

At the center of this effort was a man who could be as comfortable in a somber cancer ward as at a raucous football stadium, who once told a church audience: "You want to know about suffering? I'm a season ticket holder for the Jets."

The remark drew laughs, but it underscored Hudson's serious side, too. He managed to put words on subjects that were often the most difficult to speak about. Often, he did it with a smile.

To know Hudson was to know an anomaly, however. While his ministry focused on death, he was hardly a morose man. Every inch of him seemed to speak of an active life, from his habit of bouncing on the balls of his feet as he waited for a meeting to begin to his preaching style, which ranged from the rat-tat-tat delivery of a cabdriver to the hilarity of a stand-up comic to the subtle eloquence of a Shakespearean actor.

His deepest sentiments came in the course of speaking about dying patients. He said on more than one occasion that he often caught a glimpse of God in the faces of people who die — not an easy statement to make when so many of those faces are pained and angry. "He was haunted by death and suffering," said the Rev. Frank McNulty, a Catholic priest and one of Hudson's closest friends. "He had a feel for people who faced death. He went through the pain himself."

Hudson was 15 when his father died of cancer. Two younger brothers died later — one by an accidental electrocution; the other in a hospital operation. His mother died of cancer before she was 60. "Instead of being bitter," said Margaret Coloney, "he took the pain and turned it around."

At Drew University he was given the award in memory of King after campus officials there read an essay by an 18-year-old freshman, Magaly Roig, who first met Hudson at a Catholic church in Westfield. On the day after they found Hudson's body, as Roig reflected on Hudson's death, she thought of this from one of his sermons: "Take hold of the people who you care about in life, the ones you love, and the people who love you, and cling to them."

"I remember hearing that and reaching for a pen and scribbling it down," she said. "When he spoke, his words stayed with you. He spoke from the heart."

Red's Song of Songs

New Jersey has an official flower, an official bird, even an official bug. But it doesn't have an official state song. In a state that gave birth to Sinatra and Springsteen, not to mention the Young Rascals and Frankie Valli, this is a big deal.

The voice wasn't Sinatra or even Axl Rose. But for a balding trombone player named Joseph Rocco Mascari, who goes by the nickname "Red Mascara" because he once had red hair, the voice was just fine.

The song, well, is another story.

Somewhere in a moment of unabashed civic pride, Red Mascara, a chemical worker who played jazz trombone on weekends, penned a song that he called "I'm from New Jersey." That was 32 years ago. John F. Kennedy was running for the White House. The Beatles were four years away from their American invasion. Bruce Springsteen was just another skinny 10-year-old.

But if you happened to stumble into a political gathering near Mascara's western New Jersey hometown of Phillipsburg in 1960, chances are you could hear him. Today, Red is 70, retired, but still singing:

> *I'm from New Jersey,*
> *and I'm proud about it.*
> *I love the Garden State.*
> *I'm from New Jersey,*
> *and I want to shout it.*
> *I think it's simply great.*

Obviously, this is no ordinary lullaby. To sing of New Jersey is to see beauty beneath the image of garbage, highways, and TV ads with Telly Savalas urging you to come to Atlantic City. (Bay-beee!) In other words, you've got to love it.

Red Mascara loves his state so much that he feels Jersey needs an official anthem. If New Jersey had an official bird (the goldfinch), an official flower (the violet), and an official bug (the honeybee), why not a song? New Jersey is the only state without an official tune.

"I'm patriotic," says Red. "I thought it would be nice to have it."

So began a three-decade campaign to convert the tone-deaf souls in the Land of the Slow Dance — otherwise known as the state government in Trenton — to adopt "I'm from New Jersey" as the official state song.

When he wrote his Jersey anthem, Mascara already had some small success — his tunes were recorded by such modest groups as the Do-Re-Me Trio and the Three Clefs. But "I'm from New Jersey" has been his passion.

Of course, not everyone was moved to swoon. Walter Kern, then an assemblyman from Ridgewood, noted in 1986 that Mascara's song seemed "inappropriate, considering the dignity the state has attained." This was before Kern went on to the dignified status of pleading guilty of witness tampering in a state ethics probe of his own law practice.

Then there is the 1972 reaction of Governor William T. Cahill. After hearing the song, Cahill reportedly proclaimed those two words that every songwriter surely dreads:

"It stinks."

Cahill's statement, accompanied by his veto of the bill to adopt the song, was the closest Mascara ever got to his dream. The Assembly and the Senate had overwhelmingly endorsed the song. For the final passage, Red even took a six-piece band to Trenton and crooned "I'm from New Jersey" from the Assembly gallery.

Bills to endorse the song are introduced almost every year, but support seems especially strong now. The Senate bill has 31 co-sponsors. The Assembly version has 66. And Governor Florio has shown some support in the past. He was a co-sponsor when he served in the Assembly in 1970 and 1972.

Red has seen such hopeful signs before. And then, after support seemed to slip away, he always came back. In a way, he's a fixture in Trenton. Oh, yeah, the guy with the song about Jersey.

"They have to be ready," he says. "Just like the nation is ready now for a national health plan, the time has to be ripe. I just have to wait until they're ready for me. I'm always hoping it will be my year."

So says the trombone player who has been trying for 30 years.

Last Hurrahs

No elected official in American history served longer than Frank Rodgers. Officially, he didn't retire, though. He just decided not to run again for mayor.

Frank Rodgers, Democrat and mayor, is calling it quits.

Oops. Mistake.

"I'm not quitting," says Rodgers. "I'm just not running again."

This semantic footnote is important to the man who has ruled over the hard, Hudson County industrial landscape of Harrison since the days when America was the only nation in the world to have a nuclear bomb — 24 consecutive, two-year terms.

To quit in this town is to walk out with your job unfinished, and Frank Rodgers will have nothing of that. He intends to retire gracefully when his term ends this year. He is 84.

It's time, he says. Forty-eight years is a long time. When he was first elected he was only 36 and just out of the Army's World War II counter-spy service — an apt prelude to Hudson County politics.

Rodgers made his first challenge on Palm Sunday, 1946, refusing to back off the ticket even when pressured by Hudson's Democratic boss, Frank Hague. He announced his retirement last week, on St. Patrick's Day. If nothing else, the man has a sense of poetry.

He also retires with a record. *The Guinness Book of Records* says he has served as mayor longer than anyone else in American history. And for Harrison, one mile square with only 13,425 residents, this is a bit of a coup. The town can boast of having been listed twice in the Guinness book — the last time for something far less prestigious, however. Two decades ago, the town was named as having "most bars, per capita."

Today, there are 45 bars left, where once there were 72 to serve the triple shifts of factory workers.

But over the years, the factories moved out. RCA is gone. So is Crucible Steel. Along Harrison Avenue — just around the corner from "Frank Rodgers Boulevard" — the old bakeries and clothing stores started by Irish and Italian immigrants now share the block with a "Dentista" and Hong's Gift Shop.

Frank Rodgers endured, however. "You go where the people take you," he was saying one day recently.

Rodgers leaned back in his desk chair that sits beneath a framed 1960 photograph of him with John F. Kennedy. He ran a hand through his gray hair, then thumbed the lapels of his three-piece blue suit.

"My secret?" he asked himself, repeating a question. "I don't know. I like to ring doorbells, I guess."

When Rodgers ran for reelection, he walked the streets of his town, exchanging hellos with the couples on front stoops or with the kids who played basketball with hoops nailed to telephone poles. Harrison is one of those towns where neighbors still mark parking spaces by putting kitchen chairs at the curb. Rodgers' secret was ringing doorbells.

"He's the godfather to everyone in town," says florist John Pereira. "He brings in services and jobs."

"He listens to people's problems," says his first and only secretary, Marion Borek.

And one more thing: Frank Rodgers has never been accused of political scandal. He was never paid more than $1,000 a year in salary. For the last 10 years, he did his job for free.

But two years ago he stopped walking the streets. Rodgers, who earned his living with county and state political jobs, broke his right kneecap, and during the 1992 campaign he was laid up in bed. He won by only 111 votes. In a town where Democrats outnumber Republicans 3,296 to 223, this was the political equivalent of a small earthquake — not enough to knock down buildings, but enough to make them shake.

And so Rodgers wrote a two-page letter to the town. "Harrison is a very special community. We are a family," he wrote. "It has been an honor to dedicate my life to your needs and dreams."

He knew every doorbell, too.

Pressed Flowers

We have many ways to organize our memories, from scrapbooks to hand-written journals to computer disks. But sometimes this process is as haphazard as life itself.

The father sits downstairs in the silence of a room he calls his office and listens to the rustle of a daughter packing for college. He wonders how time passes so fast.

Fifteen years ago on this weekend, he and his wife moved into the house with two small girls. Back then, the weather was skin-glistening humid, just like it has been this past week. Back then, the living room was filled with boxes, too.

But back then, the boxes were filled with toys and baby clothes. The daughter's boxes now are filled with CDs, computer equipment, a hair dryer, a dictionary.

The father notices his own dictionary, sitting in its handy spot to the left of his computer. It is a special book to him — and not just because he desperately needs it to check his impossibly bad spelling.

Over the years, the father found another task for his dictionary. He kept his daughter's memories there.

We all need special places for our memories, special harbors where we can anchor old photos, old newspaper clippings, old letters. Some of us turn to scrapbooks or albums or cedar chests — even safe deposit boxes.

Long ago, the father turned to his dictionary — a stocky Webster's New World edition that began with the word "A" and ended 1,557 pages later with "zymurgy." Randomly and with no long-range plan in mind, he began to press dried flowers in the pages.

These were not ordinary flowers from the garden. On page 679, next to the word "imprint," he placed the white carnation his older daughter gave him when she graduated from eighth grade. On page 1124, next to the word "reliquary," he placed another white carnation, this one from his younger daughter when she graduated from eighth grade.

In all, the father pressed 10 flowers in his dictionary, all brittle pieces of the heart now, each of them a special key that unlocks an important moment in the special time lines that families draw through life, some-times in a meandering course, but nonetheless in a course just the same.

The father smiled at how he had not followed any plan in placing the flowers in his dictionary, say, with the oldest flowers at the beginning of the book and the newest at the back. Instead, the father stuffed the flowers randomly in the pages, not even noticing if he had chosen a page with a meaningful word.

Over the years when an important occasion with his daughters took place and when some sort of flower was exchanged, he would take a souvenir flower for himself and crudely press it for weeks between paper towels and a stack of books. After the moisture left the petals, he would open the dictionary and slip the flower between the pages with a piece of scrap paper on which he made note of the date and significance of the flower.

He turns to page 257 — a page with the words "civil engineering" — and notices the yellow rose from his older daughter's high school graduation awards ceremony only a few months before. He flips through a few hundred pages to a white carnation from a special school breakfast that he and both daughters had attended years before.

The father smiles again. These are not fancy flowers. No orchids or birds of paradise. The years are marked by solitary roses and carnations, occasionally with a few stalks of baby's breath. And yet, in these ordinary, common flowers, the father has placed a most extraordinary, uncommon memory — his own, often unplanned life with his daughters.

Over the years, he often planned to take these flowers from the dictionary and place them in a frame to hang on a wall where everyone could see and notice and remark about them. But he never got around to that sort of formal safe-keeping. Life, he has learned, doesn't allow too much time for marking important dates in such formalities.

Life gives you random moments you try to save, even now as one daughter heads to a college dormitory and the other follows her heart and dreams of a life as a dancer.

This is why the father keeps the flowers in his dictionary on his desk. Each time he turns its pages, in search of a spelling or a definition, he knows he will find something deeper, lasting, too.

PART TWO
PLACES

Boardwalk to Nowhere

Many towns have something that is a source of humor. In this town, the government built it.

If you study a town long enough, you can find signs of dreams that just didn't work out.

In tiny Bogota in central Bergen County, when people discuss unfinished dreams, they usually point to a 200-foot-long expanse of lumber, chain-link fencing, and pipes that looks out on the Hackensack River.

To locals it is "the boardwalk to nowhere."

If truth be told, the structure on the western edge of the town's eight-acre Olsen Park really is a boardwalk. It is made of boards, and it's designed to be walked on. You can even gaze upon the unmighty Hackensack River as it flows under a low, steel bridge, past the walls of a new hockey rink, and southward under a railroad bridge and past a concrete plant.

The view does not exactly conjure up a Jersey shore boardwalk at sunrise. But occasionally a real seagull drops by Bogota's boardwalk. And just this past spring, a white egret took up residence in the river mud flats.

But real people on Bogota's little boardwalk are as rare as snow in July. And this mysterious phenomenon is part of an ongoing town joke.

"There are more garbage cans than people," said Wolfgang Albrecht Jr., Bogota's recreation director when the boardwalk dream was conceived and now Bergen County's recreation director.

There are two garbage cans, by the way. And the town's current recreation director, Eric Schubiger, concedes that he actually has found someone "once in a while" who eats lunch on the boardwalk.

But most people who visit the site, he says with a hint of mournfulness, just sit in their cars in a nearby parking lot and look at the boardwalk as if they fear being arrested if they venture near it.

Albrecht, who like many in Bogota chuckles at the irony of the town's trying to construct a boardwalk overlooking what otherwise is a body of water that doesn't inspire you to break into "Ol' Man River," tries to explain how this started. "We had a vision," he says, "and it hasn't been fulfilled yet."

Bogota's current mayor, Steve Lonegan, puts it a little more harshly.

"It's a monument to incompetence," he says. "It should be put on a postcard as an example of what you shouldn't do. The boardwalk from nowhere to nowhere."

Needless to say, Mayor Lonegan is pleased to tell everyone who will listen that his Republican administration is not responsible for the boardwalk. Indeed, when he ran for mayor in 1995, he featured the boardwalk on campaign fliers as a reason to toss out the Democratic mayor, Leonard Nicolosi.

Lonegan won. And now he chortles: "That boardwalk got me elected."

Nicolosi will tell you, however, that the boardwalk helped get him elected, too.

When Nicolosi ran a decade earlier, he was pledging to carry out the town's dream to refurbish its park. Times, as they say, changed.

"It's affectionately known as the boardwalk to nowhere," says Nicolosi. "Even my kids call it that. I always have to swallow hard when I hear that."

If you listen to him, you can understand Nicolosi's sadness over this. The boardwalk was part of a larger dream the town had envisioned for its park. But, as with many dreams, years and money can take a toll.

In the early 1980s, Bogota's Oscar Olsen Park was long overdue for an overhaul. The baseball field needed new grass. The basketball court needed new baskets. The road and parking lot needed paving.

Like many towns at the time, Bogota applied to the state for Green Acres funds — which the state was quite happy to dispense, but with one condition: Bogota had to do something about the riverfront in Olsen Park. Indeed, if Bogota demonstrated that it would improve its riverfront, the state would be more inclined to give it Green Acres money.

Here is where the dreaming went into overdrive.

Bogota was one of the few towns along the Hackensack River with a boat launch. Actually, it was just a ramp into the river from Olsen Park. But with the vision of Green Acres funds dangling before them, several town leaders felt that the park might be a site for a small marina. The idea coincided with an even larger dream by towns in the area to create a Lake Hackensack in central Bergen County, with all manner of canoeing and bicycle paths.

Wolfgang Albrecht remembers that Bogota wanted to be at the forefront of the movement to create Lake Hackensack. "Let's celebrate the river," he says, echoing a theme of the time. "It's not the prettiest river, but it is our river, and we didn't want to turn our back on it."

Needless to say, the plan to dam the Hackensack River and create a lake never came to pass. But Bogota's river plan, says Albrecht, "took on a life of its own."

The idea for the boat launch grew into plans for a boardwalk, with a gazebo where concerts could take place.

But while planning for its park refurbishing project, which would eventually cost $830,000, Bogota discovered it didn't really own the park. The state did, because the river once flowed through the park. Years ago, Bogota took over the park by filling it in. Before it could finish its park, the town had to persuade the state to sign over the land.

As for the boardwalk — well, the state would sign over the land and release the money only if the town improved its riverfront. "Passive amenities" is how former Bogota administrator Joseph Rutch described the plans for the river.

Rutch, now director of Bergen County's community development office, remembers feeling a sense of pride at Bogota's plans. "It was kind of unique at the time," he said.

But to follow the state guidelines, Bogota found itself spending $160,000 of its $830,000 on rocks for its riverbank and wood and fencing for its boardwalk. There just wasn't enough money for the gazebo.

Today, if you go to Olsen Park, chances are you'll find children on the baseball fields or the basketball and tennis courts. But look under the stand of poplar trees and toward the river, and you'll likely find an empty boardwalk that begins on a grassy knoll and ends on a grassy knoll, its macadam path winding toward the parking lot.

"It's going to sit there as a monument to half-finished projects," says former mayor Nicolosi.

But that doesn't stop some people from dreaming.

"Put a gazebo on it," says Wolfgang Albrecht. "It's a home run."

So Long, Fat Man

No greasy spoon lasts forever. When the end comes, sometimes it's an occasion for joy.

Business was getting thin anyway. Fat Man knew that. So after the last of the dozen or so Friday lunchtime patrons paid up, Frank "Fat Man" Perretti closed his 21-seat greasy spoon for good.

On Hamilton Street in Paterson, this was something of an event.

To mark the occasion, Fat Man gave away his dog-eared menus. For the last time on the stereo, he played his scratchy stack of Dixieland jazz records by Wilbur De Paris. Then he washed the 27 unmatched glasses, emptied the stainless-steel coffee urn, wiped the mustard-yellow counter, took the tea bags from a rust-spotted tin can, smoked his last Ray Del Ray cigar, told his last dirty joke.

"Everybody says this is a landmark," said Fat Man, who once tipped the scales at 342 pounds, but is now a trim 205. "Just leave me a $20 bill, and forget about it."

If you lived or worked in downtown Paterson, Fat Man's was not just another place to grab a hero and a Coke. It was lunch-hour vaudeville. For 32 years on Hamilton Street and for five years before that on Main Street, Frank "Fat Man" Perretti was emcee, prankster, cook, cashier, and bottle washer.

Now it's time to move on. The city health inspectors ordered improvements — or leave. Fat Man is leaving.

Next Saturday, Fat Man turns 83. He may work in a supermarket to supplement the Social Security checks that support his wife and dog. He also wants to perform more stand-up comedy. For $100 a night, Fat Man will tell jokes. But there's a catch. Fat Man performs at "stag parties and bachelor affairs only." Fat Man doesn't want to spread himself too thin.

Fat Man, who dropped out of school in the fifth grade to become a bellhop, refuses to call himself a retiree, but on that last Friday lunch friends gave him a retirement cake anyway.

"Put candles in it," someone yelled.

"How 'bout this cigar?" Fat Man shot back.

In between jokes, Fat Man served up 35-cent coffees, Taylor pork roll sandwiches "without grease," and triple deckers called "Gangplank" and "Chipmunk."

He's never charged for tomatoes and lettuce. "We steal it," his sign outside said. And Fat Man never charged sales tax. He paid it out of his own pocket. "They don't bother me," his sign said. "I don't bother you."

Plates, cups, glasses, and silverware never matched. Neither did the clientele. Judges sat with messengers, lawyers next to bookies. The waiter, half Italian and half Sioux, was called "Tonto" even though his real name was Joe Battalia.

Fat Man was the glue.

And no one was safe from barbs. To be insulted by Fat Man was to enter into a fraternity. The nastier the insult, the deeper the terms of endearment.

"I give out the abuse," Fat Man said. "What the hell, they expect it."

On good days, Fat Man might play his X-rated Tubby Boots album, "Thin May Be In, But Fat's Where It's At." Sometimes he served soft drinks in a glass that featured a woman in a raincoat. When the glass became cold from the ice, the raincoat disappeared, and the woman stared at you in her birthday suit.

"In here, you're liable to run into everything," said Fat Man.

And so on that Friday, Fat Man turned to Frank Antonucci and shouted: "He's so dumb, he thinks the Long Island Sound is a big noise!" Antonucci, who was nicknamed "Ho Chi Minh" by Fat Man but looks more like Paul Bunyan, shrugged sheepishly and smiled.

"I come here because of him," Antonucci said, paying his bill and shaking Fat Man's hand.

"Thanks," Antonucci told his friend. "You made life enjoyable in this miserable town."

Said Fat Man: "Don't let the door hit you when you leave."

Antonucci didn't. But you could tell he wished he could come back again and give it a try.

Baby Jaqueline

In the late 1990s, America came face-to-face with a problem long ignored – infanticide. The stories of middle-class girls from the suburbs killing their unwanted babies filled the papers. Here's a story from a forlorn city that barely attracted attention.

Baby Jaqueline died in an alley in Paterson where the morning sun draws long shadows and you can still find a cross of faded palms and wilted mums and a rain-soaked pink teddy bear that someone left behind in her memory.

Fourteen months ago Jaqueline Lucero Garcia's life was crushed on that somber, silent patch of Paterson.

Mom gave birth on the third floor of a house with pale green aluminum siding, then tossed Jaqueline out a window and into the alley where garbage cans sit and candy wrappers wrestle with the March winds. Maybe Jaqueline took her first breath in that three-story drop to the concrete. Maybe not.

A boy named Miguel found Jaqueline with her umbilical cord still attached. People remember that.

"The kid, Miguel, came in and said a baby was lying in the alleyway. I went out. The baby was blue. I couldn't look at her too long. You see, I have two kids of my own."

The man behind those words is John Grubb, and these days you can find him serving coffee and bagels in a delicatessen next to the alley on Paterson's Carlisle Street.

A few days after Jaqueline's body was found, Grubb's youngest son celebrated his first birthday, so you can understand why he has a hard time forgetting that scene of the blue baby. Even today, his voice falls off when he speaks of it.

"People still talk about the baby," Grubb was saying one recent morning. "Especially when there is something about that other baby."

The "other" baby, of course, is the one making all the news now, the story of the high school sweethearts from the wealthy and ordered ways of Franklin Lakes and Wyckoff, Brian C. Peterson Jr. and Amy S. Grossberg, whose newborn son was found dead in a Delaware garbage dumpster two months before Baby Jaqueline's head was crushed in the fall to the alley.

In a perverse way now, the deaths of those two infants — and others, too, including one who died last spring at a senior prom — seem intertwined, as if they are part of some alien quilt of misery in these days of job growth, declining crime rates, and mutual fund mania. But if these tales of infant killings are anything, they are reminders that our efficient nation is still capable of inhumanity and death that seem too meaningless.

To understand the power of that inhumanity and the questions it raises, all you have to do is go to Carlisle Street now.

"I can't believe she did what she did," said Timothy Hanlon, who is only 11 but speaks like an adult. "Why didn't she just put the baby up for adoption?"

Tim Hanlon was talking about Baby Jaqueline, but he might as well have been talking about the son born to Amy Grossberg in November 1996.

Around the corner from the alley where Baby Jaqueline died sits Paterson's School 7. Today, students will tell you how they marveled at all the television news crews that came to their neighborhood in January 1997 to tell the tale of the baby in the alley. "We couldn't believe it," said Faby Sanchez, a 12-year-old sixth-grader.

But in these quieter days now, when the TV cameras never come around anymore, students look back in a different way, too. "If the teacher asks us to write a report about something bad that happened, we write about it," said 11-year-old Brian Walsh, another sixth-grader.

Baby Jaqueline's mother, 23-year-old Bacilia Lucero, who came to America illegally from Mexico only months before her baby's death, was initially charged with murder but ended up pleading guilty to aggravated manslaughter after admitting she tossed her daughter out the third-floor window. "I feel bad for everything that's happened," she said at her sentencing in December, "and above all, I feel bad because I don't have the little girl."

Her accomplice who opened the window for her, Juan Diego Lucero, 21, a cousin who also emigrated illegally from Mexico, also proclaimed his sorrow when he pleaded guilty to reckless manslaughter. But last month, when he was sentenced to five years in prison, he added one footnote: "It was a very stupid thing."

Such words do not fully explain what happened in that alley on Carlisle Street. But they shed light on the inhumane enormity of that death and how it will always be linked in some tragic way to the story of Brian Peterson and Amy Grossberg.

"People compare this to that Grossberg baby," said Evelyn Rios, a 35-year-old mother of five, as she stopped by John Grubb's delicatessen on a Wednesday morning. "It shows the difference between rich and poor people. Those two kids from Delaware are out now on bail. The lady who threw her baby out the window hasn't seen the street yet. She never got to go to the baby's funeral."

Not that the appearance of a mother at the funeral for her dead baby would make any difference or that it might help the rest of us find a way to understand this tragedy. But Evelyn Rios has a point.

On that Wednesday, by the alley where Baby Jaqueline died, life went on in its most ordinary way. The newspapers were left by the curb to be picked up for recycling. Across Carlisle, yellow buds on the forsythia bushes were popping.

In the shadows of that lonesome alley of death, the cross of palms that someone once left for Baby Jaqueline months ago had been knocked down by the wind or by stray animals and was lying now next to a plastic lid from a coffee cup that someone had discarded. The pink teddy bear was lying facedown, a sprig of wilted petunias taped to its stomach.

If you turn it over, the bear is still smiling and its arms are still open, seeming to reach out for a hug.

Hoffa Goes Deep

It's New Jersey's great, unsolved mystery. Where in the world is Jimmy Hoffa's final resting place? Some think it's Giants Stadium. Some even hear voices.

Matty Butler never thought it would come to this. Most days, he pushes a broom through the stands in Giants Stadium. But on a recent Wednesday, he was faced with a higher calling.

Matty Butler was told he was cleaning Jimmy Hoffa's grave. He tried not to laugh.

Officially, Butler, 68, of North Arlington, swept the soot from Section 107, just off the corner of the western end zone at Giants Stadium, just below the Bud and Marlboro signs. But then *Playboy* magazine stepped in, and Section 107 became more than just another set of bleachers.

Playboy says Section 107 is Jimmy Hoffa's eternal end zone. You could say the former Teamsters boss has all-season tickets there. Unfortunately, he paid scalpers' prices, courtesy of the mob.

Hoffa's final resting place — if we can believe a *Playboy* interview with mob hit man Donald "Tony the Greek" Frankos — is in the concrete beneath the 40 rows of Section 107. Frankos, who is in a federal witness protection program and was paid an undisclosed fee by *Playboy* for his story, says the mob shot, dismembered, and planted Hoffa in that spot in 1975, before the stadium opened.

Maybe we should beware of a hit man bearing gifts, especially if his name is Donald but he answers to "Tony the Greek." Then again, this news could tell us much.

Consider "The Fumble." Section 107 overlooks the part of the goal line where Herman Edwards of the Philadelphia Eagles scored his famous touchdown in 1978 after recovering a fumble that Giants fans say was the low point in team history. That fumble seemed a ghostly act. Maybe now we know why.

Maybe now Giants linebacker Carl Banks knows why he hears voices when he's near Section 107.

"Oh yeah," said Banks, at his locker beneath Giants Stadium. "We were in a goal-line stand near there once. I heard somebody talking. Maybe it was Hoffa."

It should be noted that Carl Banks, besides having a talent for planting his helmet in the ribs of quarterbacks, also knows how to plant his tongue in his cheek. And it should be noted that Jimmy Hoffa has turned up in more places than Elvis. But who's counting? Inquiring minds love this.

If Hoffa's grave wasn't in a Jersey City garbage dump below the Pulaski Skyway, it was in a Florida swamp. Hoffa supposedly went to Florida in a barrel after taking a shortcut through a wood chipper.

But for those who didn't believe the Florida or Jersey City connections, there was always the trash compactor in Detroit, the concrete shoes in the ocean off Key West, and the foundation of the building in Cadillac, Mich. Take your pick.

Matty Butler knew most of the choices. And as he leaned on his broom, dragged on a cigarette, and looked over Section 107, he wiped the sweat off his brow and laughed. He also seemed to be measuring whether Section 107 was big enough for a man like Hoffa.

"Was he a large man or a small man?" Butler asked.

Pete Cardiello, 74, of Jersey City, another stadium janitor, walked over with an answer.

"I saw him in the movies, and he wasn't real big," said Cardiello. "But those mob guys are professionals. If they wanted him to disappear, he would have disappeared."

And not take up too many seats, either. Matty Butler pondered that. "Hoffa's really buried down there? I really don't want to walk on it. But we have to clean it. It's our last stop today."

A few rows over, Alonzo Bodin, 75, of Jersey City, switched off the hose he was using to wash down the concrete steps.

"Sometimes I think I'm stepping on him," said Bodin. "I hear all the rumors. But if you listen to them, you go crazy."

Alonzo Bodin turned the hose back on. He had a stadium to clean, a real game to prepare for.

Common Ground

What happens when a town long regarded as a model for racial harmony suddenly becomes engulfed in the fires of racial hatred? Suppose it's the town you now call home? For three years, I chronicled the travails of Teaneck, N.J., after a white police officer shot and killed a black teenager — a spark that touched off long-simmering racial tension. Here is a column about two men who tried to heal some deep wounds.

Racial harmony doesn't always arrive in loud bursts of revelation, with trumpets and cymbals. Sometimes it comes from a quiet exchange between people that begins with a hello and a gift of a garden tomato.

In Teaneck, a tomato changed hands more than five years ago. Art Gardner, a back yard farmer with a harvest to complement his name, gave a juicy, red beefsteak to Manny Landau, who was walking by.

It was the first meeting between the two men. But in a subtle, basic way that defines trusting, genuine friendships, that first meeting helped lead to another meeting last week that has brought a dose of racial understanding to Teaneck.

Art Gardner is black. Manny Landau is white and an Orthodox Jew. In Teaneck there was a real fear that blacks and Jews might square off in a suburban version of Crown Heights.

A group of black activists planned to march past five Teaneck synagogues during Sabbath services on an upcoming Saturday. The march was actually a response to a protest demonstration by the militant Jewish group Kahane Chai outside the Teaneck homes of Leonard Jeffries, who has provoked outrage over his anti-Semitic remarks, and the Rev. Herbert Daughtry, who has been accused of defending assaults by blacks against Jews in Crown Heights.

The Kahane group, which follows the bigoted teachings of Meir Kahane, an anti-Arab Zionist who was assassinated last year, still plans to march. But local black activists in the African Council canceled their march past synagogues. The reason: Teaneck's Jewish leaders denounced Kahane Chai.

The Jewish leader who helped forge the compromise and stepped forward to criticize Kahane's group was Manny Landau. The man who helped Landau contact local black activists was Art Gardner. In fact, Gardner's living room was the setting for leaders of the African Council and Jews to meet and settle their differences. The group sat in chairs in a loose circle. Behind them on one wall was a poster of Martin Luther King and an inscription: "An American with a dream."

A few days before, Landau knocked on Gardner's door asking for help in making contact with the African Council. It was not unusual for Landau to be talking to Gardner. In those years since they first met over a tomato, Gardner, a gym teacher at the high school, and Landau, a psychologist, had immersed themselves in community causes. Most recently, both had joined an informal dialogue between local blacks and Jews. But that group did not include the younger activists of the African Council.

Gardner knew one African Council leader, Bill Jones. "He was in my gym class years ago," Gardner said.

So Art Gardner called Jones. A day later, the groups were in Gardner's living room, sharing their differences and misconceptions.

The African Council assumed local Jews secretly invited Kahane Chai. No, said Manny Landau. In fact, the majority of Jews do not support the group.

"When the Jewish community said they had nothing to do with Kahane, that was a major breakthrough," said the African Council's Harold Eatman.

Both sides know their careful peace is not perfect, nor may it be lasting. A violent outburst by Kahane Chai could destroy it. But both agree they've made the basic contact that could lead to more — something like that gift of the tomato years ago.

"We're not friends per se," said Eatman. "But at least we know who we're talking to. At least we have a base to build on."

"Common ground" is how Manny Landau put it.

"A sigh of relief," said Art Gardner.

Seasonal Clothes

Chronicling the change of seasons is no easy task – especially when you're the only one wearing clothes.

HACKETTSTOWN — Carol, the strawberry blonde with the smoky voice and the pack of Newports within reach, describes herself as the sort of devout Methodist who usually starts each Sunday in church. But as she sits just now at a picnic table in the hills of western New Jersey, she is describing the naked truth about the end of summer.

"I have to put my clothes back on," says Carol, whose outfit on this day consists of three gold chains around her neck, a pair of sandals on her feet, and absolutely nothing else except sunglasses.

If the end of summer, signaled by the Labor Day holiday, is torturous for children who must shed the emotional and mental skin of vacation and return to school, consider the plight of a nudist colony whose members must now put on their real-world costumes.

"Back to the world of clothes" is how Maria, a 51-year-old computer analyst from Secaucus, puts it. "Disappointing," adds 73-year-old Stan Schwartz of Flemington, a former private investigator and one of the few nudists who would allow his full name to be used.

While some might find them archaic in these days of *Baywatch*-style bathing suits that reveal most everything, nudist resorts persist nonetheless. New Jersey is home to three nudist colonies, but nudists say they also congregate in several other spots, including stretches of the Gateway National Recreation Area at Sandy Hook.

Here, in the leafy hills of Hackettstown, on an estate with a century-old Victorian house, the Goodland Country Club and Spa claims some 500 regular members who pay as much as $700 a season each for the privilege of strutting their stuff under groves of birch trees and across a grassy meadow that leads to a swimming pool where the solace is broken occasionally by the snort and grind of a tractor-trailer truck on nearby Route 46.

The nudists here range from corporate executives to warehouse workers and teachers, would-be novelists to gas-station attendants and retirees. They come to play volleyball and Ping-Pong, picnic over fried chicken, or just to read the stock tables in a newspaper. Most say they do not size up each other's bodies, though some admit to stealing an occasional glance. "Look, I'm not blind," says Stan Schwartz.

But if you ask this disparate lot about the coming of the cold months of autumn and winter, each seems to express a similar sentiment.

"Devastating," says Brenda, a 54-year-old writer from Westchester and one of a handful of African-American nudists here. "For me, Labor Day is like the end of the year. September starts a whole new year. It's a time of restrictions."

Her solution: "I go naked in my apartment."

◆ ◆ ◆

It is midafternoon now, and the September sun tries mightily to warm the woods at Goodland. A thermometer on the outside of the bathhouse inches past 81 degrees.

The gravel parking lot is dotted with four-wheel-drive vehicles, many of which follow Route 46 into Hackettstown and make a turn by an intersection dotted with a muffler shop, a diner, and a video store. By the Victorian house, a hummingbird floats by a rosebush.

"For many people, winter is misery," says Goodland's owner, Jack Kozilius, a 62-year-old German immigrant who has worked as an advertising salesman and language instructor and says he bought the nudist park 24 years ago because "I thought this was a nicer way of making a living than owning a funeral parlor."

On a nearby knoll, Maria, the computer analyst, sweeps the porch of the cabin she rents for the summer and arranges a table with candles and a *Woman's World* magazine.

"When it's cold enough to wear a sweater or a jacket, it's too cold," says Maria, wearing only a T-shirt.

"I miss it a lot" during the winter months, said Mark Holley, a 27-year-old forklift operator from Mount Olive. "You find yourself longing for the summer months."

Indeed, Holley says he enjoys nude sunbathing so much that on unusually warm days in February, he has driven to the beach and stripped down to the buff.

In a lawn chair overlooking the pool, Harold Smith, 67, a former welder and mechanic from Boonton, squints into the sun. Brenda's husband, Jim, hands him a research paper he fetched from the Internet about the descendants of the racially mixed community of former slaves and Native Americans in the Ramapo Mountains. "You have all sorts of interesting people here," said Smith. "You don't find any dumb nudists."

Which is one reason Smith says he dislikes winter so much. "Depressing," he says, pondering what life will be like with reduced daylight, leafless trees, and threats of snowstorms.

Carol the Methodist, 55 and a former switchboard operator for an Englewood Cliffs firm who says she was raised "completely straight" in Bergen County, leaves her chair by the pool and stops by a picnic table where Peter and Maggy of Bergenfield are eating a lunch of cold chicken, tomatoes, and bread.

"In the summer, I'm a full-time nudist," says Carol, who spends winters in Florida and lives in one of the cabins at Goodland in the summer with her second husband, whom she met here.

"This is the real you," she says, not at all fazed that she is sitting across the table from a fully clothed journalist and photographer. In the outside world, says Carol, "you go back to putting on your pretenses. With clothes come pretenses."

For Carol, nudism is as much a mental exercise as a physical one. There is, of course, the decision — and then the act — of shedding her clothes, she says. But with that, she says, comes a mental freedom and peace that is hard to duplicate among people who wear clothes.

She admits, however, that she leads a double life "in a manner of speaking."

"Up here, people don't judge you by what you do," says Carol. "People get to know you and like you for who you are, not what you are. They don't ask you what your last name is or what you do. Up here, you're not judged by that. In a dressed community, you are. There is no way to put on airs while you're naked."

Peter and Maggy, both 62, nod in agreement.

"To take your clothes off, it's no big deal," says Peter, a former marketing manager who is wearing only a baseball hat and sandals. "When it gets cold, you put on clothes."

But, adds Maggy, smiling as she slices a tomato, without clothes "it's total freedom. It's total freedom, not to be encased in something."

Many head to warmer places for vacations. Maria plans to return to Jamaica and a nude resort. Carol says she turns the heat up in her Florida home and goes nude indoors.

But Stan Schwartz, who has no travel plans yet, says he is hoping for a warm autumn.

"If this were late September or October and it was a nice day," he says, "there would be guys up here listening to the Giants and Jets games."

Death on a Sidewalk

Death is a staple of news stories. But sometimes one man's passing makes you stop and wonder how such a thing could happen.

Friends say he fought in Vietnam, once worked at a drug store, and had a wife and a daughter. But Larry Magill loved the street.

On a lonely, cold Sunday, he died there.

On the sidewalk, behind Jim's Luncheonette, two blocks from Jersey City's Journal Square, Larry Magill froze to death as the mercury dipped to 18 and a 10-mph wind blew in from the west. A day after the authorities removed his body, you could still find his last possessions there: a two-day-old newspaper and a half-empty cardboard cup of black coffee, its plastic lid still in place.

Officially, Larry Magill, 41, goes down in the books as another homeless statistic, the first in New Jersey to die in this season's cold spell, the seventh in the New York metropolitan area. Surely, he will not be the last. And for that, we should be ashamed.

This nation proudly marshals its technology, political muscle, and money to save whales trapped in Alaska's ice, but it seems incapable of preventing people from freezing to death on city sidewalks. Indeed, we are no longer shocked at the vast number of our homeless people — or that some die so cruelly.

Larry Magill's death was front-page news in a Hudson County paper, but it was overshadowed by a story about a real estate salesman who went, as the banner headline proclaimed, "from newsboy to millionaire."

So much for our values.

On the morning after his body was found, you could find a few of Magill's friends walking by the spot where he died at Newark Street and Summit Avenue. On a speaker outside a nearby clothing store, you could hear "The Twelve Days of Christmas." At a grocery store, you could hear clerk Ray Diaz say that he didn't even know one of the neighborhood's homeless people had frozen to death.

"What can I tell you? They all look the same," Diaz said. "I don't have time to talk to the homeless people."

Police say Magill was found shoeless and bare-chested, and without his blue Air Force–style, hooded jacket. His friends say he may have died after thugs took his jacket and he sank into a drunken stupor.

But no one knows for sure. The day after his body was found, the pavement that became Magill's deathbed was still home to six cigarette butts, a blue button from Magill's jacket, and a matchbook from Bill and Ted's Sportsmen's Bar in Newark.

"He was happy being a drunk. The streets were his choice," said a homeless man named Richie, adding that he drank with Magill the day before he died.

On a lark that day, Richie says, he scrawled this message in black marker on the mustard-colored wall above the spot where Magill froze: "This is the end of dopers and drunks, all dead but too stupid to lay down."

On the same wall, Richie says, another homeless man wrote this: "May God give me one X-mass gift. A fast and quiet death and a free bus ride to heaven."

Richie said Magill was too drunk to help write any messages — or understand them.

"He wanted to sleep. He went to sleep," Richie said. "I told him to go to the Port Authority bus station. He wouldn't. His mind was shot."

Last winter, Magill and Richie "camped" in an abandoned house. This year, Richie found an apartment. Magill went to the streets.

Joe, another homeless man, says Magill's mother and ex-wife came around, trying to persuade Magill to find shelter. He refused to listen. They gave up.

But Magill wasn't abandoned.

Leonard Erwin gave Magill the pants he died in. Diane Fernandez gave him a lawn chair to sleep on. Manny De La Osa gave him money for coffee. On Thanksgiving morning, local residents brought him food.

For Christmas, Denise Walcott promised Magill she would make him lasagna.

"Don't worry," she told Magill.

"That's all I want," he answered, returning to his bed on a sidewalk in the richest country in the world.

The spot where he froze to death.

Trump's Neighbors

To understand Atlantic City is to tell a tale of two cities — the glitzy casinos and the neighborhoods left behind. When it opened, the Taj Mahal casino was billed by its owner, Donald Trump, as the greatest in the world. A few blocks away, life was far different.

Walk out the chrome doors of the Taj Mahal in Atlantic City, with its purple-magenta-lavender carpets and its sunburst chandeliers. Walk past the silver-turbaned "Sultan's Helper," past the impatient limousines and the hot-pink azaleas and the white stone elephants and the intense eyes of the security men.

Walk down the Virginia Avenue driveway that the Trump people insist on comparing to the Champs Élysées.

And say hello to Tyrone Gibbs.

Gibbs, 32 and just out of prison after serving 15 months of a four-year cocaine rap, is not impressed with his new neighbor's "billion-dollar dream come true."

The Taj Mahal may have 70 minarets and onion domes, 3,007 slot machines, and clerks who insist on telling you that "wonders never cease" when they answer the phone. But the civic improvements stop at the property line.

The neighborhood that Tyrone Gibbs shares with Donald Trump doesn't look like the "eighth wonder of the world." It looks like Berlin after the Eighth Air Force made a bombing run in World War II.

"This neighborhood," says Gibbs, "is gone."

On the day when Donald Trump was preparing to open his Taj Mahal, Tyrone Gibbs was standing on a patch of Virginia Avenue sidewalk outside Joe's Bar, where the door stays open 24 hours and you can hear the jukebox a half-block away.

Nearby, a dozen men sipped Bud or Bacardi. Gibbs wore a baseball cap that proclaimed what surely could be Atlantic City's unofficial theme: "Don't worry, be happy."

From his spot, Gibbs had a clear view of the Taj Mahal. And from the Taj Mahal, the best view of Gibbs' neighborhood was from the $1,500-a-night King Tut penthouse suite. Wonders never cease.

"Eighth wonder of the world?" said Tyrone Gibbs, nodding toward the casino's turrets and flags. "I'm living in one of the wonders of the world."

Gibbs' address is the Virginia Avenue Projects, a patch of brick, government-financed apartments surrounded by chain-link fencing. It's not Taj Mahal, but, like Donald Trump, Tyrone Gibbs likes Asian names. "We call it 'Little Vietnam,'" Gibbs says.

It's not a joke.

"The whole deal is that we're forgotten," says Rodney Nixon, 35, who works as a construction laborer and supports four children from three relationships. "There's a line between the casinos and the neighborhood."

Vincent Hood, 33, nods.

"They're trying to move us out," he says. "Look at this place."

Here or there, like a cactus in a desert, stands a home with a family. But most buildings are boarded up. And many lots are vacant, the result of too many fires or too much neglect by landlords.

"I used to live there," says Hood, pointing to a four-story apartment building at the corner of Virginia and Atlantic Avenues. "Sixteen families. Who knows where they're at now?"

It's the usual American urban story, with the usual cast of urban characters and the usual urban problems. The developers need land. The poor need a place to live. And too many of the young men spend their days with bottles, not jobs.

But in Atlantic City, in Donald Trump's new neighborhood, this scene goes beyond irony.

At the Taj Mahal, Donald Trump breaks even only if the gamblers lose $1 million a day in his casino. A block away, in the neighborhood of vacant lots, empty buildings, and men with bottles, no one breaks even.

And meanwhile, to get to the Taj Mahal, to lose their money, the gamblers must drive through a neighborhood of losers.

No wonder Donald Trump calls his new casino "one step beyond your wildest imagination." No wonder alarm bells ring when someone hits the slot-machine jackpot.

Village of the Darned

Towns pass laws to ban all sorts of things, from honking your horn to shopping on a Sunday. In this Jersey town, they banned cursing.

RARITAN —
Damn, this place is quiet.

But don't be fooled.

You can go to jail in this postage stamp of a town in the central New Jersey flatlands if you curse in public. The law says so.

But in the four years since Raritan outlawed cursing, no one has even been arrested for foul-mouthing off.

What gives?

"Cursing?" a 20-year-old mechanic, Steve Ackerman, said as he leaned against the outside wall of the Quick Chek convenience store on a sunny afternoon and pondered his town's ban on earthy speech. "I still curse. Everybody does. I could care less. It's a big joke."

Four years ago, in one of those nationally publicized quality-of-life moves for which New York's Mayor Rudolph Giuliani now is getting headlines, little Raritan banned cursing.

Yup. No ifs, ands, or ACLU. If you gather "upon the streets, side-walks, steps, or platforms of any store, business, house, park, church, or railroad station, bus or other conveyance, or within and around any building, dwelling house, office, place of business, factory, or private or public place" and use "profane, vulgar, or indecent language, by making insulting remarks or comments to others," you could go to jail for 90 days, pay a $500 fine — or both.

Anyway, that's what the ordinance said.

In the case of Raritan's battle with four-letter language, actions speak louder than words. And if you ask the police whether anyone has been charged with cursing, you come face-to-face with one of the strange ironies of Raritan's quality-of-life campaign.

"We've never arrested anyone just for cursing," said Raritan Police Chief Michael Sniscak.

This does not mean that Raritan's police are slacking off or have been cursed with hearing impairment. Nor does it mean that Raritan's 5,751 residents have all joined church choirs and look heavenward for angry inspiration instead of hell.

"I don't think the town has changed at all," says pharmacist Michael Phillips, who explains that he "wouldn't curse for the hell of it," but that others do. "I don't think the law has affected anybody."

Back at Borough Hall, Mayor Anthony De Cicco sits in an office where a sign tells you that "the use of profanity is the sign of the lack of spiritual growth," and tries to explain why an anti-cursing law was passed but no one has ever been arrested, even though most everyone agrees that most everyone curses from time to time. Even De Cicco, an ex-Marine who became a bartender, tells you: "I'm not a prude."

De Cicco, who has served as Raritan's mayor for 15 years, admits that he championed the ordinance as a way to dissuade young adults from congregating outside the local Quick Chek store. The borough had already enacted an 11 p.m. curfew for children, but it needed something else for those over 18. Plus, the mayor wanted to put people on notice that foul language could be a crime.

Before the anti-cursing law, De Cicco said, many young families had to walk through a "gantlet of vulgarity" as they parked their cars in the Quick Chek's lot and walked inside.

"New Jersey has the reputation as being vulgar or rude — which, to some extent, is true," said De Cicco. "It's this macho way of talking. The girls were just as bad as the boys. I don't want people to be subjected to that."

So why hasn't anyone been arrested?

De Cicco is well aware of the statistics, but is hardly miffed. He nods as if to understand, then explains one of his town's tidy little secrets.

"We can't stop people from cursing," he said. "But there are many times when an ounce of prevention is worth a pound of cure."

The main business district in Raritan runs for 10 blocks along Somerset Street. On one end sits the town's post office. On the other, separated by blocks of two-story, wood-frame homes long since covered with aluminum siding, stands a statue of the town's most famous son, World War II Medal of Honor winner John Basilone.

Along Somerset Street, you can walk by a place that repairs vacuum cleaners, a shop that makes trophies for baseball and bowling teams, a tailor named Gino, a bakery bedecked with signs announcing St. Patrick's Day, a place that sells guitars, a Roman Catholic shrine to the Blessed Sacrament, and a beauty salon called Sophisticated Lady where a woman named Hope Venerus holds court between washes, cuts, and hair spraying.

She sighs and rolls her eyes when asked about the ban. "It was a big thing initially," she says of the onslaught of media attention four years ago. "Now, no one talks about it anymore. And life hasn't changed at all."

Venerus happens to be president of the local Chamber of Commerce. She also happens to be something of a reluctant critic of the cursing ban — not necessarily because she likes to talk a blue streak, but because she knows human nature. And no human law can stop human nature.

"You're always going to have cursing," she says, gently spraying the hairdo of a middle-aged customer. "You're always going to have people pushing the limit."

A short walk from Venerus' beauty salon sits a mini-mall that the mayor claims is the epicenter of the cursing problem. And here lies yet another irony of life in Raritan: For all its notoriety in the eyes of the mayor, the Quick Chek is the town's magnet for fans of those dolls called "Beanie Babies."

Inside, across from a deli case and next to the bananas, dozens of the stuffed toys sit on a counter. And searching through a cardboard box for some hard-to-get Beanies, Mary Musto — "call me the Beanie Baby Queen" — is asked to ponder the cursing problem.

She frowns.

And laughs.

"Do I think cursing has stopped? No," she says. "Do I think anything's changed? No."

A Beanie Baby customer, Carol Kent, a nurse who grew up in Paterson and freely admits she knows a curse when she hears one, still laughs at the reaction of a friend when she announced she had taken a job in Raritan.

"My friend told me that if I stubbed my toe, I better not curse," said Kent. "So if I stub my toe, I have to say 'fudge' instead of . . .'"

Kent doesn't finish the sentence, but you get the idea.

Mary Musto listens and laughs, then suggests what may be the final irony of this talk of cursing in Raritan.

"Why did we pass that law?" she asks. "To get on the map."

The Old Corner (Micro) Bar

The old gin mill ain't what it used to be. Not in these days of boutique beer and microbrews. Not when you have something called the Fraternal Order of Foam.

It was a big moment one summer evening at Andy's Corner Bar in Bogota when Harry and Patty strolled in the side door and announced to the regulars:

"Tonight we break 100."

They were not talking beer mugs. Or bowling scores. Or golf. Or darts. Or the number of peanut shells they could stack on the bar.

Harry and Patty Pfaff of Fairview had chosen this night to cross into the nirvana of suds life at Andy's, and provide yet another bubble of proof that the gentrified Nineties are transforming the habits of one of the last bastions of working-class America: the shot-and-beer neighborhood pub.

That night, the Pfaffs chugged — oops, sampled — their 100th different microbrewed beer in a year, from breweries as small as a garage and as far away as the Czech Republic.

No Carling or Rheingold here, thank you. To reach that foamy pinnacle, the Pfaffs' tastes (and tolerances) ran from Wild Goose to Flying Dog to Hurricane Reef to Dixie Crimson Voodoo to Rasputin Russian to Jersey Shore Gold. And that's naming just a few of the beers listed on the four-page card that microbrew fans at Andy's keep on file like employee time cards to be marked each time they drink.

At Andy's, those who manage to survive 100 different microbrews achieve a singular honor: membership in the Fraternal Order of Foam. Their name is engraved on a plaque on a wall at the bar. They take home a windbreaker.

"The challenge," said Patty Pfaff, 37, a medical assistant in a physician's office, "was to find something we haven't had yet." Harry Pfaff, 37, a Nynex communications executive, nodded. "Variety," he said, "is enjoyable."

For the rite of passage to the 100th brew and in honor of the July Fourth holiday, Harry and Patty both chose a Liberty Ale. It was just after 10 p.m., and the event was framed in the sort of sociological schizophrenia that has accompanied the new beers into the old bars. The tavern TV was locked on sports (a baseball game between the Rangers and Rockies), but James Taylor was moaning "You've Got a Friend" from the jukebox. Above a smoky mirror from the days when drinkers chased their shot of whiskey with a beer, an old Budweiser sign looked down on a microbrew beer tap shaped like a goose neck and a display of small bags of Wise potato chips.

"You'll get the windbreaker in September at the party for everyone," said bartender Tom Gibbons as he smiled and took out a pen to mark the latest microbrews on the Pfaffs' beer cards.

While a mere ripple in the long river of beer history, this brief milestone at Andy's is significant for what it symbolizes. Once regarded as little more than a cute weekend hobby by beer lovers who concocted odd brews in basements and bathtubs, microbrewing has blossomed into what could arguably be called a pesky fly on the back of the muscular American beer business.

Today, the scores of microbreweries that produce some 350 different kinds account for 1.5 percent to 3 percent of all beer sold nationwide, according to industry figures. Such numbers are hardly cause for the stout giants at Budweiser, Coors, and Miller to break into a sweaty foam. But at places such as Andy's, microbrews have been the equivalent of a pacemaker for a tired, sputtering heart.

Only a few years ago, Andy's was barely paying the rent, said owner George Gray. On almost any weeknight now, the oval bar is packed, mostly with fans of microbrews. The regulars range from plumbers and electricians to lawyers, doctors, and Broadway musicians.

In another generation, when bleary-eyed men gathered in corner bars in the evenings to forget about factory jobs and trade tales about old boxers and new girlfriends (some of them actually true), beer was something of an afterthought. You could drop $2 on a sweaty bar and drink all night — and still go home with enough change to buy coffee, a roll, and a newspaper the next morning. Microbrews were like foreign films — rare, exotic, maybe a little unmanly, and known for a bitter aftertaste.

"Half of the beer we sell now is microbrews," said Gray, who not only pours the beer at Andy's but is the sort of drinker who can taste the difference between a Naked Aspen, an Old Peculiar, a Big Indian, a Big Muddy, and a Big Shoulders. "Budweiser still helps to pay the bills, but the microbrews give us a new niche. This is a form of entertainment. Some people go to the movies. Some people come here and sample the beer."

Gray, 48, took over Andy's from his father (and tavern namesake), Andrew Gray, in 1990. "We were strictly a shot-and-beer neighborhood bar," said Gray, who began working with his father in the early 1970s. "A guy came in on weekends and played the organ and we had a movie screen where we would project the words to the songs. Everybody around the bar would sing along."

As for beer, Gray said the tastes of the regulars ran from Ballantine to Schaeffer — and not much wilder than that. A 10-ounce glass cost you 15 cents. But in the mid-1970s, Andy's took a radical step and raised the price to 20 cents, then 25 cents. "One day we lost the old crowd," Gray said, "and the old crowd never came back."

What changed was a few customers bringing in a bottle or two of odd microbrews — or even home-brewed concoctions. Gray noticed customers seemed to like sampling the exotic, so he installed extra beer taps alongside the dependable sellers like Budweiser.

Today, as if to underscore the change taking place, Andy's has a Web page on the Internet, which includes nicknames of the regulars and advice on different brews. As for the price, microbrews at Andy's go for $2.50 or more, which means that drinking 100 different microbrews in a year requires more than just a hardy set of taste buds — it's a small investment.

For the Pfaffs — and the more than 150 others at Andy's who are members of the Fraternal Order of Foam — price is hardly a factor, though.

"There are some people who like to go to the same place in Wildwood each year for two weeks," Harry Pfaff said. "We like to sample different types of beer. That's us."

Down the bar, Edward "Skip" Mullen looked on and smiled as Harry spoke.

Mullen, 46, of Teaneck, a survey technician by day, is a charter member of the Fraternal Order of Foam by night — and largely regarded around Andy's as the tavern's equivalent to Norm on the *Cheers* sitcom.

But while Norm would routinely call out "beer" to *Cheers'* affable bartender, Sam Malone, Mullen is likely to ask for a Warsteiner. Wiry enough to look like a runner (which he insists he is not), Mullen also is about half the size of the beefy Norm.

Sitting next to Mullen was Charlie Kovacs, Andy's version of *Cheers'* Cliff Claven. Kovacs, 41, a senior project computer manager for a food manufacturer, drives several nights a week from his home in Lyndhurst to sample the microbrews at Andy's.

Indeed, Kovacs and Mullen have become such regulars at Andy's that they have special brass plaques to signify their spots at the bar.

On many nights, the two trade stories about beers. Mullen, who claims to have sampled 2,500 different microbrews and plans his vacations around stops at small breweries, said he has even sampled beer with chili peppers in it.

"I'll try anything once," Mullen said.

Kovacs chuckled as he listened. His worst experience, he said, was a lemon-flavored beer that foamed up in his mouth.

As for Andy's, Kovacs speaks of the bar as if he were borrowing from the lyrics to the *Cheers* theme song. "You kind of look forward to coming here," he said. "You get to know all the regulars. It's like a family."

Another member of the fraternal order, Jim Roselle, 35, of Ridgefield, claimed, "My problem is I went to Germany on business." After that, he would only drink microbrewed beer. He's even taken the extra step of brewing his own at home. As for the American beers he used to drink — "they taste like water," said Roselle, an engineer.

"I usually look forward to the fall so I can sample the pumpkin ales," said Alexi Browne, 37, of Teaneck, a videographer. "I actually look forward to the changing seasons so I can sample the different beers that come out."

To a dyed-in-the-hops Bud drinker, this might sound otherworldly. But to George Gray, it's evidence that beer drinking has come full circle.

"We once had 20 breweries in New York alone," he said. "This micro-brew craze reminds me of the time when we used to have a choice of all sorts of local brands."

A Question Called Camden

What can you say about a street with a prison on one end and a demolition company on the other? In Camden, one of America's poorest cities, I set out to find an answer. It was 1993, the middle of the gubernatorial campaign, and the candidates were all but ignoring cities and focusing their efforts on voter-rich suburbs.

Luis Samuel Plaza has these dreams: He wants to keep his two sons off drugs and away from stray bullets. He wants to stop arsonists from burning down an abandoned home he just bought.

And one more thing: He would like Governor Florio to leave his office on State Street in Trenton and pay a visit to his turf for a few hours.

Plaza's turf is State Street in Camden, one of the poorest streets in one of America's poorest cities.

On this gritty mile of hardship, there is a prison at one end and a demolition company at the other. In between, amid burned-out houses, welfare moms, and gangs that mark their turf with graffiti murals to dead comrades, are people like Luis Plaza — hardy, hopeful, and, yes, a little haggard.

"You can get everything here, from drugs to weapons," says Plaza, 41, standing outside his wife's beauty salon and across from the boarded-up, two-story home he purchased for $5,000. Someday, he hopes to turn the building into a small restaurant — that is, if it isn't torched first by gangs that have turned Halloween Eve's "Mischief Night" into an excuse to set fires.

Plaza, a landscaper who converted the trashy lot behind his home into a patio-garden by collecting broken bricks from demolished tenements and by planting banana trees and rosebushes, came to Camden 25 years ago from Puerto Rico.

He is one of the few here who actually have seen Florio in the flesh, even though both the governor and his Republican challenger, Christine Todd Whitman, have passed through Camden during the current campaign. But, as Plaza is quick to add, his Florio sighting was in a suburb where Plaza had a landscaping job.

In a way, it's symbolic of the campaign: The candidates have focused on the suburbs; the cities feel forgotten.

"People may tell me they want to move, but I have to try to make a difference," Plaza explains. "If everybody just leaves here, this would go like a jungle. I would like to see the governor come here and care for this jungle a little."

Inside her beauty salon, Elly's Cuts and Curls, where a sign still advertises back-to-school discounts, Plaza's wife, Elizabeth, echoes her husband's hopes. "We are trying," she says, "to make the effort."

She and her husband are quick to concede, however, that the odds are long for turning Camden around — or even getting politicians to visit.

On State Street, voter registration is less than 40 percent. Election Day turnout runs even lower, officials say. What's more, few outsiders pass through this Camden neighborhood, unless they come to buy drugs or they get lost on their way to the aquarium or the house where poet Walt Whitman once lived. If the outside world catches a glimpse of State Street and Camden's nine square miles at all, it's usually from a car while hurtling across the elevated steel and granite ramps to the Ben Franklin Bridge a few blocks to the south of Plaza's home.

And yet, here on State Street is a searing portrait of America's underside and a reminder during this gubernatorial campaign of the decay that grips New Jersey's cities because of crime, poor schools, and chronic joblessness among the underclass.

Once a bustling industrial town, with almost 100,000 residents, Camden's population has dwindled over the last four decades to its current level of about 87,000. About 16,000 poor whites still live there. The rest are poor blacks and Latinos.

Almost a quarter of all of Camden's adults are unemployed — a rate that is three times higher than the state's. Half the children live in poverty. More than half grow up with only one parent. The rate of violent crime is five times higher than in the rest of the state. The rate of teenage deaths — mostly from gunbattles between drug gangs — is 100 percent higher. Child abuse is almost 400 percent higher.

For all its troubles, though, Camden will always be part of any campaign that Jim Florio is in, if only in name. Here, where Democrats outnumber Republicans 12 to 1, Florio built a power base that took him to Congress and eventually to the governor's mansion.

Today on State Street, however, you don't see Florio campaign signs. It's hard to find a fan.

"Tell Florio he doesn't deserve a second term," says Michael Jones, 39, who is out of work and spending the day waxing a friend's car. "He's doing nothing for Camden. We need jobs."

Jobs. It's a common cry here.

Down the block from a graffiti message that proclaims "Snitches are Bitches" sit three women. All are single. All collect welfare. All find fault with Florio's plans to force welfare recipients to find jobs.

"They say they want people off welfare," says Towanda Swain, 21 and the mother of a 9-month-old daughter. "Why should I get off welfare if I can't get a job? I was upset that her father was not around. But there's never been a day when my daughter goes hungry. Anyway, my mom did it with me. I didn't have a father, either."

The other women nod. Crystal Coleman, 27, worked in a nursing home in Philadelphia. But trying to raise a 3-year-old daughter without a husband leaves little time to find a job or money for day care. Like many neighbors here, the women worry about the neighborhood.

"The abandoned homes just sit here," says Coleman, gazing down the block and counting them off. "One, two, three, four, five, six."

Swain glances next door and describes how drug addicts set a home on fire three months ago. "It's scary," she says. "We're afraid to sit outside. You never know if there will be a shooting."

"A woman was shot in the leg a few weeks ago," says the third woman, Margarita Vargas, 34. "Around the corner, there was a drive-by shooting two weeks ago."

"When it's dark," says Coleman, "we're in the house."

The women point down the block to a graffiti mural on the side of a building that depicts four young men. All were shot to death by drug gangs. The youngest was 14, the oldest 18.

Around the corner were two more murals. One, for a young man nicknamed Gadget, bore this epitaph: "Died making peace between two friends."

"When you die in Camden," says Towanda Swain, "they give you a wall."

"Pretty soon," adds Crystal Coleman, "they'll run out of room and start painting on the street."

One father who is trying to play a part in his son's life is Obanion Gordon. He is 35 and earns a living by selling homemade clocks from a vending cart in Camden's central business district. Each night, he returns to State Street.

"It seems that all the jobs go to people from outside the city," he says, wrapping a thick arm around his 2-year-old son, Ogbonna. "They come into town, then leave at 5. I stay because I'm trying to make the neighborhood better."

What remains, he admits, are many young men who turn to drugs. "Drug pushing is the biggest employer in Camden," says Gordon. "You can't get drugs out of a community without offering other opportunities. It's a way of life here. Some people want to make the neighborhood better, but I realize the environment is a teacher, too."

On State Street, the environment is ruled by the sound of gunshots.

"I've been shot at before," says Jerry Hack, 25 and a fledgling barber. "I've felt one go right past my head once. At night here, it's a war zone."

Near a mural to a slain drug dealer — "In memory of Carlos" — Sandra Perez, 34, pushes her 2-year-old daughter, Betty, in a stroller. "I usually don't come outside," she says, rushing past, her eyes sweeping the block. "All day, I just stay inside. It's dangerous. I wish someone in government would come here and do something."

As she stops to talk, Perez points toward the tenements, with their broken windows and sinking roofs. "Horrible," she says. As salsa plays from a boombox down the street, her gaze shifts toward a group of young men.

"Too many drugs," she says, nodding in their direction. "This needs to be cleaned up."

The young men down the block include two drug dealers, who give their names only as "Ponche" and "Garfield." For now, they rule State Street.

"I deal drugs because I can't get a job," says Ponche, wearing new Reebok sneakers, a purple sweatshirt, and a gold wrist chain.

Ponche, 23 and just back on the street after 18 months in prison for dealing cocaine, holds court at Fifth and State Streets. On a nearby stoop, with an empty bottle of Colt 45, sits Garfield.

Garfield, 32, peels back his shirt to show a red scar the size of a thumbnail on his shoulder. "I was shot three weeks ago," he says. "Got into an argument with a guy in a car over $40."

Ponche and Garfield both say their customers are usually local blacks and Latinos, as well as white suburbanites who pull up to the curb in their cars for a quick cocaine buy. Ponche reaches into his pocket and pulls out a wad of rolled bills to prove his point. Nearby, three teenage boys on bicycles wait. They act as runners and lookouts.

"Where could I get this with a real job?" Ponche asks. "On a good day, I gross about $800."

Garfield adjusts a black bandanna he wears on his head, and asks: "Do you prefer I stick somebody up or sell drugs?"

Ponche says he has tried to apply for jobs, some as far away as Cherry Hill. "But when they see the Camden address," he says, "there is no job."

Garfield nods. "If there were jobs, there would be no drugs."

At that moment, a gray Ford Escort pulls up to the curb. It's not a drug customer, but Ponche's wife and his two daughters: one 6 months old, the other 4 years old.

Ponche reaches into the car and picks up the 4-year-old. She is dressed for a party, in a white smock with red trim. Ponche holds her in his arms and smiles proudly.

"Do you know why I sell drugs?" he asks. "I do it to support her."

The girl starts to cry and Ponche puts her back in the car and waves goodbye. As he returns to the street to look for customers, he is laughing.

"In five years," he says, "if I'm not dead, I'll be selling drugs."

A Lonely Parade

*On the day America cele-
brated its victory in the
Persian Gulf War, I found
a mother in Newark whose
son never came home.*

For every brassy victory parade amid the fluttering torrent of ticker tape on Broadway, there is inevitably the quiet loneliness of a mother like Deborah Talley, who lives on a dusty dead-end street in Newark where weeds grow on a vacant lot with a bent basketball hoop.

Talley didn't go to the mega-event in New York City, dubbed "The Mother of All Parades." She was home on Triton Terrace in Newark with her wilted daisies from Memorial Day, her yellow ribbon, and her memories of her son Robert, who was killed in the Saudi Arabian desert.

After a war, we have our victory parades. But we also have our mothers' tears for sons like Robert Talley who don't come home.

Robert was only 18 when he was killed, the youngest casualty in a war in which only 146 Americans died in combat and another 122 died in auto accidents or from other "non-hostile" causes.

A year ago this month, Robert Talley graduated from Newark's Barringer High School. By August, he had enlisted in the Army, hoping he could earn enough money to go to college and become a doctor. Just after Valentine's Day, his Bradley Fighting Vehicle was hit by a rocket mistakenly fired by a U.S. helicopter.

"Friendly fire" is the way the Pentagon describes Robert Talley's death. Bitter is the mood Deborah Talley, 37, has tried to fight ever since, especially on this day.

A friend asked her to go to Manhattan to watch the parade. But Deborah said no. She didn't even turn on the television.

"To be honest I don't give a damn about the parade," she said. "I'm happy the soldiers came home. Don't get me wrong. But why should that parade mean anything to me? Why should I take part? My child isn't coming home. It's nice for those coming home. But . . . "

Deborah Talley's voice trails off, and she draws an imaginary circle on her dining room table with an index finger and gazes out a window. For a few moments, the only sound is the whoosh of trucks 100 yards away on Route 21.

"I feel left out, like I'm on the outside looking in," she continues. "I brought him into this world, helped him grow up. That's a part of me that won't be coming home. What can you say?"

Deborah Talley knows the answer to that question: There is nothing you can say when a son is killed by accident in a war. She will tell you the experience is surreal and that sometimes she thinks the footsteps on the stairs are Robert's. And then she falls silent again.

She turns to a shelf and her pictures and wipes a tear from her eye.

"Yes, that's him," says Deborah, pointing to a framed portrait of Robert as an 18-year-old Army private. His jaw is set. His eyes are determined, confident.

Deborah Talley holds the picture for a few moments, then reaches for the flag the Army folded into a triangle and gave her when they buried her son. And then, she again reaches for the shelf and Robert's black uniform name plates bearing the word "Talley" along with a brass circular insignia inscribed with "U.S.," and two gray badges that say "rifle" and "grenade."

"Pieces of metal," she says. "Don't mean nothing to me."

She worries now about her other sons, William, 17, and Ronald, 12. And she promises that, if there is another war, she will do everything to stop them from enlisting.

"The government got one of my sons," she says. "It won't get the other two."

As for herself, Deborah Talley says she is "holding on" and "taking things slow."

On the day of the "Mother of All Parades," a mother in grief walks downstairs to check her mail and scan her empty street.

"I'll get through it," she says. "I will."

War and Survival

One day, in an otherwise empty barbershop, I discovered that the man who had cut my hair for years harbored a painful secret. He had been a barber at Auschwitz.

Jacob Swierdlow points to a black-and-white photograph, faded and grainy, that sits on a lace tablecloth atop the dining room table of his Fair Lawn apartment. His index finger leads you past an iron gate and a courtyard, to a brick wall and the shadows.

"This is where they shot the prisoners," he says. "The black wall, they called it."

His finger moves to the right, to a building and more shadows. "This is where I worked. When we heard shots, we got very quiet."

On the 50th anniversary of V-E Day, as the world remembered the heroics of old soldiers and generals and political leaders, Swierdlow, now 75, widowed and a grandfather, contemplated the power of luck. His is a war story of personal survival, without weapons, amid uncommon horror.

He did not spend the war in a foxhole, in a bomber, or on an aircraft carrier. He endured more than two years of a killing field called Auschwitz, working in one of the 40 satellite slave labor sites that ringed the infamous concentration camp and its gas chambers where up to 1.5 million Jews and others were executed. A key to survival, he says, was a skill he learned from his uncle in the Polish city of Bialystok. He was a barber.

To be a barber at Auschwitz was to occupy a front-row seat to the daily horror of the Nazis — their sly combination of manipulative vocabulary combined with hair-trigger cruelty. Barbers were responsible for the shaved heads (and bodies) of prisoners — a dehumanizing regulation if ever there was one. In Swierdlow's case, he occasionally was ordered to trim the hair of Nazi guards, too — a cruel joke, considering that the men he was making look good were doing their best to destroy his people.

He concedes that his talent kept him from the gas chambers. "I wanted to live. That's what kept me going," he says. And yet, imagine the inner conflict. Swierdlow's eyes well up at the thought.

It was impossible to pick up a gun and fight back, and yet living required that you blot out the evil around you. Swierdlow's dormitory overlooked not only an execution pit, but a building where the Nazis carried out medical experiments on Jewish women. "I can barely think of it now," he says. "The screams and what they did. We tried to not listen."

This is not an easy story for him to tell. Inevitably it requires Swierdlow to ask himself how he survived and others did not. Of the 60,000 Jews from his hometown, fewer than 1,000 survived the war.

"You mean, why was I lucky?" he asks in an accent still laden with the hard consonants of his native Poland. Swierdlow pauses as he asks himself the question. He begins to cry. "I don't know," he says finally.

He refuses to call himself a hero. And yet, he traded haircuts with the Nazis for extra food for his Jewish comrades to augment the paltry diet of watery soup at noon and a tennis-ball-sized piece of bread for dinner.

He left Auschwitz on a forced march with some 58,000 inmates, passing through three other camps before finally being liberated by Soviet soldiers on May 9, 1945. He was drafted into the Red Army as a barber, later marrying a Ukrainian woman, and finally making his way to Israel in 1961 and the United States in 1964.

He cut hair in the Bronx for 20 years. These days, you can find him in a barber shop in Teaneck called Chubby's, where Frank Sinatra sings on the stereo all day and Wildroot is not a garden plant.

You will know Jacob Swierdlow by a tattoo of six digits on his left forearm, 100588 — the inky reminder of how his humanity was stolen by a force called Nazism. As humiliating as the tattoo is, he refuses to remove it.

"I'm proud of it," he says, "because I survived."

The Last Good-Bye

I spent a year chronicling life in a homeless shelter. One night, the shelter shut its doors.

There are few good-byes at a homeless shelter, no hugs, no promises to write or call.

But one night, as the azaleas bloomed and the calendar turned from April to May, a shelter in a Hackensack church shut its doors for the warmer months, and the regulars took time to ponder some of the basics of life without roots or promises.

"Where am I gonna sleep tomorrow?" asked a 55-year-old man named Brian who suffers from lung cancer and drug addiction and who wears a hollow-eyed look under a New Jersey Devils cap. "I haven't the faintest idea."

Brian's nightly home for parts of the past six months was a mattress on the linoleum floor of a hall at Hackensack's Christ Episcopal Church. Called "Peter's Place," the shelter is for those homeless souls who are barred from other local shelters because of addictions, mental illness, or a refusal to abide by rules that require them to hunt for a job or apply for welfare, organizers explain.

"This is for people who have fallen through the cracks, the most desperate of the homeless," explains the Rev. William Parnell, the rector of Christ Church. On this night, he adds a postscript, however. "This is a sad time for all of us."

Peter's Place, which was named after a longtime homeless-aid worker, only has so much money. No other church or organization is stepping forward with an offer of space. And so, on this night, the regulars at Christ Church are trying to say good-bye to the two dozen or so homeless people until November 1, when the shelter promises to open again.

It is a ritual that seems out of place, perhaps — this attempt to bid a fond farewell to men and women whose daily life is mostly a path of despair. And yet, it is part of the hidden life of America's homeless. Sometimes a shelter must close its doors.

It is 9:15 p.m. now. The homeless regulars gather on a deserted sidewalk across from the Hackensack post office, by a building that serves as a drop-in shelter. Earlier inside, a few watched *Wheel of Fortune* and

Jeopardy! A few others just sat blankly at tables. On a wall, a sign invites them to a Narcotics Anonymous meeting. The nearby counter is home to jars of instant coffee and non-dairy creamer.

On many nights at the pre-shelter, the homeless can take showers before heading to Peter's Place at 10 p.m. But tonight, there are no showers. Someone walked off with the towels that had been donated.

"That happens sometimes," says Marge Bueschen, a volunteer from St. Anne's Church in Fair Lawn, who chaperones the pre-shelter.

Maybe one of the homeless took the towels for a makeshift bed on the street somewhere. Bueschen doesn't know. "It's the end of the road tonight," she says, nodding across the room where a Tom Cruise movie, *The Firm*, now blares from the TV. "Tonight the group was a little quiet, though a few were talking about where they would go."

Outside, on the sidewalk, a 60-year-old man named Frank, who explains that he was evicted from his Fairview apartment when he lost his job as a pest controller, pulls on a cigarette and somberly says he'll head for a park with a sleeping bag "if worse comes to worse." Another man, Gary, says he just wants to "get out of the rain." Another man, Joe, a former health aide, shakes his head and says, "No idea."

Yet another — a 25-year-old named Kelly who is one of the few with a broad smile — laughs and says: "I was thinking of decking a cop and getting arrested."

"Don't do that," says another man, 41-year-old Eusebio, who lost his home, in a Moonachie trailer, when he lost his warehouse job.

At 9:35 p.m., a police car rolls to a stop by the curb — another regular ritual here. A window on the police car rolls down and a booming voice inside orders the men to "stop blocking the sidewalk" — which is otherwise deserted.

The men look, nod, and shuffle a bit. The cop rolls on. The men stay.

Just before 10 p.m., the group walks to Peter's Place, passing a few members of the church choir and a Bible study group who have just finished their meetings inside. The homeless carry orange cards — passes that entitle them to a spot at Peter's Place.

Once inside, the homeless seem almost businesslike in their routines. Each goes to a closet and fetches a mattress, then drags it to a spot. Then, each fetches a blanket and pillow.

Brian and Joe drop their mattresses by a bulletin board that announces a church cake sale and a picnic. Gary drops his underneath a clock. The half-dozen women who have come this night drop their mattresses behind a partition with a sign that proclaims "Hosanna."

At about this time, the night's first crisis of sorts evolves.

One of the homeless regulars, a 33-year-old man named Pat, announces he wants to leave. Robin Reilly, a client advocate at Peter's Place, puts an arm around Pat and tries to convince him to stay.

Reilly whispers that she suspects Pat wants to head to a local tavern. What's more, he just got out of jail after being arrested for public drunkenness. "Please don't leave, Pat," she pleads. "Why don't you stay here?"

Pat smiles and heads for the door.

Moments later, Reilly is standing in a storage room. In a stack by a wall sit plastic boxes, each a little larger than a hat box, each with a name scribbled on a swatch of masking tape. "Tommy." "Teresa." "Mike C."

Reilly explains that the boxes hold some of the regulars' belongings. "This is as much as they are allowed to keep," she says.

On this night, she is offering something else. She carries out plastic trash bags, each one filled with a makeshift quilted sleeping bag, sewn together by volunteers from old blankets and bedsheets. "We call them People Keepers," says Reilly. "Maybe this will help them."

Parnell explains that when it first opened in 1996, Peter's Place was only supposed to cater to homeless people when the temperature dipped below 40 degrees. "But we found that just didn't work," he says.

Over the next few years, the shelter grew in scope and promise. Today, some 200 volunteers from area churches lend a hand, too, cooking or chaperoning at night. Thanks to donations and grants, the shelter employs five workers.

At 10:45, one of those workers, Jose Gonzalez, flips the switch on a bank of fluorescent lights — the signal to the homeless that they have only 15 minutes until the room will be darkened.

At a table, Frank and Eusebio finish a card game. At another table, another man reads a "Batman" novel.

A man in a Knicks hat walks to a bathroom carrying a toothbrush. A woman combs her hair.

Another Peter's Place worker, Debbie Doyle-Levi, was not scheduled to work tonight but she came anyway. "I just feel this is my extended family," she says. "When someone doesn't have a home, it makes me a little humble, too."

At 11 p.m., Gonzalez flips the lights again, and the homeless head for their mattresses. "I won't be here tomorrow morning," Doyle-Levi calls out. "But I love you all."

◆

Morning comes early in a homeless shelter. At Peter's Place, Gonzalez flips the lights on at 5:15 a.m.

In the kitchen, where Gonzalez kept watch all night, a black-and-white television is tuned to an *I Love Lucy* rerun.

In the shelter, Eusebio is one of the first up. He heads for a bathroom with a toothbrush. Moments later, he returns with a telephone book. "I'm looking to see if I can afford a motel," he says.

Other men and women are up now, each dragging their mattress back to a closet.

At the front door, someone is knocking.

It's Pat, smelling like he took a bath at a brewery. An off-duty police officer picked him up and dropped him off. Once inside, Pat heads for a table with coffee and donuts.

The television now is tuned to a morning news show, and the homeless gather around to check the weather. One man asks if the Knicks won. Jose Gonzalez wipes down mattresses with a bleach cleaning solution. One of the homeless men grabs a broom and sweeps the floor.

A woman in a purple sweater sits at a table with a cup of coffee and explains, "I slept in the street for two years. I'm not worried now."

Across the room, everything she owns sits in a baby stroller.

"You got to do what you got to do," says one man who says he lost his home in a messy divorce that left him bankrupt. He says he feels lucky, though. He has a job driving a taxi.

Just before 6 a.m., the group drifts out, one by one. The eastern sky is now streaked with the dawn. A garbage truck cruises by.

Later that day, Eileen Wiest, program coordinator of Peter's Place, is also cruising the streets, passing out those homemade "People Keeper" sleeping bags to anyone who needs one.

Walkin' the Keys

Sometimes in the center of poverty, it's possible to find richness. I found it one day in the Paterson Library, where, besides books, you can check out the public piano.

Andre Brown sits at the piano as the morning sun peeks over a window sill. His fingers take a random walk on the keys.

Ping. He hits a solitary, careful note. Then a chord. *Hmmm.* And then, a hop, a skip, and a jump of serendipity. *Ping. Blink. Hmmm.*

"Nice, huh?" he says. "And a grand piano, too."

Brown smiles at the oddity. Here, on the second floor of the main branch of the Paterson Library on Broadway, down the block from a crack house, the Sweet Dreams laundry, and a liquor store where winos gather each morning with the rush hour, sits a shiny Steinway piano that anyone can play, no strings attached — except, of course, for the 264 that the library dutifully keeps tuned.

If there is a token presence of peace in this city of hardship, this may be it — a public-access piano. The library bought it in 1971 for $5,388.

Marian McPartland, the jazz pianist, has been here to finger-walk the keys. But she had an audience.

Most days, it's one player in this empty room, playing to an audience of portraits from the library's art collection. Above the piano hangs a painting of a young woman, casting a woeful eye. Next to her is a young boy, a satchel thrust joyfully over his shoulder.

Some days, a homeless man plays his saloon repertoire. Other days it's a jazz buff. Most days, it's Andre Brown.

He is 19 and a graduate of Passaic Vocational and Technical High School. Someday he wants to open a nightclub — and for that reason he takes business courses at Passaic County Community College.

His heartfelt dream, however, is to be a singer. He even has a name for his style — "Power soul." And when he sits before the piano, he admits it's hard not to dream.

"A piano," he says, "is my love."

He plays haltingly now, hardly in the league with Marian McPartland or even the jazz buff or homeless man he passes occasionally when he comes to the library. When he comes here, Brown learns as much as he dreams. It's been a long time coming.

He remembers his grandfather's house and the stand-up piano that he banged on as a young boy. He also remembers his first serious urge to learn piano.

It was five years ago, in junior high school. At the time, he was enrolled in a public school in East Orange that offered music courses. But the piano classes were filled. Brown settled for the guitar.

Then, 18 months ago, he happened to wander into the library's assembly room. There, by the flag, sat a piano with a cover over it.

"I never saw a piano before in a library that anybody can play," he explains. "It blew my mind. A piano in the middle of what people call the ghetto."

Brown will tell you that he meditates at the piano. "I close my eyes, and I swirl around in the darkness," he explains.

He also wonders about the real world outside the library's walls. At the library piano, he has written songs about young girls who run away from home and live on the street, about a man who finally has a family, about deception in a love affair, about hard struggle.

Outside on this sultry day, a boy and a girl play catch in a schoolyard. A group of men argue loudly as they stand by a car. From an apartment window, a baby cries. On a corner sits a trash-filled oil drum.

But all that may as well be in another city. In his room, by the piano that anyone can use, Andre Brown can be alone with his dreams.

Sometimes he arrives as early as 10 a.m. and stays as late as 5 p.m. At the piano, Brown has been known to lose track of time.

"Sometimes, they have to open the door and kick me out."

It's a mark of pride. Sadness, too, for the hard world still outside.

Grand Canyon

Crime crosses all boundaries. This story began with a gas station robbery in the heart of a city. It ended in a suburban church.

In a white clapboard church, under an azure sky, a golden sun, and maple trees whose leaves were shedding their summer's green for autumn's orange, city met suburb. It was not a happy moment.

A victim of a city slaying, Gary Donnelly, was eulogized in the suburban community of Emerson that he called home. And as 114 relatives and friends at the Emerson Bible Church sobbed or just hung their heads in the grief of the moment and tried to sing such hymns as "How Great Thou Art," a minister asked why. It was not an easy question.

"Why? That has to be the question," Pastor Gregory D. Stephens said as he stood before Donnelly's wooden casket and the nine floral arrangements in the background. "Why Gary? Why?"

Pastor Stephens paused, then answered his own question: "Because we live in a broken world."

The slaying of Gary Donnelly is one of those crimes that transcend geographical boundaries between cities and suburbs. In a way, it's also one of those senseless crimes — much like those in the movie *Grand Canyon* — that cause people to wonder just what is happening to their world.

Here are the facts:

Gary Donnelly, 24, was supposed to be married in about two weeks to a woman he met at Rutgers University when they were students there. The Rutgers chapel was reserved for their wedding. They were scheduled to seal the deal on a condominium.

But one evening, as he left his sales job at a Saturn auto dealership in Jersey City, Donnelly stopped for gas at a nearby Texaco station. So did a group of eight youths from Newark.

It should be noted that these youths, who were driving two Acuras, had their own line of work that night. Police say the gang had stolen the Acuras from Garden State Plaza in Paramus. To get to Paramus from their homes in Newark, they had stolen another car. And before dropping into the gas station, police say, the gang had also robbed five people in Jersey City — two 13-year-old girls of coats and jewelry and three men of $135.

The nightly score was three stolen cars and two armed robberies, from Newark to Paramus to Jersey City. And it was only 9:45 p.m., not even time for Channel 5 to broadcast its nightly parental public service message: "It's 10 p.m. Do you know where your children are?"

At the Texaco station, Donnelly pulled up to the pumps as the youths were robbing the attendant at gunpoint. Police say one youth turned, saw Donnelly, and fired a shot. Donnelly died at a hospital, a single bullet in his left side. The youths fled. The cars were recovered later in Newark and identified as stolen from Paramus.

What this slaying tells us is that drive-by crime is no longer confined to cities or their residents. This year, Paramus Police Chief Joseph Delaney expects a 15 percent increase in stolen cars at malls in his town — a jump of 150 thefts.

"Most thieves will be from Newark," he says. "That's where we find the cars afterwards."

On the morning of his funeral, such statistics of crime and punishment meant little to Gary Donnelly's mourners. They remembered him as a diligent leader of the church youth group, a young man who stayed out of trouble. Mostly they sobbed.

As Pastor Stephens ended his eulogy still asking the haunting question of why such a killing took place, and after Gary's cousin sang a gospel song called "Every Heart Is Breaking," there was yet one more song to be played.

At the request of Gary's fiancée, Anne Marie Buchner, the organist played "Somewhere" from that musical about boundaries and senseless crime, *West Side Story.*

"We'll find a new way of living.

"We'll find a way of forgiving.

"Somewhere."

O. J. and Us

Someone once said that malls have become the modern-day Main Streets. On the day O. J. Simpson was acquitted, I found myself in the TV department at Macy's at a Paramus mall.

We stood together between the stacks of crystal wine glasses and the bags of potpourri, a few steps from the ceramic wedding statues and a painting of two angels. Before us 69 television screens were tuned to that courtroom in Los Angeles.

It was 1 p.m. in the Macy's in Paramus, about as central a place as there is in the cultural life of northern New Jersey. We were white, black, Latino, and Asian, young and old, male and female, more than 100 in all. And when the verdict came in, some gasped, some cheered, and some walked away cursing. Most were quiet. It was that different, this aftermath.

There are moments when history comes knocking — and then you wonder: What next? What meaning should be drawn from it? How do you go on? Are you relieved or confused that something so monumental has ended so fast, with so much unanswered?

"My mother's going to go into withdrawal," said George Herrero of Bogota, describing his mother's daily habit of watching the O. J. Simpson trial. For himself, Herrero is left with a deeper predicament in some ways — cynicism. "This just means that money can get you out of any situation," he said.

"My heart was beating," said Oscar Vasquez. "But now? We just have to go on. You can't look back. Everyone's glad it's over."

Not everyone. Seated on a step in front of one of the Macy's screens, Lila Ginsberg, who is white and lives in Fort Lee, watched in silence, then shook her head from side to side as the meaning of the verdict became clear.

"I'm really distressed," she said, walking away with her sister. "I've really lost respect for our judicial system. It will further divide our country by race."

Just a foot away from Ginsberg stood a black man, Richard Cardwell of Teaneck. As the verdict was read, he leaned against a friend, his body sagging.

"He came here to support me, I think," said Cardwell. "He knew it would be emotional."

Cardwell, a computer consultant, followed the trial each day on television, even taping daytime court sessions so he could watch them when he arrived home at night. "I guess I'll have to find something else to do with my time now," he laughed. "But this obsessed me."

For Cardwell, the reasons are personal. Before starting his own business, Cardwell had been an IBM account executive. He had met Simpson during an IBM convention and admired him and the inspirational speech he gave. Cardwell had also been the victim of what he felt was racial discrimination by the Los Angeles police.

It was 1981, and Cardwell was in Los Angeles for an IBM meeting. For dinner, he and three other IBM executives — all of them black — took a drive to a Mexican restaurant in a rented Mercedes-Benz.

On the way back to their hotel, they were stopped by police, ordered out of the car, and frisked — then told to go on. "We were a bunch of IBM guys in white shirts and suits," said Cardwell, his voice rising as he recounted the story. "There was no reason to stop us."

It was such an experience that partly drew Cardwell to the Simpson case. And now? "I think the country has renewed its faith in the justice system," he says.

It went like that at Macy's, back and forth. A 28-year-old female attorney turned from a TV in disgust. "Right now, I want to get out of the law profession," she said. Nearby, Bill Hudson of Ridgewood said: "I think O. J. did it. But there was reasonable doubt, too."

It was a case as confusing as it was captivating. And the aftermath may be more of the same. As the crowd filed out, a young woman turned to her friends and smiled.

"This is history," she said. "We'll always remember we were here, watching the TV in Macy's. But we'll always wonder about it, too."

Like most of us, she left in silence.

The Day the Music Died

When a theater is reduced to rubble by the wrecking ball, something deeper dies, too. So it was with a Jersey rock-and-roll palace.

Chris Miller saw the crane and the wrecking ball, and suddenly the rock-and-roll memories played again in his head. He parked his truck. The delivery of electrical parts would wait.

It was a rainy spring morning in Passaic, and the old Capitol Theater was dying. Chris Miller wanted to pay respects.

All week on Passaic's Monroe Street, the mourners have come to watch the crane turn the Capitol into ragged piles of timber and brick. Like 29-year-old Miller, who is from South River in Middlesex County, a few stand by themselves. Others knot in small clusters by the tuxedo shop across the street or down the block by the X-rated book store as the theater walls tumble and secrets pour out.

On this morning, a plastic Christmas tree spilled onto a pile of plywood. The tree is broken now, a silent relic to those days when the theater had enough life to celebrate holidays.

A few onlookers, such as Ray Boria, 49, cheered this scene. "Oh, it was so disgusting," he muttered.

But most stared sullenly, wondering what's being lost here. In a city where empty stores seem to outnumber parking meters, the death of a theater is more than just another pile of broken bricks. One of the last theaters to die in Passaic was replaced by a McDonald's. Another is now a parking lot. The Capitol is supposed to become a mini-mall.

Chris Miller heard this news and just shook his head.

"They tear down a building," he said, "and put up a shopping mall. People can't afford it, but they do it anyway."

Nearby, 56-year-old John Mika of Passaic leaned against the tuxedo shop wall, his eyes following the swinging crane. "It's a sad day," he said. "I'm just bringing back all the memories."

Mika remembered how a quarter got you a bag of peanuts and another quarter got you into the movies. "For half a buck," he said, "you could enjoy yourself all day."

In the 1930s, the Capitol hosted vaudeville acts, including the Three Stooges. Then came the movies.

And when big movie houses died in the 1970s, rock-and-roll revived the 3,200-seat Capitol. The Rolling Stones played here. So did The Who and Bruce Springsteen. The last concert was March 11, 1989, with Duran Duran.

After that came the fires.

"You felt like they were performing at your house. It was more personal," said Chris Miller of the concerts. "You felt if you yelled, 'Good song,' they heard you."

"It had that musty odor, too," said Mike Apuzza, 30, of West Paterson, a substitute teacher.

That old smell still hung inside the theater, as Curt Phillips of Garfield and Jim Zangara of Clifton stood by a side door and mused about how the fires scarred the murals and the Romanesque arches by the stage.

"It was our Willowbrook," mused Zangara, referring to the name of a nearby mall as he shined a flashlight across curved rows of broken seats and wet carpet.

He is 35 now, but on this rainy morning he was 12 again, remembering how his aunt would drop him and a brother off to spend Saturday afternoons in matinee mischief.

"Yeah, me too," said Phillips, 42. "My favorite seat? Center, about the fifth row. Then, when I got bored, I'd head for the balcony."

In the balcony, if you were a kid in the Fifties, you threw candy on the patrons and dodged the angry prowling of ushers. But on the day the wrecking ball came, there was no candy. The floor was littered with cracked plaster and strips of an X-rated film with a woman in a black negligee — another secret relic.

"You can't replace this," said Jim Zangara.

"No," said Curt Phillips. "A piece of Passaic just died."

To be replaced by a mall.

The Land of Plenty

The murder-suicide of an elderly couple seemed out of character in a town as tranquil as Mountain Lakes — until I drove there one sunny afternoon as the oaks and maples were starting to put on their autumn coats and learned about a once happy life that became so sad.

MOUNTAIN LAKES — Three days before she drowned herself and her wheelchair-bound husband in their backyard pool in this idyllic Morris County town of tall trees, narrow lanes, and stout stone fences, 80-year-old Betty Schell drove to the local library. Among the books she selected was a Tom Clancy novel, *Without Remorse*.

If she wondered about the tragic irony of that title and the story of a man who leads a double life, she didn't say. When she dropped by a friend's house for coffee that day, Betty Schell seemed to exude the same portrait of grandmotherly stability and sweetness she always did, chatting easily about herself and her husband, Emil, who had been immobilized by a massive stroke four years before.

"She was just her old self," said Roland Sterner, a friend since the 1950s. "Ordinary."

But over the next few days, Betty Schell laid out an extraordinarily careful plan that seemed out of character to those who knew her.

She canceled her Saturday morning bridge game. She penned notes to police and her family of four sons and eight grandchildren. Late in the afternoon on an otherwise quiet Friday in September, she told her husband's nurse to leave the house on an errand.

Alone in the ranch home with her husband of more than half a century, police say, Betty opened the back door and rolled her 82-year-old husband to the edge of the pool, where she had planted red begonias earlier in the summer and where an empty green Adirondack chair still sat on the following Monday, seeming to beckon visitors.

Taking a rope, she tied her husband's hands and legs to the chair, looped the other end of the rope around her waist, and pushed the chair into the pool.

Prosecutors say the note she left proclaimed her "devotion to and love for her husband" but also the sadness that "they could not live life as they wished."

Officially, police list this as a murder-suicide. In Mountain Lakes, the residents see it less coldly. As library director Peggy Bulfer put it, "She did it for love."

"They were so devoted to one another," said the town's mayor, Duke Smith. "You just knew them, that whatever they did they did together."

• ◆ •

To say that Betty and Emil Schell were pillars of their community is something of an understatement.

Each week, Betty brought freshly cut flowers to the library. Each Saturday, after he retired as a mathematician at IBM, Emil met with friends to discuss retirement investments.

One summer, Emil challenged his town to a chess match, playing eight games at once in a town park and winning them all. He was on the school board. She joined the League of Women Voters and the local College Club. He kept an extensive collection of Duke Ellington records.

"That was one of his loves," said Smith.

Another was gardening. When he ran — unsuccessfully — for the Borough Council in 1972, Emil referred to his penchant for tilling the soil in his campaign literature.

"I enjoy mulching leaves," he wrote on a leaflet. "This is not everybody's idea of fun." Three days after their deaths, a rusted hoe and rake leaned against the back wall of the couple's empty home.

For most of their lives, the Schells lived in a three-story, white stucco mansion on a hill, framed by flowers and overlooking Mountain Lake and, beyond, the lights of New York City.

According to one local legend, silent film star Mary Pickford once lived in the house when Mountain Lakes was a country refuge from the bustle of New York City. In the Fifties, Sixties, and Seventies, when local community groups needed space for meetings and parties, the Schells donated the use of their home.

"I met them very early," said Smith. "They were one of only a dozen Democrats in the borough when I moved in in the Fifties. They were old, New Deal Democrats who admired [President Franklin Delano] Roosevelt and grew up in the era of social change."

The active life slowed four years ago, when Emil's stroke left him unable to speak, walk, or do almost anything without assistance. Two years later, the couple traded their mansion for a smaller ranch house. The move down the mountain symbolized how much their lives had changed.

"Mountain Lakes is a lot like a lot of suburbs," said the Rev. Larry Kalb, pastor of the Community Church, where Betty was a member. "The social life revolved around homes."

With Emil's condition, much of life in Mountain Lakes passed by the Schell house. To compensate, Betty became well known for her jaunts about the 3 1/2-square-mile borough of 3,900 residents. She had tea each week with a group of friends. And in summer, when the flower garden bloomed, she regularly left bouquets of flowers at the library.

In turn, librarians put together packages of books by such authors as Edgar Allan Poe and Mark Twain that Betty would take home and read to her husband.

In the days after the deaths, friends had donated a floral arrangement to the library in memory of the Schells. The bouquet of sage and ferns sat on the library's main desk, flanked by announcements for the garden club and a children's soccer league.

The Schells' deaths have left this town perplexed. There were none of the usual signs common to suicides by the elderly. While somewhat isolated, they did not seem lonely. Nor were they short of money. Emil's career as an IBM executive had left them well-off.

"There was no hint of despair," Kalb said.

Five days before he died, Emil marked his 82nd birthday. For the occasion, his friend Roland Sterner stopped by the house and gave him a bag of fresh corn.

"I'd talk to him," said Sterner, "but all he would do is grunt and smile. I can see where she had had it up to her teeth because Emil was just a shell of his former self."

But as well as he thought he understood his friends, Sterner realizes there was a side to them that the town never saw. Until now.

"We all agree we didn't know Betty," he said, "and we didn't know the Schells."

A Little Girl Named Megan

The murder of 7-year-old Megan Kanka is one of those crimes that resonated across America, inspiring the spate of legislation known as Megan's Law. What follows are two columns. In the first, I went back to the scene of the crime; in the second, I went to the prison where sex offenders are sent for rehabilitation.

This summer, 11-year-old Judyann Tomko stopped walking by herself on the quiet streets of her town.

"I am afraid," she said, "to be alone."

Judyann knew Megan Kanka.

In this 40-square-mile piece of Central Jersey flatlands where split-level homes now sprout on old farms, murder is as rare as the solstices — on the average twice a year among the 86,000 residents, police say. But the rape and slaying of 7-year-old Megan Kanka one year ago, allegedly by a convicted sex offender, has changed life here in ways residents say they are just beginning to understand.

You can find the change in small footnotes to life — Judyann's fear of venturing outside by herself. Or you can find it in larger trends — a doubling in volunteers, from 200 to 400, who offered to designate their homes as "safe houses" in case children fear being followed by a stranger.

But in Hamilton this is an especially somber time to mark how life has changed — and in this case, with a double-edged sword of emotions. On a Wednesday, neighbors were cheering the state Supreme Court ruling upholding the so-called Megan's Law that requires convicted sex offenders to register with local police after they leave prison. On a Saturday, they tearfully commemorated the first anniversary of Megan's killing.

Last July 29, Megan walked across the street from her two-story, cream-colored home to play with a dog, only to be raped and killed, allegedly by a paroled sex offender who was her neighbor.

In a brown house around the corner from Megan's, Judyann sits at the kitchen table with her brother and grandmother. It was on the Tomkos' front lawn that the petition drive for Megan's Law began. Judyann and her 8-year-old brother, James, set up a picnic table a few days after

Megan's death and asked people to sign a petition to enact a law allowing police to publicize the names of convicted sex offenders. "Together," the petition said, "we can prevent another senseless loss of life."

"I feel good for what I did," said Judyann, describing the petitions. "But now . . ."

Her voice trails off, and her grandmother, Gerry, picks up.

"It's almost like you feel you're a prisoner in your own home," she said. "The kids are afraid to go out anymore."

It was not supposed to be this way here. To drive into Hamilton is to pass the brick-and-mortar evidence of a town's attempt to retain its down-home quality in the midst of suburban sprawl. It is a town of front porches and flowerpots, of swept sidewalks, American flags on the front lawn, of gardens with statues of the Blessed Virgin.

It is now a town known mostly for one crime, even though the cold reality indicates that the town is virtually crime-free. Its rate of 1.5 violent crimes per 1,000 residents ranks far below the statewide average of 6.4.

"I moved here from Jersey City because I wanted a safe place for my kids," said Jesse Thatcher, the crime prevention consultant for the 100-member police department. "In some ways, there is a positive result in having people now becoming more aware of who their neighbors are."

But when awareness leads to fear, can the result be considered positive?

On Barbara Lee Drive, where Megan Kanka grew up, pink bows adorn trees and porches in her memory. The house where she was killed is gone now, bulldozed after it was purchased by the local Rotary Club. Residents are trying to turn the property into a quiet park — "Megan's Park," the sign reads.

On an otherwise pristine July afternoon, Peggy Easton, who lives next to the future park, stood on the edge of what will be a small lily pond and sighed. "It's brought us together as a community," she said. "But it's torn apart the family."

Easton not only knew Megan, she knew the man charged with killing her, 33-year-old maintenance worker Jesse Timmendequas. "He once helped my husband take a TV antenna off the roof. I never had any idea who he was."

Easton tells the story of that fateful day. She has committed it to memory. Megan, dressed in matching blue shorts and shirt, was reported missing around 7 p.m. By midnight, police had scoured the neighborhood, but were focusing on the house that Timmendequas shared with two other men — both former sex offenders — and the elderly mother of one of the men. A detective had spotted torn, blue clothing in the house. The clothing turned out to be Megan's.

As she tells the story, Easton recalls her last moment with Megan.

"The night before she died," said Easton, "Megan came over to our garden. She took some tomato seeds and asked whether a plant would grow if she planted them in her back yard. This summer, a tomato plant sprouted where she planted the seeds."

Down the block, Lesli Cetrulo takes groceries from her car. She, too, remembers Megan. The memory brings tears to her eyes.

"We now look out for each other more on this street," she said. "But this just killed our neighborhood. We're not innocent anymore."

JULY 30, 1995

In a room where an air conditioner rattles in overdrive as it tries to fight off the relentless humidity, five men sit in a circle of chairs. On the other side of a door, along a corridor bathed in yellowish light, guards talk loudly, their voices rendered hollow and indecipherable as they echo off the tiled walls. Beyond a window, coils of concertina wire gleam in an orange sun. Beyond that sit the towers, gray and silent reminders that every movement is closely watched.

The men are here, in a special prison of low brick buildings on a parched, treeless piece of landscape by Route 1, because they have molested children. They are in this room on the second floor of the Adult Diagnostic and Treatment Center — the prison's official name — because they have volunteered for therapy to learn how to control their predatory urges when they are set free.

But while every second of their present lives behind bars is monitored, it is the future on the outside they worry about now that the state Supreme Court has given its seal of approval to Megan's Law, the package of legislation named after a 7-year-old Hamilton Township girl who was murdered one year ago, allegedly by a convicted sex offender and former inmate here.

Two of the men in this room knew Jesse Timmendequas, the 33-year-old maintenance man who has been charged with raping and murdering Megan Kanka. (Three years later Timmendequas was convicted and sentenced to death.)

"He was a coward," says Mike, 55, a former contractor from Atlantic City who is serving 20 years for molesting his stepdaughters. "It's unfair we're all judged by what he did."

Under the new Megan's Law, sex offenders would be required to register with local police departments after they leave prison and possibly face public exposure in their new neighborhoods if local prosecutors judge them to be dangerous. The prospect has divided constitutional lawyers, police, and therapists, who wrestle with issues ranging from invasion of privacy and vigilantism by fearful neighbors to the cost of monitoring the whereabouts of hundreds of men long after they leave jail.

Parents of young children raise an equally compelling and reasonable argument — the right to know if a sexual predator is living on their block.

The debate, however, underscores yet another issue that cuts to the heart of what drives compulsive sexual predators to act out their dark urges: Would public exposure drive these men further underground? Would anybody really be protected as a result?

A man named George, his red hair receding slightly, leans forward and speaks: "I would be so afraid somebody would find out about me."

The other men in the circle of chairs nod in agreement.

"And if they did find out," says George, "I'd just move out of state. I wouldn't have a choice. I would be forced to run from one place to the next. My greatest fear is I'd have to start my life over."

Another man — Charlie — cuts in.

"I was a master manipulator," he says. "If I want to molest anyone again, I'd just move to California. But I also know that moving away would be the worst thing for me. I need to be around friends who can support me and keep me out of my offensive cycle."

George, unmarried, a 42-year-old machinist from Central Jersey, was a Boy Scout leader when he was caught fondling three boys. He is serving a 15-year sentence. Charlie, 34, the father of a son and daughter, who worked as a sound engineer in South Jersey, is serving 12 years for sexually assaulting two neighborhood girls.

Avenel — as the Adult Diagnostic and Treatment Center is called by those who work there — is one of only a handful of prisons nationwide that have been specially set up to treat sex offenders. There are 740 men here now, from physicians and ministers to those judged mentally retarded. Some are fondlers and flashers. A few are murderers. Their sentences range from two years to life. The vast majority — unlike the rest of New Jersey's prison inmates — are white, well-educated, and over 30.

It is here at Avenel that the hard work of understanding sexual predators takes shape. And yet, therapists who work with these inmates agree that it is a new science, akin somewhat to trying to discover cures for obscure viruses.

All the men in Avenel are judged to be repetitive and compulsive — two traits that are considered ominous among sex offenders. But there is no special pill they can take to stop what they do, no guarantee that when they leave they will be rehabilitated.

Dr. Nancy Graffin, who directs psychological treatment at the prison, compares it to alcoholism or drug addiction. "Every man who leaves this institution needs to continue in treatment," she says. "You don't cure alcoholism. You don't cure drug addiction. You don't cure repetitive and compulsive sex offenders. You have to get them into ongoing treatment."

Psychologists such as Graffin are part of a growing movement that believes one of the most effective ways to control sexual predators after they leave prison is to encourage them to enter programs akin to Alcoholics Anonymous where they can discuss their problems without fear of being publicly shamed. "We work very hard with these men," she says, "to break the pattern of secrecy."

But the belief that these men need lifelong therapy has partly fueled the grassroots movement that resulted in Megan's Law. If sexual predators are never really cured, say the law's proponents, then why shouldn't the public know who they are? What is more important — the privacy of sexual molesters or the safety of children?

The questions have constitutional, scientific, and common-sense implications — some of which are contradictory.

"As a mother I would want to know if a sexual predator was living across the street," said Graffin. "But as a professional psychologist, I can understand the dangers of exposing these men to public scrutiny. It would drive them further underground, which would fuel their most dangerous tendencies."

Charlie, the sound engineer, puts it this way: "Secrecy is the enemy of sex offenders. But secrecy and privacy are not the same."

The balance between allowing sex offenders to seek counseling for their most troubling urges while maintaining their privacy is delicate, notes Graffin. The life of a sexual predator is lived mostly in secrecy, she says.

"And shame," says Charlie.

"The feelings of guilt got to be too much," said George, the former Boy Scout leader.

"I hated myself for what I was doing," added Mike, who explains that shame drove him to try to commit suicide. "I put a 12-gauge shotgun to my head and pulled the trigger. I missed."

When he leaves prison, Mike vows to enroll in voluntary counseling programs offered free by the state in Trenton, Red Bank, Avenel, and Paterson. But he wonders if the public's anger toward sex offenders will spill over to demonstrations and even violence.

"I don't want these clinics to face the same problems as abortion clinics," he says.

Another man, Pete, 58, a former postal worker who molested his daughters, says he feels he would be able to handle the notoriety if he returned to his hometown and was publicly singled out by local police. "But I don't know if the public could," he says, wondering whether his neighbors would give in to possible vigilantism.

"I can understand the public's anger against us," said Joe, 42, a research biologist who has served four years of a seven-year sentence for abusing his son and daughter — actions, he says, that were the result of his being abused as a child. "But I'm afraid the movement toward more punishment will only do away with treatment for us. What's lost in the arguments over Megan's Law is the concept of recovery. My biggest fear is that people like me will feel ostracized. The key to recovery is maintaining relationships."

"If I get out I should be required to get treatment," says Mike. "Make it mandatory."

"And if a man refuses, put him back in jail," says Charlie. "If there's a man you have to notify the neighborhood about and he is not being treated, get him locked up. Don't give families a false sense of safety."

The Tree of Life

The old apple tree in the back yard never seemed like much — until it started to die.

Trees tell stories and teach lessons. Their growth rings remind you how hard the rain fell one summer, how dry it was the next. Their bark bears the old scars of violent lightning strikes, of muscular hurricanes, of icy blizzards.

Sometimes trees can tell you about people, too.

The father thought of this as he looked at the apple tree one day in his back yard. The tree is dying.

The tree was already aged when the father moved with his wife and daughters into the house back when Reagan was president and Lebanon was a military quagmire and hardly anyone knew about AIDS.

The apple tree's trunk was already as wide as a garbage can, its lower branches as stout as wharf pilings. Its leafy umbrella stretched skyward almost two stories. Its twisting, gnarled roots seemed to explore every corner of the back yard. Its bark, grooved and knotted like Churchill's brow, seemed capable of every expression and mood, from mirth to wisdom.

Each spring, the tree wore a white blossom blanket. By summer's end, it laid a carpet of red apples on the grass. One year the father collected almost 20 bushels.

And here, the tree taught the first of its lessons.

When the father paced the yard and picked up apples, his daughters helped, too. Each girl followed with a small bucket, racing from one red bauble to the next.

The father didn't realize it then, but the tree was teaching the daughters how to count — one, two, three, four apples. "Look how many I picked up, Daddy . . . I have more than her, right?"

Of course, the father credited himself for inventing this math lesson disguised as yard work. Back then, the father didn't understand the tree and what it could do.

By the next summer, the tree taught the daughters how to climb. The father also liked to think he taught this lesson, stepping from one thick branch to the next, then jumping down amid a tide of laughs.

But it was the tree who was the real teacher here, its quiet, unbending stability lending just the right level of encouragement that builds a child's confidence as she reaches for a branch on her own and discovers she can balance on it.

The father knows now that he can't really teach confidence, not like he can explain shoelace tying or bed making. But back then this apple tree could teach confidence — just by being there.

The tree became a secure canopy for a summer sandbox where the daughters learned how to share toys and space with each other. It shaded a birthday picnic where the daughters learned early lessons about friendships, good and bad, long and short. It served as a "third base" in games of Whiffle ball. One of its thick branches held a wooden swing made by the father's father — a reminder that simple, imperfect gifts, made by hand and heart, are sometimes the most valuable.

Each fall, the apple tree became a stage where the daughters watched hyperactive squirrels perform acrobatics with acorns from the nearby oaks. Each spring it served as a pit stop for the gang of pushy blue jays that passed through the neighborhood on the long flight north to Canada. "Daddy, do birds really fly that far?"

And then the tree taught its most important lesson — this time to the father.

The tree had begun to slowly die. First a branch fell, then another. Then a fungus invaded. Then rot set in here and there. The tree still gave birth to spring blossoms and summer apples, but each year's crop seemed smaller, less vibrant.

The father trimmed branches. He mulched the soil. He watered. He sought advice from friends who knew apples from oranges. The tree would revive, then falter a little more.

Several years ago, the father thought it might be time to cut the tree down. It was becoming ugly now. No more thick canopy. Almost no apples.

And then, one morning, he heard a shrill series of squeaks, like a cabinet that needs oil.

He walked nearer and listened, then noticed a hole in a thick branch, weary with rot. The father fetched a ladder and peered in.

A nest of baby sparrows.

That was two springs ago. This year, the father thought perhaps it was again time to cut down the tree. The cancerous rot was spreading.

And then, he saw another hole, another nest.

The tree will stay, the father has decided, until it dies on its own. Maybe it has more lessons to teach, more stories to tell.

PART THREE
SIGNS

Land of the Toxic Belch

Shutting down a tollbooth on the New Jersey Turnpike takes more than just an act of nature — or God. In this case, it took a toxic cloud.

The rotten egg smell hits you a mile up the turnpike, just before the cigarette billboard in Elizabeth conveniently announces, "Where the flavor is."

You pass by the sewage treatment plant and under the electrical wires and their Erector-set stanchions. And then, as the angled pipes of the Exxon Bayway Refinery loom over the old slaughterhouse, you arrive at the tollbooths in the Land of the Toxic Belch.

Count your change.

Take a whiff.

But don't bother holding your nose. It doesn't work.

Bill Armstrong can tell you that. He's a toll taker at Exit 13, and normally the exhaust fumes from the cars and trucks and the area's rotten-egg odor don't bother him.

"Part of the job," says Armstrong, 41, who has spent the past four of his 19 toll-taking years at Exit 13. "What are you going to do? You got to make a living."

But one day, Armstrong found he couldn't breathe and make change at the same time. The smell in the air knocked him and 16 other toll takers all the way to Elizabeth General Medical Center.

This time, it wasn't the usual rotten egg stink that turnpike drivers know is the most identifying characteristic of Elizabeth. The smell burned Armstrong's nose, squeezed his chest, made him dizzy.

"We were saying, 'My God, we know this place stinks,'" said Frank Barton, who was in the next tollbooth that day and went to a doctor the following morning. "But this was something we never smelled before."

Doctors gave Armstrong oxygen, a blood test for carbon monoxide poisoning, a chest X-ray, an electrocardiogram, and advice to "get some fresh air." But as he walked out, Armstrong fainted again.

Environmental officials told us that the odor was from a toxic belch, some sort of industrial burp of bad air. But within 24 hours, the state Department of Environmental Protection was announcing it was giving up the search for the source. The odor was gone.

No stink. No search.

"The only way we can find a culprit is to sniff it back to the source," said John Hagerty of the DEP. "It's not like a dead body. We had nothing to go on."

That may be true. But it would be nice if the state agency assigned to protecting the environment would at least fake some concern.

Exxon, meanwhile, promised everyone that it had checked its refinery and found no cause for alarm. This may be true, too. But then, Exxon's credibility is about even with Teddy Kennedy's.

"We don't think it came from our operation," said Exxon spokesman Douglas Walt. "The best we can determine is our operations were completely normal."

The bottom line here is that something belched, 17 people went to the hospital, and now life is supposed to go on.

At the tollbooths, Bill Armstrong stood inside the office and leaned against a wall with an Exxon calendar and a poster of an American flag that said "Honor America and help fight heart disease." He looked out at the snorting trucks and the white smoke rising from a refinery stack and wondered about his future.

"You don't know what it's going to do to you down the road," he said. "You don't know what's coming."

We don't know. But we do know this much:

The area around Exit 13 stinks — and that's not because of the hard work of men like Bill Armstrong. It stinks because we tolerate it, as we drive by and roll up our windows or ask the toll takers, "How do you stand it here?"

We also know that we have had a warning disguised as a toxic belch. Sometimes warnings teach us a lesson. So far, we haven't learned much except how to forget.

Grayness on the Edge of Town

New Jersey maintains a special relationship with rock-and-roller Bruce Springsteen. But that relationship is getting old.

The future of rock-and-roll stands before me, and it's an ironic sight to behold.

No, dear baby boomers, the future is not the hoarse-toned, carotid-bulging, Jersey-born-in-the-USA Bruce Springsteen — as a music critic suggested a generation ago.

The future stands now in Row 5 of the Continental Arena. It is well past 10 p.m. on a weeknight, and our man is soaking up the holy wash of a Springsteen rock sermon about girls, guys, cars, the night, loneliness, dreams, amusement parks, the road, and forlorn love.

Mister Future's hair is deserting him, but what remains is trimmed neatly, especially those gray wisps around the ears. He sports an expanding, spare-tire midriff, sagging jowls, and a weekend tan. He wears khaki pants and a white golf shirt with the name of an electronics firm embroidered over his heart. His wrist is home to one of those desk-clanging, Rolex-like watches with a metal band that resembles a bicycle chain.

He is, as they say, settled.

But on this night he is on his feet, dancing and pumping the air with his fists. And, with Saint Bruce leading the way on stage, Mister Future is singing in a full-throttle-wake-the-babies-don't-care-what-it-sounds-like chortle:

"Tramps like us, baby we were born to run."

Tramps?

Rock-and-roll may be an industry built on stars, but the chemical equation doesn't end there. It's also an industry of fans. And — how do I put this gently? — the fans are not as trampy as they once were.

They arrive in sport utility vehicles. They sip Absolut vodka in the parking lot. They chat on cellular phones. They pay almost $70 for the good seats — and that's after they fork over $10 for parking, $5.25 for a beer, and $30 for the souvenir T-shirt.

And, yes, some of them see the ironic humor in this. In the words of Springsteen loyalist Ed Myers, a 37-year-old real estate appraiser from

Hamilton who carries a business card with phone, fax, beeper, cellular, and e-mail numbers: "I hear a song and I'm driving down the shore with the top down on my car again. I feel like a kid again."

As he says this, he answers a call on his cellular phone.

Many rockers can spark feelings of youth and freedom and occasional recklessness. But Springsteen's fans seem a special breed. That Springsteen himself will turn 50 this year and that the rocker who gained fame for songs about the working class is now worth $90 million is part of the irony — and the humor, too.

We watched this happen when Sinatra grew old. The fans lost their Mack-the-Knife, rat-pack-wannabe swagger, traded bobby socks for leisure suits, got married, moved to the suburbs, and warned their kids not to go to Woodstock.

In another corner of their lives, they kept searching for the magic nonetheless. And so, when Sinatra would arrive in Atlantic City or at the Meadowlands, those fans would follow. But the event was not just about the music. The event was about sparking that old youthful chemistry.

With Sinatra gone now, here come Springsteen's "tramps."

Picture this: It is just after 5 p.m., a Wednesday. You are strolling through the parking lot of the Continental Arena. The Jersey sun is sinking into that section of Giants Stadium where Jimmy Hoffa is reportedly buried. There is not a piece of shade to be had.

But no matter. The parking lot is jammed with Springsteen fans and, if wheels are a barometer of success, this group is doing well. Jeeps compete for space with Explorers and BMWs.

As he describes his Springsteen loyalty, Ed Myers toils over a high-tech propane burner, grilling a feast of lobster tails and filet mignon for a group of friends who have set up a bar in the trunk of a Saab. Myers is something of an old hand at this. On this night, he is attending his sixth show in Springsteen's 15-show run.

But he is far behind his friend Chris Burek, 36 and a self-employed salesman from Allentown, N.J. This is Burek's 10th show. It is also Springsteen's 10th show.

"He's one of us," says Burek of Springsteen, suddenly correcting himself a bit. "Well, he's not really one of us. I don't make $90 million. But we all feel like we're 15 again. His songs mean something to you and it's personal. He has the ability to bring out those thoughts that you can't articulate. Everybody's been 15 or 16, and young and stupid. He makes it all right."

"It's a part of my life," adds Cindy Mathews, 37, a mortgage appraiser. "It's America."

Across the parking lot, Jeff Skalecki, a 28-year-old Bell Atlantic salesman, is on a stage with a microphone, singing a better-than-average rendition of Springsteen's "Hungry Heart."

"Everybody needs a place to rest; everybody wants to have a home."

The crowd of 200 mouths the words. Nearby, booths set up by the arena to evoke the feeling of Springsteen's Jersey Shore let patrons play boardwalk games. Here, you can shoot BB pellets and win a stuffed tiger. There, you can aim a squirt gun. A few steps away, you can measure your strength by pounding a mallet. Skalecki walks off stage, smiling.

"This crowd grew up with him," he says of Springsteen. "They now have their big-boy and big-girl jobs. But seeing him reminds them of their youth."

He pauses, then adds one more thought about Springsteen: "He's a great salesman and everybody's buying."

It is after 9 p.m. now, and Springsteen is in a full sweat. He has pounded through such anthems as "No Surrender," "Prove It All Night," and "Darkness at the Edge of Town." The whole arena seems to be singing, pumping air, swaying hips, playing air guitar — even tossing an occasional bra on stage.

Springsteen will announce later that this is a "rededication" to rock-and-roll and to the E Street Band that he formed in his Asbury Park days of the early 1970s. From his seat on the side, Peter Bidgood, who moved to Colorado after graduating from Fairleigh Dickinson University, talks of another type of values.

"The connection is family," he says, "and the way he brings us together."

It's almost 11 p.m. now. Springsteen has left, as has most of the crowd. On the arena concourse, Mel Bleemer, former accountant, strolls to his car with his wife, Reggi. He too has found something valuable here.

"I came fully expecting to go home with a headache," says Bleemer, of Cranford. "I was sorry to see it end."

Bleemer is 70, by the way.

And one more thing: He saw Sinatra, too.

Letter from the Abyss

Suicide is not painless – as the theme song for M*A*S*H suggested. Someone is always left behind. When a California man killed himself, his mother in New Jersey tried to come to grips with it.

Lenny Yedziniak said he owed everyone an explanation. So just before he popped the pills that killed him, he scribbled his final messages in a notebook.

There were notes to his parents in Saddle River, to his brother, to his grandmother, and to his new girlfriend.

But from his home in northern California, Lenny Yedziniak penned his longest note to a 4-year-old girl with a lively smile and blond bangs — his daughter, Christine.

"To you, most of all, I beg forgiveness," the 32-year-old Yedziniak wrote to his daughter, who lived with her mother in Hawaii. "Drug use brought me to the level of life I'm living today."

There was more.

Yedziniak pleaded with Christine to be honest "even if it may cause you to be punished or embarrassed."

He advised her to stay off alcohol. "If you do that," he wrote, "you shouldn't have any problem staying away from all drugs."

And, finally, he hinted at his own despair. "I had one more chance to have a real meaningful life, and drugs blew it for me. I was going to reenroll [in college] this spring to get a teaching credential which would permit me to work with kids in wheelchairs. But I lost it all. So don't use drugs for fun ever please.

"Maybe I'll be lucky enough to get reborn as one of your lifelong friends or something. That'd be cool. Man, I love you, Christine. Please don't be angry with me. Just don't do dope. Please don't be mad at Daddy for going away forever. There is really no other choice."

On a rainy afternoon, before a fire in the living room of her Saddle River home, Lenny's mother read her son's notebook again and groped for answers.

It was not easy for her. Along with the note for Christine, there was a final message to her.

"My suicide," Yedziniak wrote his mother, "is not meant to hurt you. For one thing — you'll never have to see me fail again."

Yedziniak's mother shook her head. She could do nothing else. How do you explain how your son got hooked on cocaine and sank to the bottom when other young men got jobs, got married, raised children? How do you accept it?

She said she always did her best. She sent her son to prep school, gave him extra money, welcomed him back even when he went months without calling.

And now this.

"I knew he was smoking pot and he drank more than he should," she begins, describing what she learned of her son's jump from marijuana to cocaine. "But . . ."

Her words trailed off.

"Most kids were doing it," she continues. "They never got hooked. And Lenny got hooked."

Another victim to the junk we stupidly call "recreational drugs."

Lenny Yedziniak scribbled his last words around 6:30 p.m. on December 8 in the apartment he shared with his new girlfriend. Only a few weeks before, he wrote in an upbeat Thanksgiving card to his parents that "everything appears to be rolling in the right direction."

He had a new therapist to help with his addictions. But he had troubles, too. He had lost his taxi driver's job.

But suicide?

"I really couldn't believe it," his mother said, remembering the call.

After writing those final messages, Lenny took a blanket and a pillow and drove his 1972 Ford Maverick 30 miles up the California coast to a grove of redwoods. He drank a half-quart of milk and, the local coroner said, swallowed as many as 60 chloral hydrate tranquilizers and an unknown quantity of two other tranquilizers, Lorazepam and Dilotid.

Five days later, hikers found Yedziniak's body in the grove. It was the same spot where he and his girlfriend planned to be married.

Today, his ashes are scattered there.

Battling Bedsheets

I once saw a Klan cross burning on a vacant farm field in Alabama. In New Jersey, the Klan doesn't hold cross burnings; they call them "cross lightings." And when they feud, they call the ACLU.

It's not easy being a white supremacist, even if you're a wizard with a pointy hat and an empire to run. People make fun of you and point fingers. Sometimes they steal your fire.

Such is the plight of Richard Bondira, grand wizard of the Invisible Empire, Knights of the Ku Klux Klan, in New Jersey.

Poor Richard. He lays claim as the one, only, and authentic KKK Invisible Empire grand wizard in the state. He would like you to feel sorry for him. He feels put upon.

Being grand wizard means you're supposed to be in charge. And normally that's not much of a problem, since most people don't have the mental dexterity to run an invisible empire. Usually only a few people are dumb enough.

But along comes Joe Doak.

Doak, of Clayton, a town in Gloucester County, says he's grand, too.

What bugs Bondira is that Doak also lays claim to being the one and only guy in charge of New Jersey's Invisible Empire. These being hard times for Kluxers, there's not room enough in this state for two top hats.

Only Joe Doak is not a grand wizard. He's a grand dragon. This means he's a step down on the Klan scale, and ought to listen to the wizard.

But Doak, by day a cashier for Philadelphia's subway system, says Bondira is not a wizard at all, not even an official, sheet-wearing member of the Invisible Empire.

Doak says Bondira is a fraud who was "banished" from the Invisible Empire for being too much of a pain in the sheets.

Bondira, 38, of Oxford, in Warren County, explains that he voluntarily split from Doak's group and founded his own Invisible Empire — and filed copyright papers in his own name — long before Doak's crowd organized.

And you thought the Bible was complicated?

"Joe Doak is a joke," Bondira says. "He's a fraud, a phony. He is claiming he is a grand dragon. What kind of proof has he got? Doak is the grand imposter. I'm the grand wizard."

And wizards are supposed to be the only Kluxers who can appoint grand dragons.

Enter the imperial wizard, J. W. Farrands of Shelton, Conn.

Farrands says he's the guy in charge of the Invisible Empire and that Bondira is merely a maverick.

"We don't even answer Bondira," Farrands says. "He's such a fool. He stole our name. He's nuts. Did he get a little wild with you on the phone?"

No, just loud.

It should be noted that the Ku Klux Klan is not the World Boxing Federation — or even the World Wrestling Federation.

If one joker claims the title, you can't call Don King or Andre the Giant to arrange a bout in an Atlantic City casino and settle matters.

Why not a lawyer then?

Bondira says even the ACLU turned him down. Poor guy. And he says Doak has the audacity to send out literature using Bondira's symbol for the Invisible Empire.

"We have a right to go out and fight for the good name of this organization," Bondira said.

Richard Bondira would like you to know that he does not permit violence in his Invisible Empire. His boys never threaten blacks or Jews. And they never burn crosses.

"We call them cross lightings," Bondira says. "We're an educational, non-profit, private, fraternal order."

Being a grand wizard, Richard Bondira also is smart enough not to embarrass himself by revealing how few people actually join the Klan. "It's a secret," he says. "And you can't have a secret organization without secrets."

By contrast, Bondira says it's no secret that Doak is recruiting "all the white trash."

"I'm not after quantity," Bondira says defiantly. "I'm after quality."

And grand wizards know quality when they see it.

Squirrel and Me

I love animals — really. I just wish they wouldn't drop in unannounced. And when they do, why can't they behave?

I stand in my attic, face-to-face with a squirrel, fat, furry, and probably pregnant. In my left hand, I wave a dust mop. In my right, a squirt gun.

America may be at peace, but this squirrel has chewed its way into my attic. I have decided to draw a line in the attic dust.

The squirrel laughs.

Actually, the squirrel hisses. But I have come to believe that a squirrel's hiss is really a laugh, haughty and mocking, which translates into:

"Hey, jerk, nice attic. Love the dust. Now, why don't you go downstairs and let me raise my family in peace? Otherwise, it's the mother of all battles."

I wondered about rabies and the headlines if I was found curled up and babbling with my mop and gun. Then, the squirrel hissed again.

I pulled the trigger.

I realize animal-rights types are probably hissing as they read this. So be it. I, too, love animals. It's just that I prefer a wall between the animal kingdom and me. Outside, they're cute. Inside, they're coats.

Anyway, it's a Saturday, and I'm a little desperate. This strange ballet began at 6:30 a.m., when I first heard the squirrel, who had already scratched through gutter, siding, and shingles, and was now working on its final obstacle, a wood beam.

As the sun climbed above the trees, I climbed a two-story ladder to check the damage. The squirrel watched me from a nearby gutter, its tail twitching and a smile creasing its face.

Trust me on the smile.

I banged the gutter. The squirrel didn't flinch. I climbed down and threw a stick. (The stick clanged into a neighbor's garbage can.)

But at least the squirrel left. I climbed up again and sprayed insect repellent on the hole. (It was all I could find at 6:30 a.m.)

Within the hour, the squirrel was back. I waited for a hardware store to open, figuring I needed something besides bug spray.

"Oh yes, squirrels," the hardware man said. "We get 'em every day. Big problem. Dried animal blood does the trick. Spread it around the hole. They hate it."

I passed on the blood, and instead bought metal screening to cover the gutter and steel sheeting to cover the hole. But first, how do I get the squirrel out?

"What you need is pest control," the man at the animal shelter said.

In the Yellow Pages, you can find companies with such inspiring names as "Animal Busters," "Exit," or, my personal favorite, "Bliss Exterminator." Most specialize in "all your exterminating needs." I was impressed.

Nonetheless, I phoned a man recommended by the shelter. He suggested a "long-term plan" with a "humane trap," and "transporting the animal to a spot 10 miles away so it can't find its way back."

He also wanted $200 and "at least a week" to do the job.

It was now almost noon, and I was not looking forward to a long struggle. I turned to a daughter: "Do you still have your squirt gun?"

My strategy was simple: Drench the little bugger. Worry later about the attic.

And so, I squirted — and squirted. I emptied two guns. I also screamed "GET OUT" and shook my dust mop a lot.

The squirrel stayed put.

Hiss. Hiss. Laugh. Laugh.

I finally reached for a box of mothballs and threw handfuls. The squirrel was not impressed. She even picked up a ball and chewed. She also hissed more.

I thought again of rabies. So I climbed down, figuring maybe I would try the "long-term" trap.

As for the squirrel, I think she finally got tired of living in a wet attic that reeks of mothballs. An hour later, she was gone.

I patched the hole, but a few days later — at precisely 6:30 a.m.!! — she was back. She scratched at the patch, but gave up. I guess she finally got the message. I've drawn a line in the attic dust.

Between Tears

How do you find peace in a racially charged community? After a white cop shot and killed a black teenager in Teaneck, N.J., a town long regarded as a model for racial harmony, I embarked on an unsettling journey into the frayed state of race relations. Part of this journey included a trial where a verdict didn't bring closure but deepened the divide.

One side of the courtroom seemed to lift upward, gasping and cheering, breaking free finally in a sigh of pent-up relief at the news that Officer Gary Spath was not guilty. The other side sobbed, collapsing into anger.

In a way, the end of the Gary Spath trial in Courtroom 138 was the perfect metaphor for this two-year ordeal that has divided races, communities, people.

On one side, euphoria.

All-right!

The other side, anger.

No. No. No.

If there was any common ground in this loud moment of anger and joy, it was in the tears.

Gary Spath, charged with manslaughter after he killed 16-year-old Phillip Pannell almost two years ago, bear-hugged his attorney, Robert L. Galantucci, as the jury foreman pronounced the verdict and the cries of joy filled the court-room. And then, tears rolling down his cheeks, Spath walked to the first row of the spectator seats and hugged his wife, Nancy, her eyes also teary.

Six seats away in that first row, there were also tears. But they were as different as the versions of truth in this case.

Thelma Pannell, the mother of the 16-year-old black youth who was shot in the back by Spath in a Teaneck back yard almost two years ago, bent forward, her sobbing rising in volume as the cheers subsided on the other side of the room.

"Why Lord Jesus?" she cried. "Why? No. No. Why Lord Jesus, why?"

By her side, her sister, Dale Monroe, stood, shaking her right fist at the jury box, her face convulsing in the portrait of anger and rhetoric that has seemed to follow this case since that day in April 1990 when Spath fired his gun because he thought the teenager was trying to pull a gun from his coat pocket and shoot him.

"How the hell could you do this?" she yelled to the jury as a sheriff's officer stepped in front of her, asking her to sit down, and the jurors looked on in silence. "My sister has suffered for two years. Not guilty? I'm getting my sister out of here. We expected this anyway."

Thelma Pannell rose from her seat and on the arm of a minister, the Rev. Stanley Dennison, and other supporters, she walked from the courtroom, still crying.

"No. No. No. Why? Why?"

"That's all right," said Monroe. "It'll be taken care of. What did you expect from an all-white jury?"

Inside, the judge ordered a poll of the jury.

Aye. Aye. Aye.

It went like that 12 times, an "aye" for each juror.

And outside, still sobbing, Thelma Pannell's voice cut through the walls, an echo of anger for each affirmation of not guilty.

"No. No. No. Why?"

In the coming days, there will be much said about the truth in this verdict and the righteousness of Gary Spath's story of self-defense as he chased a teenager who had a gun in his pocket. Likewise, there will be much said about why the state of New Jersey prosecuted this case so hard, so long.

The real story of this case, however, lies somewhere in that portrait of tears, between the gut-level anger and the gut-level joy. What's deeply tragic here is that the truth lies in division.

"I know it's difficult for everyone concerned," said Judge Charles R. DiGisi.

Outside the court, one of Spath's friends and supporters, the Rev. Bart Aslin, a Catholic priest, noted that verdict day was the Catholic Feast of Our Lady of Lourdes. Among other things, it's a feast that commemorates healing. "I knew he would be acquitted today," said Aslin.

Farther down the hall, her voice still choked in sobs, Thelma Pannell also looked to religion for comfort. "Why Lord Jesus? Why?"

There may never be an answer to that question of why. But later, at his attorney's office, perhaps Gary Spath described the end of his own ordeal better than anyone could:

"It's like being the winning pitcher in the ninth inning of the seventh game of the World Series."

One side wins. One side loses. Between the tears, sometimes there is solace.

He Couldn't Be Helped

The picture was splashed on newspaper front pages across the nation – a group of Miss America contestants and a homeless man who had been sleeping under a boat on an Atlantic City beach. Here is the story of the family that tried to save him.

It's hard to miss the white wall plaque hanging just inside the front door of Joan and Ray Burke's house on Gray Street in Bogota. The plaque announces, "Friends welcome."

Maybe Jim Robinson read that plaque when he walked into the Burkes' house that first time two months ago. Whether he understood the message is something else. Says Joan Burke: "I don't think Jim even knew it was there."

The first time the world saw Jim Robinson was September 10, a Sunday. Robinson's face was on the front page of Sunday newspapers across America, one of those candid images that speaks to us in a language that transcends words and yet burns our conscience.

The scene was an Atlantic City beach. Robinson, 42, homeless and wrapped in a blanket, was sitting in the sand next to a lifeguard rescue boat with another homeless man. In the background were 51 Miss America contestants in bathing suits, one woman for every state and the District of Columbia. Beauty queens and the beasts — a snapshot sermon about homelessness in the land of plenty.

Some of the beauties seemed shocked. Some giggled. A few seemed perplexed. Robinson, his shoulder-length hair falling in his eyes, seemed sleepy, embarrassed. He had spent the night under the boat. For most of the summer, the sand had been Robinson's bed. The boat was his umbrella.

But that morning, the Miss America contestants were scheduled to pose for publicity shots with the boat. To take the picture, police roused Robinson and his friend.

Some 100 miles to the north, in Bogota that Sunday morning, Ray and Joan Burke were eating breakfast when they saw the newspaper picture. They knew immediately it was Robinson.

Joan Burke, 50, a telephone company worker in Hackensack, is Robinson's cousin and godmother. For months she had worried about him. She had been close to Robinson's parents, who lived in Westfield. Now that they had died, she felt responsible for him.

In January, the Burkes drove to Atlantic City to see Robinson. He was a cabbie, but living in a flophouse. The Burkes offered help. Robinson refused.

In July, the Burkes heard that Robinson had lost his taxi job and was sleeping on the beach. A few weeks later, the phone rang. It was Robinson. A few days after that — on their 28th wedding anniversary — the Burkes drove to Atlantic City, this time offering Robinson a place to live. He refused.

Then the photo appeared. The next day, the homeless man Robinson had been photographed with died. Robinson checked into a hospital, then phoned the Burkes to see if they were still offering a bed.

So began the rehabilitation of Jim Robinson. He made the papers and the TV news — the touching story of the homeless man trying to put his life together and the middle-class family helping him.

Ray Burke, 52, a retired New York City transit cop, drove Robinson to work at a Bergenfield book publisher. He took Robinson to Alcoholics Anonymous meetings. Joan Burke loaned money to Robinson, cooked his meals, washed his clothes. Joan and Ray even canceled a Poconos camping trip because they were worried about Robinson.

But this story of Good Samaritans did not end happily, despite the best efforts of the Burkes.

Robinson, still troubled by his alcoholism and fired from his job for making too many personal phone calls, left by bus for Atlantic City. He never said good-bye or thank you, never called to say he was OK.

The Burkes were left with their anger and disappointment.

"Some people think we're crazy," said Ray Burke. "But if you don't try, what do you gain?"

Said Joan: "Right now, we feel stung. But we would probably do it again. You always go back for more."

If more of us were like that, maybe there wouldn't be so many Jim Robinsons.

Gathering the Memory

That mystery of terror known as the Unabomber touched New Jersey on a December Saturday in 1994 when an advertising executive opened a package and a bomb exploded. Ten months later, Tom Mosser's friends gathered to cement his memory.

There is unfinished business when death comes suddenly. It has been that way for nine months, since advertising executive Tom Mosser was killed in the kitchen of his home in North Caldwell, the victim of a national mystery called the Unabomber.

On a hot August Monday, hundreds of Mosser's friends — and those who have come to admire him — gathered on a golf course along the Palisades Cliffs in a narrow sliver of a town called Alpine.

An FBI agent took a vacation day and flew in from San Francisco and the Unabomber investigative team. Several cops came from North Caldwell. Peter Max donated a painting.

The golf outing raised $200,000 for the Tom Mosser Foundation, which provides, among other things, scholarships for minorities at prep schools.

But the poignancy of the day wasn't cemented until just before noon, when a young woman with shoulder-length auburn hair stepped into the harsh sunlight that baked the pristine fairways of the Alpine Country Club.

That Monday was a hard day for Susan Mosser. On the previous December 10, a package bomb exploded in the home she shared with her husband — the same day they had planned to buy a Christmas tree.

On the Sunday before the golf outing, Susan had to summon what happiness she can manage these days to throw a birthday party for 2-year-old Kelly Mosser, the daughter who was playing in the next room when her father was killed.

"Today we're really trying to perpetuate his memory," said Susan Mosser, brushing away a tear as she sat at a picnic table. "We have to make new memories. Today will be another new memory."

Tom Mosser's legacy is now unavoidably linked to the horror of terrorism. He is, officially, a victim of the Unabomber, whose handiwork is often described in the coldest of terms — 16 exploding packages across the United States since 1978, leaving three people dead and 23 others injured. But on the golf course, the depth of this loss emerged in a way that cannot be captured in numbers.

Susan Mosser talked about her golf bag. It was a Mother's Day gift from her husband. Kim Mosser, their 14-year-old daughter, said she was using some of her father's old clubs. Playing alongside Kim was Steve Gallagher, a police officer from North Caldwell.

"He was the man who came and told me Tom was dead," said Susan. Gallagher and his wife are now godparents to Kelly Mosser.

It is those human connections that seem to percolate through each story about Tom Mosser and his memory. Mosser was a public relations and advertising man, a success in a business of hype, hyperbole, and bragging. And yet, when people talk of him, they do not brag of his achievements, though there were many.

They speak of his heart.

"He was educated by the Franciscans," said Freeman Miller, "and I think he lived those rules all his life."

Julie Slavitt Karlitz remembers how Mosser went out of his way to thank her publicly for her work on a public relations seminar to help market the Olympic Games. "He was like Johnny Carson," she said. "Johnny Carson isn't loud and flamboyant, but in his quiet way, he brought out the best in people."

Julie's husband, Herb, also remembered Mosser's soft-spoken, reserved demeanor. "But when he spoke," said Herb, "he had something to say."

On that August Monday, his friends and admirers spoke for him.

"It means someone has not been forgotten," said Mark Weiss.

Susan Mosser put it another way. She had just slapped a golf ball down a fairway and stepped back into the shade again.

"We're trying," she said. "We don't give up easily."

One for the Road

Economic hardship can drive a man to do unusual things. In this case, it drove this unemployed man to make himself into a human billboard. Needless to say, there was a law against that.

The desk job was routine, maybe too easy. Denis Kallimanis of Hackensack wanted more. But not much. Just $18,000 a year, with benefits. He also wanted a challenge.

He got none.

The résumés were out. But the phone wasn't ringing. And now it was August, and only two weeks left before his stint ran out as a temporary marketing clerk for a jet airplane manufacturer in Teterboro.

It was time to get desperate.

"Everybody's out on the road," Kallimanis reasoned. "Even the Beatles said, 'Why don't we do it in the road?'"

The road it was.

One day after work, Kallimanis, 33, headed for Route 17. He pulled into the Shop Rite in Hasbrouck Heights, just south of where Route 46 feeds into 17. Too busy. He moved on.

A mile south, Kallimanis parked the car near the White Castle hamburger place. He bought a soda and two hamburgers, then walked to the edge of the highway, near a jug-handle. He wore his blue interview suit, a white shirt, and a red tie: his conservative, business look.

And in his hands, he held his new résumé — a 3-by-4-foot piece of white cardboard with this message in foot-high black letters:

"I NEED A JOB."

Kallimanis propped up the sign on the grass, then stood by, trying to look respectable, unthreatening. His mind was a mental tennis match of damned-if-you-dos, damned-if-you-don'ts.

"I said to myself, 'This is crazy. No, this isn't crazy.'"

Fifteen minutes passed. A car finally stopped. A man from an office supply firm rolled down the window and handed Kallimanis a business card. Not much, but a start.

Another man drove up, announcing he worked for a "financial services company."

"What company?" Kallimanis asked suspiciously.

The man gave the name. Kallimanis already knew it as a fly-by-night outfit.

"Thank you," Kallimanis said.

The man laughed as he drove off.

There was also an exterminator, who began by asking: "Hey, what's with the sign?"

Kallimanis wasn't in the mood for small talk. Anyway, the message on Kallimanis' sign was hardly as cryptic as the Oracle of Delphi.

"Can't you read?" Kallimanis answered. The exterminator nodded.

It went that way. A few drivers, pushing through the muggy rush hour, merely gave a thumbs-up sign. Others shouted obscenities. Fewer still stopped. Nobody had a job that fit Kallimanis.

There were more people from office supply firms, one who ran an employment agency, another who sold insurance, another, phones. There was even a plumber.

"I could do that," Kallimanis said. The road teaches confidence.

Kallimanis has sold men's suits. He's trained and managed sales-people. He's ordered merchandise, balanced budgets, soothed irate customers. He had a year of college and some data processing classes. His hobby is computers.

When he took the temporary marketing job at the airplane manufacturer in January 1988, he was told to organize the filing system. He did. In fact, he did it too well. These days, he is so efficient he claims to be able to finish a day's work in 30 minutes, tops.

He spends the rest of his time reading magazines or dreaming or fuming in frustration.

Kallimanis placed a classified ad in the "situations wanted" column of a weekly newspaper. He got 40 calls — 38 from people also looking for jobs. He also mailed résumés to the 40 largest companies in the area. He got one response. Thanks, but no thanks.

His stint on Route 17 lasted two days. But it wasn't frustration that sent him packing. It was the cops.

New Jersey highway laws say you can't solicit on the road. It's too dangerous.

You need a billboard.

Woodstock Mother

The Woodstock music festival in 1969 was not a time of joyous revelry. Two people died there, one of them from New Jersey. On the 25th anniversary of the festival, I set off to find the mother who lost a son.

Henrietta Mizsak remembers her son Ray's youthful look on the August day in 1969 when he left her Hamilton Township home near Trenton to catch a train for Woodstock.

He wore bell-bottom jeans, a T-shirt, and sandals. His hair was just beginning to creep over his ears. He paid for his train ticket with money he had earned from cutting lawns. He was 17. It was the last time Henrietta saw him alive.

Ray Mizsak was killed at Woodstock early on the morning of Saturday, August 16, 1969. In all the wide-eyed hoopla surrounding the 25th anniversary of the concert, his 73-year-old mother wishes someone would remember that.

Two people died at Woodstock. One succumbed to a drug overdose. Ray Mizsak was crushed by a dump truck as it rumbled along the edge of the concert site in Bethel, N.Y., to haul away garbage. Mizsak had wrapped himself in his sleeping bag and retreated to a quiet spot. The truck driver never saw him.

In the years afterward, as the concert came to be seen as a mythic blend of idealistic karma, rock music, and hedonism without consequences in that fuzzy concept known as "Woodstock Nation," Ray Mizsak's death was reduced to an obscure piece of trivia. For his mother, a housewife who had five other children, this is a painful thought. "Most people," she said, "couldn't care less. It was just a big drug party."

This has been a summer of memories and anniversaries. It began with D-Day, then moved to the Moon landing, and continues now with Woodstock. With D-Day and the Moon landing, we were reminded how danger framed each event and its memory. At D-Day, thousands were killed. In the decade-long race for the Moon, rockets blew up. Several astronauts died.

Woodstock has been cast far more benignly. It's as if 400,000 mostly white, suburban kids frolicked in mud, smoked grass, got naked, listened to music — and then returned to college and career paths. Some portrayed it as the Baby Boom's last brush with innocence.

That summer, Ray Mizsak spread his youthful wings. In September he would start his senior year of high school. He spent his free time listening to records by Crosby, Stills, and Nash and Creedence Clearwater Revival. He took up painting, mostly in a modernist style, his mother says. He talked about opposing the Vietnam War. He had no specific college plans, just a yearning to travel.

Ray's father, a carpenter, promised to buy him a ticket to California after high school. "Then he said he wanted to go to Woodstock," said Henrietta. "He said it was an outdoor concert. What could be wrong with that?"

When he died, Ray's only identification was a Social Security card with his name but no address. His parents weren't notified until 12 hours later, when a cousin who was a Trenton police sergeant noticed the name on a police wire.

"Today, for me, there's nothing to glorify about Woodstock," said Henrietta. "I've felt bad for weeks thinking about it."

An autopsy revealed that her son had not taken any drugs or alcohol. A hearing cleared the truck driver who killed him. "It was an accident," said Henrietta. "Ray was just in the wrong place at the wrong time. What could we do?"

Her husband has since died and is buried next to her son in a Princeton cemetery. At the Woodstock site, a plaque rests on a cement block to pay tribute to the rock bands that played there. There is nothing for Ray Mizsak, though.

A few weeks after their son died, Henrietta drove to the site with her husband. "We just wanted to see it," she said. "It looked like a farm field that had been trampled."

They asked where their son had died, but no one knew the spot. Even then, no one remembered.

The Paper They Signed

Courtrooms are stages for all manner of human pain. One day, I stumbled on a divorce case that still remains one of the most pathetic I have ever heard about.

The wife sat on the left with her lawyer. The husband was on the right with his. Between them was a piece of paper. The pre-marital contract. Best-laid plans.

This wasn't Donald and Ivana Trump of Trump Tower. This was Stella and Edmund Jacobitti of Maywood.

But it was a messy divorce just the same.

Stella is 64 and has multiple sclerosis. Ever since her husband filed for divorce, she has also lived with two other indignities, Medicaid and Meals on Wheels. Edmund is 83, a retired physician with $5 million in assets. He doesn't want to part with them.

Like the Trumps, the Jacobittis have a written pre-marital agreement that is supposed to give them a quick, wash-your-hands, uncomplicated divorce. But that's where the similarity ends.

If the Trump pre-marital contract goes through, Ivana gets $25 million and a 40-room mansion in Greenwich, Conn. If Stella Jacobitti is forced to swallow her pre-marital paper, she gets nothing. Zippo.

Stella Jacobitti didn't even get a wheelchair from Edmund until her lawyer, Gail Mitchell, went to court to get one. The judge, Conrad Krafte, had no trouble ordering Edmund to supply the wheelchair, but he drew the line at forcing Edmund to pay for Stella's adult diapers. That's how low things have sunk in this divorce case. Stella has her medical needs. But Edmund has a pre-marital agreement and a bonfire of inanities for his defense.

The marriage was the second for both of them. Her first ended in divorce. His first wife died. When she married Edmund in 1975, Stella says, she never even read the pre-marital agreement. "I was in love," she says. She laughs when she thinks back.

For Edmund, Stella quit her teaching job and worked for no salary in his medical practice. They had 11 years before her multiple sclerosis was diagnosed. A year after that, they separated.

At the time, she was in California, visiting her son and undergoing medical tests. When she didn't return after a month and took half of a $32,000 joint checking account, Edmund filed for divorce.

He asked the court to enforce the pre-marital contract. Stella balked.

She doesn't want Edmund's fortune, just something for a dignified life — about $60,000 a year. Edmund has offered $24,000 a year — but only from a trust he controls. One of his main concerns, says his lawyer, Albert Cohn, is keeping Stella's son from sharing this fortune. When it comes to Stella's son, Edmund's bonfire burns bright.

"It's absurd," says Stella's son, Bill Westerfield, 39, who now cares for his mother at his home in Vermont. "It doesn't do me any good to make my mother more dependent on me by taking her money."

And so the horror show continues. The divorce case that began in 1987 and may yet run as long as *Les Miserables* played for a few days recently at the Bergen County Courthouse in Hackensack, in a room with more echoes than spectators. This time, there was a new judge, Andrew Napolitano, but the dilemma was the same.

Edmund's legal papers say Stella is guilty of extreme cruelty, not the least of which is calling him "cheap" in front of friends. Stella says he refused to pay for eye exams or provide enough fresh food.

Napolitano listened for two days. Then he ordered Stella to undergo a psychiatric exam to determine if she's competent. She passed the test, her dignity intact but her case delayed two more weeks.

Stella says Edmund made a "god out of his money." Edmund refers all questions to the pre-marital agreement. "That is the issue," he says.

One time, these two were in love. Maybe they even talked softly to each other and dreamed about growing old together. But that was back when they signed their pre-marital agreement. Long ago.

Stolen Cars, Broken Dreams

I decided to cover the 1996 election without ever laying eyes on Dole or Clinton. Instead, I went to a variety of communities and chronicled ordinary people facing some aspect of American life. In Newark — America's stolen car capital that year — the major concern was whether you would wake up and find your car.

The line forms in a room without windows, with walls the color of light coffee and linoleum the color of eggshells. By the door, a hand-scrawled sign warns, "Do not enter until we call next."

On a recent morning, Steve Kasyanenko, a Paterson teacher, was "next" — and not happy about it.

"I'm taking the day off and she's taking the day off," he said, nodding to his wife, Anela, an Irvington teacher. "And it's not too pleasant."

Here, on the second floor of the Newark police station, it's another day in one of the most frustrating chapters in America's long-running crime saga. The room is called the "auto release" department, but it is known as the place where victims of car thefts show up each morning to learn what happened to their piece of internal combustion machinery. Is it damaged? Intact? Totaled?

"This is the third time my car has been stolen," said Kasyanenko, who lives in Maplewood and drives a 1991 Honda CRX sports car — one of the most popular targets of car thieves in North Jersey.

He was phoned by police and told to come to Newark. But he was not told what happened to his car, only that it was recovered. "This time the car was taken right out of my driveway," he said. "And what happens?"

He answered his own question.

"Nothing."

Kasyanenko explained that the first time his car was stolen, he was left with a $5,000 repair bill. The second time, it was several hundred dollars. In neither case were the thieves caught.

"We might as well put a sign on the car that says, 'Please take me,'" Anela said.

"This is devastating," Kasyanenko said. "In the old West, if someone stole your horse, they hung them. Today, the consequences are nil. And I have to pay the damages to the car out of my pocket."

Such personal sentiments are worth weighing in this political season. While crime is a staple of election campaigns, the political rhetoric is often framed by impersonal and wide-ranging statistics, sensational blood-soaked victims' stories of murder and rape, or attention-getting proposals to execute drug kingpins, hire 100,000 more officers, or build more prisons.

The smaller stories of Steve and Anela Kasyanenko and other victims of less sensational crimes seem lost in the tumult. And yet, while murder and other violence may scare America, it is property crimes such as car thefts and burglary that hit home most often — with numbers as much as four and five times higher than violent crimes. What's more, it is property crimes where the conviction rate is lowest.

A trek to the Newark police auto release department is a journey into the bureaucratic equivalent of water torture, with each step a drip-by-drip wound.

First, there is the problem of time. The department is open only from 9 a.m. to 6:30 p.m. and until noon on weekends. No night hours here.

Then there is the task of assembling the necessary papers such as the car's title and its registration and insurance cards. If some of those items are in the glove compartment of your stolen car, well, you have to hunt for copies in your files.

Next is the unknown. Was your stolen car vandalized? Will the thieves be caught? How much will all this cost?

And finally, there is a trip from the Newark police headquarters to one of three car storage lots on the eastern edge of Newark, where the New Jersey Turnpike passes by on a landscape dotted with hulking warehouses and oil tanks and is criss-crossed by two-lane roads that are ruled by impatient tractor-trailers. As if the pain of a car theft and a trek to this industrial netherworld isn't enough, the lots charge victims $85 storage and towing — but only if a car is retrieved within 24 hours. After that, it's an extra $10 a day.

"At my age, this is very bad. You get an empty feeling in your stomach," said Bertha Tornabene, 79, of Red Bank.

Tornabene stands in line with her granddaughter, waiting to hear the fate of her 1993 Nissan Altima, stolen two nights before from her driveway some 40 miles away. "You can't imagine what it's like to wake up and see your car is gone," she said.

She is trying to keep her hopes up and is actually smiling, as Steve Kasyanenko walks from the release department holding a photocopy of a police report with the verdict on his own car.

"Forget it," he said. "It's totally damaged." He runs his index finger down the list of problems listed on the report — a rear light missing, a headlight broken, the dashboard damaged, a front fender dented.

"It was a $10,000 car," said his wife, Anela.

"It's junked," said Kasyanenko. His problem: He had liability insurance, but nothing to cover damages from theft. What he also doesn't know yet is that the damage is worse. The thieves stripped his car of its engine, tires, and seats. But he won't learn this until he finds the towing lot.

Moments later, after learning of her car's fate, Bertha Tornabene emerges. Her face is ashen. "Look," she said, pointing to the copy of a police report and the word in large letters: "BURNED."

Lt. Henry Alston, the head of the Newark police auto theft squad, has seen the exasperated shock and humiliating dismay now clouding Bertha Tornabene's face thousands of times. He has run the department for seven years now, but says he still feels pain each time he watches another victim at that moment.

"I was naive. I had always underappreciated the value of a car to ordinary people," said Alston. "This kind of experience is terrible. And the hardest hit are the working poor — those people who might live in the projects or on the edge and need a car to get to work at a car wash or a supermarket. If they don't get to work, they don't get paid. Their car is everything to them. If a guy loses his car, he's right back on welfare."

Shirley Hay of Newark, a postal worker, didn't go on welfare. But when her car was stolen a year ago, she stayed home from work for three weeks without pay until her car was recovered. The reason: There was no bus to take her into downtown Newark for her midnight shift at the post office.

Those kinds of stories do not show up in the statistics of stolen cars. Indeed, on another floor of the Newark police department, another message about car thefts is being conveyed by public relations specialists: The numbers of stolen cars are dropping. In 1989, Newark became the car theft capital of America with a record 15,698 thefts. Last year, the number dropped to 9,865. And this year, the numbers are 18 percent lower than in 1995.

Such is the good news. The bad news is that, despite decreased thefts, an average of one car an hour is stolen in Newark each day.

Joaquin Lavordor of Union says his 1993 Honda Del Sol was stolen for a four-day joyride. It's the fourth time, he said. A woman in line listened, shook her head, and offered this story: "What happened to me? You wake up in the morning to take your daughter to school and the car is gone." Her daughter missed school.

It is almost 11 a.m. now, and Richie and Jean Griffith of Toms River are next in line. Behind them stands a lanky 29-year-old man from South Dakota, Jonathan Chronister.

The Griffiths — he is a pilot and she is a marketing specialist — lost a year-old Jeep Wrangler from a hotel near the Newark airport. Chronister, a sheet metal installer, is missing a Ford pickup truck and a boat that was attached to it on a trailer.

Chronister, on a vacation trip, stopped in Newark, thinking it would be too risky and expensive to stay in New York City with his boat and pickup truck. He figured he could park the truck and boat on the street while he stayed in the Hilton Gateway Hotel, where he was told the garage was not big enough for his pickup and 15-foot boat. "In South Dakota," he said, "I leave my keys in the truck. Nobody takes anything. Never."

Here, the truck and boat were taken the first night. And now, police report in hand, he heads out the door for the Dente Brothers Towing lot on Newark's eastern edge. What he doesn't know is how lucky he is.

Chronister will find his pickup intact — except for the stereo speakers. His boat is missing its battery and depth finder and has this graffiti message spray-painted on the dashboard: "Eat this."

His most difficult task is paying the $220 in storage and towing costs. The towing firm won't take Chronister's credit card. He heads back to the hotel ATM for the cash and is out of town by nightfall.

The Griffiths are another story.

Their Jeep looks like it has been through a demolition derby. The doors are gone. The dashboard is cracked and the radio gone. The steering column is broken. The front bumper is dented, as are both front fenders and the hood. The windshield is scraped. The top of the console between the bucket seats is torn off.

"Aggravating," said Richie Griffith.

He studied the odometer — the Jeep had been driven by thieves more than 300 miles in three days. He looked at the gas gauge — it was near empty.

Griffith figured he had enough gas to drive to a gas station. He was wrong. He made it a mere two miles and ran out of gas. It took him another hour before he was on the road again.

Steve Kasyanenko didn't even bother to try to recover his stripped Honda CRX. The damages were more than the $7,000 value of the car. Plus, there was the other matter of a $295 bill from Dente Towing.

As payment, he gave Dente Towing the title to his car.

"I didn't want it," said Kasyanenko. "I just left it."

Orphaned by AIDS

I have written my share of columns about AIDS and the people who suffer from it. But I had no idea of the depth of the tragedy until I found myself on World AIDS Day in a home in Jersey City where children with the virus are sent after their parents die or abandon them.

Rose sits on a bed with Bugs Bunny sheets and a Barbie doll by her pillow. The morning sun pours through a window as she shows me a color photograph of a woman in a white shirt and jeans, with slender hands and a wisp of a smile creasing her face.

"This is my mommy right here," says Rose, holding up the photograph, then gently placing it back on the bed. "My mommy is dead."

And her father? "My daddy got lost," she says.

Rose is only 3 years old, one of three girls and two boys under 5 years old who live on the second floor of a small corner of compassion in Jersey City known as St. Clare's House. It is to such a place that the littlest victims of AIDS come, the orphans whose parents died from the disease or are too sick to care for them now.

Rose arrived at the two-story converted house near Jersey City Medical Center in June, just after her mother went into the hospital for the last time to die. Her father, also believed to have the disease, walked out several years ago and never came back.

So far, Rose's relatives won't adopt her, and finding a foster family has been hard. Unlike two older brothers who were quickly taken in by relatives, Rose has the same problem her mother had — AIDS.

Such a story is common at St. Clare's. The face of AIDS, especially today on World AIDS Day, is a mixed portrait of many victims, from gays to heterosexual drug users — even to the relatives who are left behind. But the children of St. Clare's hold a special place in this tragic legacy.

In an epidemic where the virus is spread primarily by the foibles of human behavior, children like Rose are victims of circumstance. She caught the AIDS virus because her mother was a drug addict who used AIDS-infected needles, then got pregnant with Rose.

Rose doesn't understand the fine points of how the virus is spread to children in the wombs of AIDS-infected mothers, says the St. Clare's House manager, Patricia Robinson. So far, the only outward symptoms of Rose's illness are swollen glands around her neck. But Robinson says Rose feels a sense of something amiss. "Sometimes she cries and doesn't know why," says Robinson. "She just says, 'I'm sad.' "

Such is the difficulty of being so young and facing such a harsh future. Rose doesn't have the vocabulary yet to express her pain.

Nationwide, AIDS researchers estimate, 45,000 children have been orphaned by AIDS since 1985. In Newark alone, one study found 3,200 AIDS orphans. The numbers are expected to double by the year 2000.

At St. Clare's, Rose spends her days watching Barney on television and listening to Dr. Seuss stories read to her. The other children at the house suffer from brain damage, liver problems, and tuberculosis — all because their parents took drugs and developed AIDS.

The home was opened five years ago by a former Franciscan seminarian, Terrence Zealand, and his wife, Faye, who decided to devote their energies to helping AIDS victims after one of their friends died of the disease. Besides the one in Jersey City, the Zealands opened homes in Elizabeth and Neptune.

Most of the 200 children who have passed through their hands end up with foster families; many eventually die of AIDS. "It's difficult," says Zealand. "We go to too many funerals."

It is unlikely that Rose will live to be a teenager. Her nurses say she does not understand this yet, however. For now, she spends her days planning to visit Santa Claus. And if you ask about her family, she explains: "I have to get a new mommy."

Rose says this as she picks up another photograph, one that shows her smiling and sitting with her mother who died.

"Look here," she says. "I'm happy."

The Lonely Holdout

Every town has someone like this – someone who refuses to move or sell the family home in the face of progress. Sometimes progress never arrives, though.

FORT LEE —
Rose Mitrano smiles and tells you she sometimes thinks she lives in the country.

If you gazed out the kitchen window of her home here, you might think so, too.

Spreading southward, amid patches of scrub trees and clumps of thigh-high weeds that cover an occasional pile of bricks and cinder blocks in the heart of downtown Fort Lee, are almost 16 acres of emptiness. People who claim to know such things will tell you the land is worth $20 million now, maybe more.

Rose Mitrano puts another value on it.

"I got memories here," she says. "I have a lot of memories."

She is 75 now, and still lives in the house her father built. Once, when Fort Lee was still a town where bottled milk was delivered to your door and the horizon was not blocked by high-rises, the Mitrano house was part of a neighborhood of homes and families. "There was almost 100," recalls former mayor Henry Hoebel.

Now only one house — the Mitranos' — is left from that neighborhood.

It's been that way for almost 25 years.

"We're all alone here," says Rose.

The 16-acre patch of vacant land that Rose Mitrano can see from her kitchen sits like an oasis of possibility less than 200 yards from the George Washington Bridge and the highways that converge there in a concrete delta. Mere location automatically makes the land one of North Jersey's most valuable vacant properties. Greed has made it one of the most notorious.

In the early 1970s, developers bought up the homes in the small enclave of Italian immigrants, often paying inflated prices.

"We were offered $800,000," says Rose's 74-year-old husband, Joseph. "We turned it down."

He laughs at the thought, claiming he wanted to buy a large two-family home with the money but just couldn't find one that he and Rose liked — even with $800,000 in his pocket.

Rose explains the real reason.

"This," she says, "is where I grew up, where I've lived most of my life, where I raised my children."

You can't put a price on that.

Over the years, as family after family sold out, developers bulldozed the neighborhood into piles of bricks and ragged timber, stringing together a series of lots to form the 16-acre parcel they hoped to turn into a $270 million retail mall.

But the deal never worked out.

In 1974, developers tried to bribe Fort Lee Mayor Burt Ross in the hope of gaining municipal approval for the mall. Ross didn't take the $500,000 bait, and instead went to the FBI and exposed the scheme, even going undercover and wearing a hidden microphone to collect evidence that convicted seven investors.

In the 1980s, after the mall project had sunk into bankruptcy, New York developer Harry Helmsley bought the property for $13 million, promising to turn it into a mini-city of twin, 30-story high-rises and office towers. He even came up with an exotic name for it — "Helmsley Palisades."

But local opposition to more high-rises in an already crowded borough, combined with an economic recession that flattened North Jersey's construction trade, stalled Helmsley's plans.

This year, amid North Jersey's renewed building boom, the 16-acre parcel has again attracted speculation from investors.

"I've had a lot of calls," says Fort Lee Mayor Jack Alter.

At the Mitrano house, though, the phone stopped ringing long ago.

"It's a little lonely," says Rose Mitrano.

◆

The afternoon sun filters through the windows and Rose takes a seat in her living room, on a chair next to a table that holds a porcelain statue of a woman. Rose explains that her mother bought the statue in California.

Pictures of grandchildren sit on another table. On a wall is another photo of Rose, Joseph, and the couple's two grown sons and two grown daughters. Beyond the lace curtains that cover the windows, you can hear the faint slogging of cars, trucks, and buses lining up at the toll plaza to the George Washington Bridge.

Rose concedes that she has no regrets about turning down $800,000 and the chance to sell their home when all their neighbors did. It's one of those emotional canons of the soul that seems to make no sense and yet makes all the sense in the world.

"I wanted," she says, "to hold on to my house."

After coming from Italy, her family lived for a few years down the block — in a home that was part of the group that was bulldozed. But, when she was a teenager, her father bought the piece of land on the corner of Hoyt Avenue and Bridge Plaza, and built a two-story home with a two-car garage out back.

"It was a family neighborhood," says Joseph, who still works as a plasterer.

"They were very friendly," says Rose. "We knew everybody. Now we know nobody."

You can stand on the Mitranos' front porch and see the gray super-structure of the George Washington Bridge. But, if you lower your eyes, you take in the weed-covered rubble of a developer's dream gone awry. Look to the left and you see a parking lot for a taxi service. Look to the right and you take in the vacant 16 acres. The streets are still there. Weeds creep over the old, cracked sidewalks now, and in a few spots you can still make out the curb cuts for driveways.

But if you stroll down Hoyt Avenue where the Mitranos' neighbors once lived, the landscape takes on a silent, sorrowful feel — like one of those tracts condemned because something toxic was found in the soil. Now if cars pass by, they're headed somewhere else, usually to the bridge.

"The traffic is sometimes bad," says Rose.

"You stay inside the house, you don't hear anything," says Joseph. "It's a jungle."

He is standing now on the front porch. A magnolia and a red oak flank the sidewalk that leads from the street. A red rosebush climbs from a garden.

"We try to keep things nice," says Joseph, "but look at this."

He walks to the edge of his driveway, where he stacked a pile of news-papers weeks ago to be collected in a recycling drive. The papers were never picked up — and were recently flattened when a truck drove over them in an attempt to beat traffic from the bridge.

"We don't even get a street sweeper anymore," says Joseph.

He is silent at the thought, taking in the scene for a few moments, then walking inside to be with Rose.

"Before it was like a family," he says. "Now it's not a family."

Rose nods.

"It's like living in the country," she says. "I wish there was something we could look at. But I'll stay as long as I can."

American Dreamers

Pedro and Marcia had one request of America. They wanted to be forgiven for sneaking into America as illegal aliens. They even paid taxes on the jobs they worked.

Pedro and Marcia sit at the kitchen table of their two-bedroom apartment in Belleville. The morning sunlight cascades through a window and sweeps across the living room. Outside, traffic glides by, passing a fruit market, a store that sells Italian ice, and a string of frame homes swathed in aluminum siding.

Marcia stubs her cigarette in an ashtray and opens her wallet.

"Look," she says.

It's an array of credit cards. Pedro nods. "I just got a Gold card," he says, his voice still bearing a trace of his Brazilian homeland.

Marcia opens a folder with Social Security cards and the couple's tax returns, then sweeps a hand toward the living room, where a TV-VCR unit faces a couch and a coffee table that is home to a stack of books that includes a college anthology of English literature.

She points to the window. "Outside, we have a Toyota Corolla. We bought that on a bank loan because we worked hard to establish credit. And this condo — we own it, too. But . . ."

The word hangs there ominously.

Pedro and Marcia, both 29, are living the American Dream — except for one important piece. They are illegal aliens. And in the next few months, depending on the decision of a federal immigration judge, Marcia may be deported to Brazil. Pedro may not be far behind.

Theirs is a story you don't often hear amid the rhetorical tumult that passes for America's debate over immigration laws. It's a story of two young people who came to America to work hard, who deliberately paid their taxes even when they could have cheated, of how they legally obtained special Social Security cards that are given to non-citizens who want to open bank accounts, of how they established credit and married and bought a two-bedroom condominium, and of how they refused to take welfare.

"We pay all our bills," says Pedro. "We never took anything from the government."

But this story has another side, too. One day, Pedro and Marcia knew they would have to ask America to forgive them for the way they arrived — as illegals. They hoped it would mean something if they lived solid, upstanding lives. But so far, America has been unforgiving.

Pedro and Marcia, who agreed to tell their story only if their full names were not used, work six days a week — he, earning $23,000 a year parking cars at a Manhattan garage, and she as a $25,000-a-year assistant manager of a pricey New York City restaurant.

Marcia and Pedro admit they made a mistake: They came on tourist visas and remained illegally. It's a common ploy for immigrants who do not want to wait (sometimes years) on a list to get into America. But what makes Pedro and Marcia different is that they tried to rectify their mistake. Few illegals attempt that, deciding instead to live anonymously for years.

It was 1994. Marcia had been living in the United States for four years, mostly working as a waitress and baby sitter. Her goal was to establish her citizenship. But how?

A couple whose child she cared for had offered to sponsor her efforts to gain legal residency. But it would take too long — perhaps 10 years, requiring her to work for the couple that long in a role not unlike that of an indentured servant. Marcia researched immigration law on the Internet, even logging into the Library of Congress at one point. She asked friends for advice. Eventually, she got the name of a Miami lawyer used by other Brazilians.

He said he would help her file the correct papers and get her "green card," the first step toward legal status. She paid him $2,500.

A few months later, after meeting him at the New York City office of the federal Immigration and Naturalization Service, she walked away with a temporary work authorization permit and a formal immigration number. It was May 1995. Pedro decided to hold back filing his papers.

"I was so desperate, I almost went back to Brazil," Marcia said. "I didn't ask any questions. I guess that was my mistake."

Nine months later, in February 1996, Marcia and Pedro were married by the Belleville municipal judge. "It was Ash Wednesday," Marcia remembered. "It was the only morning we could take time off. As it was, I came home, changed clothes, and went to work. The judge was busy."

"And," says Pedro, "we are busy, too."

A month later, in March, thinking her immigration papers were in order, Marcia headed home to Brazil, her first visit since she came to America. Pedro, still officially illegal in America, remained here.

Marcia returned to New York City on her birthday. She got off the plane at John F. Kennedy International Airport and showed her Brazilian passport with what she believed was an official stamp by the INS allowing her to reenter America. She was told to go into a room where a man was already handcuffed to a chair. She didn't leave for seven hours.

So began a journey into the legal system that handles immigrants. Her new lawyer, Raymond D'Uva of Newark, concedes that hers may be a difficult case to win. A judge, he said, could even issue a deportation order.

"Unless she can establish that she has a right to be here, she's got a problem," said D'Uva.

The INS has charged Marcia with fraud because of the papers that were filed on her behalf. D'Uva suspects that the other lawyer, who has since disappeared, either had a friend in the INS create phony papers for Marcia or that he gave the name of a fictitious American husband.

The INS has not concluded its investigation, and so it is not entirely clear how this other lawyer filed Marcia's papers. When Marcia came through customs at Kennedy Airport and was asked the name of her husband, she answered honestly. "I told them it was Pedro," she said.

"Maybe she was just a little bit naive," D'Uva adds. "Most people know that you can't just pay somebody some money and get a 'green card.' What she should have done is nothing. She should have laid low. I believe she didn't know what she was doing. But it may not matter."

Says Marcia: "Even if I prove I am innocent of fraud, I'm going to be illegal again."

Such is the dilemma. Marcia and Pedro admit they could have easily established citizenship by having a baby. American-born children automatically are citizens. Often illegals use that as a way to gain legal status here.

Marcia shakes her head at that. "We didn't want to start a family for the wrong reasons," she said.

She adds that she had plenty of other chances to slip through the cracks in the law and establish her citizenship, and even could have asked several friends to marry her temporarily and allow her to establish citizenship, and then divorce. "I wanted," she says, "to do things the right way."

Marcia and Pedro could also go underground — to simply not show up for the INS hearing and go about their lives as anonymously as possible. With so many illegals and only a limited number of INS agents to ferret them out, they would probably get away with it. They've decided against that, too.

"We don't want to live like fugitives," says Pedro.

"Look at all we've tried to build here," says Marcia. "We are middle class here. In Brazil, there is no middle class, only rich and poor. And we'd be poor there."

She turns now toward their living room. She is silent for a moment and seems to fight back a tear.

"I love this country," she says. "I really do. But . . ."

The thought — like their lives now — remains incomplete, just hanging there in limbo.

The Fallen Brother

*Burying the dead can some-
times take on a special meaning for the living, especially
among those who fight fires.*

Firefighters remember.
So when they took Wally Bitner's broken body on his last call through Paterson to his funeral, amid the somber flourish of bagpipes and the mournful beat of drums, the men who fight fires and call themselves brothers because of it unlocked their memories.

Ed McGrady remembered hamburgers.

"We had hamburgers for lunch that day," he said, recalling the July 1989 afternoon when he last saw Bitner standing on his own. "And then the call came in."

The false alarm.

Walter "Wally" Bitner, 38, died on a recent Saturday, after his paralyzed body finally lost a fight that began with that false alarm in 1989.

It had been a hard nine years. And if you had any doubt about that, all you had to do was look into the eyes of the more than 200 Paterson firefighters lining Main Street outside St. John's Cathedral, their right hands snapped in salute and their faces framed in hard worry, as Bitner's coffin rolled up on a firetruck.

"It's a strange feeling," said McGrady, now a captain with 15 years in the fire service. "It's a brotherhood thing. It's sad to see a brother like that."

The bagpipers, a collection of police and firefighters from across New Jersey who call themselves the Emerald Society, broke into the Irish funeral tune, "Going Home." An hour later, as Bitner's coffin was carried out of the cathedral, they played "Minstrel Boy." In between, at a funeral Mass that touched the solemn and the personal, a church soloist sang, "I have loved you with an everlasting love," and Bitner's friends talked of his simple calling to become a firefighter and the complex tragedy that took his life.

"It's a hard thing to understand," said Deputy Chief William Flynn, standing inside the cathedral as clouds of incense floated toward the arched ceiling. "Most people think it's dangerous to run into a burning building. But just riding a truck is difficult."

"It's not a game," said Don Gilmartin, a Newark firefighter and drum major of the Emerald Society.

Bitner took his last ride on July 11, 1989. He was 28 and working at the Riverside Fire House on Lafayette Street in Paterson. George Bush was in the White House. Desert Storm was just a description in a weather report. Jim Florio was still in Congress.

"We had just finished lunch," said Ed McGrady. "And then the bell hit."

The logs say the time was 12:21 p.m. McGrady can still remember the address they were headed to. "It was 220 Hamilton Avenue," he said.

Wally Bitner wasn't supposed to be working, nor was he assigned to Engine 5, a pumper. But another firefighter needed a day off and asked Bitner to trade shifts. When the alarm sounded, Bitner, who worked in the same Riverside station but on Ladder Truck 3, leaped on the pumper truck, into the jump seat on the passenger side.

The jump seat had no door. Bitner, records show, didn't buckle his seat belt.

Ed McGrady took the jump seat on the driver's side. A driver and another firefighter hopped into the cab.

The truck pulled out of the station and onto Lafayette Street, made two quick lefts, and Bitner fell backward out onto 16th Street, swatting his head on the pavement.

"Some construction workers were yelling," said McGrady. "I couldn't even see what happened. But I knew Wally fell out."

Bitner fractured his skull and lapsed into a coma that day. He awoke six months later, paralyzed from the neck down. For the past nine years, colleagues and family say, he lived in a Mountainside nursing home and communicated with a computer keyboard pad or hand signals. A flick of the wrist meant "yes"; a nod of the head meant "no."

Bitner's precise cause of death has not been established. But last week, firefighters received word that Bitner's body was starting to break down in ways that could not be repaired. "It just seemed that everything was starting to go," said Deputy Chief James Tice.

At Bitner's funeral, though, friends talked of a robust man with a humane side. "A large, strong man" is how Chief James K. Pasquariello put it. "But as big and strong as Walter was, he was kind."

After graduating from Eastside High School, Bitner seemed to chase two dreams — firefighting and medicine. He entered Seton Hall University's pre-med program, but often spent his free time at Paterson fire stations as an auxiliary firefighter. After three years at Seton Hall, Bitner dropped out and joined the fire service.

In his funeral homily, the Rev. John Piccione, a Franciscan priest who is chaplain to the Paterson Fire Department, paid homage to Bitner's career switch. "What we do here is remember a brother who had a calling," said Piccione. "Not a job, like any job, not a career like any career, but a calling."

But as noble as Bitner's calling was, his ignoble last ride to a false alarm seemed to hover behind each phrase of every eulogy. "On that fateful day, the flames were not burning," said Piccione, "the smoke was not billowing, but from the moment Walter put on that uniform, he was giving his life to the city."

Likewise, while Bitner might have been known more as a paralyzed firefighter whose family settled a lawsuit for an undisclosed sum against the manufacturer of the firetruck without a door, his friends remembered those moments when Bitner could fight fires.

In his eulogy, Joseph Murray, who once worked with Bitner in an A&P grocery store and is now a fire department captain, remembered how an off-duty Bitner suddenly showed up at the scene of the Alexander Hamilton apartment fire in 1984 where 13 people died and 59 were injured.

"I felt this tap on my shoulder," said Murray, "and someone said, 'Hey pal, what do you need?' It was Walter."

Murray sobbed as he recalled that tragic evening.

Moments later, his eulogy over, the congregation of firefighters recited the "Fireman's Prayer," with its somber phrase, "Give me the strength to save some life." They stood in silence as 15 bells were sounded as a final alarm for Bitner. And then as Fire Captain Michael Ventimiglia sang "Amazing Grace," and as the fire hat Bitner wore on his last ride was taken from his coffin and given to his nephew, who stood with his wife, Hilda Nieves, the firefighters left, single file and in silence.

Outside, a new Engine 5 sat by the curb, white and gleaming and ready for a call.

This one had doors on the jump seat.

A Matter of Skin

Behind every landmark court case, there is a human story. Such was the case of the black and white teachers in a high school.

In the end, perhaps it was inevitable that someone had to let go of the legal rope. But who can be happy with the ending of the tug-of-war over affirmative action in the Piscataway case?

It was supposed to be a landmark decision by the U.S. Supreme Court. Instead, it was settled out of court, with the final decision late at night and the legal fires doused by a pile of money. In short — a payoff.

The case, viewed as the most important test in years on the fairness of affirmative action, dates to 1989. George Bush was president and the Persian Gulf War was almost two years away.

In Piscataway, the school board faced a vexing decision. Because of budget cuts, it had to lay off a teacher in the 10-member high school business department.

State law requires that the last teacher hired be the first to be let go. But the choice was hardly that clear in Piscataway. Two teachers were at the bottom on the seniority ladder in the business department. Sharon Taxman and Debra Williams had been hired the same day in 1980, and the school board found both had similar qualifications. The main difference was skin color. Sharon Taxman was white, Debra Williams was black.

Taxman was fired, with the school board claiming that it wanted to promote diversity in its teaching ranks and to have a positive role model for 30 percent of the students who were non-white.

But what happened next hardly brings credit to Piscataway as a place that nurtures role models.

The white teacher filed a lawsuit. And who could blame her? Sharon Taxman worked hard and played by the rules to establish her teaching career. She lost her job because of something she could not control — her skin color.

As for Debra Williams, she suffered, too. When the board cited skin color as the only reason for keeping her on the business faculty, Williams felt her hard work had been diminished. Like Sharon Taxman, Debra Williams had worked hard and played by all the rules, even earning a master's degree. But now, Williams felt her success was tied to one thing she could not control — her skin color.

Williams developed high blood pressure. She began attending meetings and declaring that she should be valued for her hard work, talent, and rapport with students. But she was left with the same humiliating feeling that far too many black professionals are left with by affirmative action — that they have to prove themselves in ways that go beyond the daily grind. "I would rather think that they kept me because I was qualified," Williams told an interviewer, adding that she feared being seen as just "another lonely black teacher needing a job."

To put it another way, Debra Williams feared she was a token.

This is what affirmative action had finally come to in America. It was no longer just a bloodless policy concept, aimed at redressing the pain of old bigotry by extending an extra helping hand to blacks. In Piscataway, two lives were tarnished.

But the humiliation doesn't end there. Fearing a loss before the Supreme Court, a civil rights coalition known as the Black Leadership Forum approached the Piscataway school board, promising to cover 70 percent of the cost of an out-of-court settlement. Piscataway said fine. The payoff was in.

And now Sharon Taxman will receive $433,500 for lost pay and pain. She got her old job back in 1992, and works in an office that adjoins Debra Williams'.

But school officials say the two teachers rarely speak. It's not that they dislike each other. It's just that each feels dehumanized by a policy that placed a higher value on the color of their skin than on the content of their character or the power of their intellect.

Sharon Taxman's lawyer described the ending right, despite the cash windfall for his client. "Anticlimactic," he said.

Driving Ambition

What's your dream? If you could quit the day job, what lark would you just love to embark on? For some people, it means getting behind the wheel of a beat-up Chevy and bashing some other guy. People actually have fun doing this.

It's another pristine autumn Saturday in the sun-washed hills of western New Jersey. The oaks and maples are just beginning to flame red and orange, but Jeff Kazista ponders beauty of another sort.

He leans over the hood of a 1971 Oldsmobile Cutlass with more dents than a teen with a bad case of acne, and tries to explain why he enjoys spending an afternoon smashing this old beast of a car to metallic bits.

"It is," he says, "better than sex."

And it is, he says with a card dealer's grin, something "you don't understand unless you do it."

Welcome to amateur day at the racetrack.

On this day when the rest of the world seemed to be at football games or raking leaves or meandering through malls and flea markets, Kazista, 31, of Westfield, left behind his job at a pet store for the Flemington Speedway and a chance to summon the Walter Mitty in his soul and pretend he was Richard Petty — a tire-burning, pedal-to-the-metal stock car champ.

It was the all-comers amateur stock car race at Flemington, and — well — it wasn't a pretty sight.

Consider the first 20 minutes: One spinout against the wall, two flat-ten-the-fender wrecks, three slam-the-brake skids.

And that was before the Monte Carlo painted like an American flag lost a wheel and another junk of a Buick hit the wall and barrel-rolled across the track, with the driver walking away.

And that was before Kazista's engine started squirting oil like a runaway lawn sprinkler and he had to drop out. "I had a puddle of oil around my feet," he said.

As bad as the oil leak was, it hardly compared to Kazista's last amateur race.

"Last time, I ended up on top of the wall," he said.

To race, all you needed was $60 in entry fees, a road car with standard tires, a factory engine, and the proper helmet, a roll bar, and guts. Top prize was $1,000 — won on Saturday by Stephen Haegele of Ivyland, Pa.

Needless to say, no one showed up with the family Mercedes — or minivan, for that matter. If you ever wonder what happened to all the muscle cars from the 1970s, look here.

Here was Tim Apgar, a Raritan police officer, with a 1973 Monte Carlo. Here was Rich Miller, a Flemington sign painter, with a 1982 Ford LTD. Here was Eric Schuster, a Pennsylvania pool installer, with a 1971 Buick LeSabre. Here was Eric's father, Buck, with the Christmas present from his son, a 1977 Chevy Impala. Buck even painted a nickname on his car that surely the folks from Chevrolet never envisioned: "The attack model."

But as rough-and-tumble as the race is, drivers insist they are not afraid — especially since they are required to buckle up with special five-point harnesses. "If you're physically scared," says Apgar, the police officer, who finished 14th and won $50, "it's not worth doing. But I've wrecked so often doing this, I wonder why I do it."

Every car had dents by the dozen. Every car had the doors welded shut. No car had a windshield. To race, you had to place wire mesh over the front window.

"I got mine at the Home Depot," said Eric Albright, 24, of Morristown, an engineering student.

Albright describes himself as a former road-raging sort of guy, who now takes out his driving aggressions on the track behind the wheel of a 1973 Chevy Chevelle he picked up for $100.

"I used to be the guy on the parkway going 90, swerving in and out," says Albright, who claims he never, ever speeds on real roads anymore.

He smiles, by the way, as he says this.

"This is where I do my legal racing," he says, pulling on a Marlboro and looking over the sun-washed Flemington track.

As for the car, he says, "you want the biggest hunk of iron you can find. It's for crashing, because that's mostly what we do."

On Saturday, he finished 13th and won $50. But before the race, it seemed doubtful that Albright would even make it to the starting line. As he revved his engine, his father, Cliff, an AT&T engineer and his son's one-man pit crew for the day, used an aluminum baseball bat to straighten a fender.

"This is no death wish," says Cliff, trying to dispel the notion that drivers of these cars are tempting fate. "It's the thrill of speed."

On Flemington's five-eighth-mile banked track, the cars reach speeds of up to 90 mph. And that's in spite of the coating of soapy water that the Flemington race organizers spray to heighten the sense of danger.

"We do things to keep the speed down," says Wendy Kennedy of the Flemington race staff, pointing to the soapy coating as well as the obstacle course of tractor tires scattered around the track like giant hockey pucks. "This is where you're supposed to have fun."

Tom Wolf, a forest ranger from Tabernacle who finished fourth in a 1977 Monte Carlo, puts it somewhat more ominously.

"It's like driving on a snowy road," he says. As for keeping his car running: "I spend all my free time at the local junkyard."

• ◆ •

Flemington Speedway opened in 1915 as a horse-racing track. The speedway's wooden bandstand, with its flaking gray paint, went up the following year.

Because of its dirt surface and because the open track was too tempting, Flemington soon doubled as a magnet for race cars. The horses stopped racing in 1955, but it wasn't until 1990 that the track was paved with asphalt.

Today, Flemington is one of only three speedways remaining in New Jersey, the only one in the northern half of the state.

But its fame extends far beyond cars. In 1992, Flemington was one of only three sites in the nation where Ross Perot held rallies for his ill-fated presidential campaign.

It's a small-town sort of place, where no one wears a tie and everyone seems to have a baseball hat advertising motor oil. In an age when television seems to have homogenized so much of American life, this place stands out as an icon to eccentricity.

In the men's room, a radio plays Christian gospel music. Under the bandstand, the local Republican organization has a clubhouse. Out back, you can set up a picnic spread under maple trees. As for the competition, there are no instant replays, no laser-guided timing devices. As the drivers lined up for the pre-race meeting, the official starter, Warren Austin, pleaded with them to not cheat.

"I don't need a bunch of fights afterward," said Austin. "I just want to drink beer with you guys after we get through."

This sort of down-home spirit is a magnet even for auto racing's stars. A month ago, Richard Petty even stopped by.

"Yeah," said Bill Mollineaux of Parsippany, a former racer turned tractor-trailer driver, "Richard and I sat right over there by the first turn and talked about the old days."

But as much as the drivers worship the stars such as Petty, it's also the sort of place where local heroes are still born, bred, and remembered despite never having received an endorsement or never having appeared on a television talk show.

"My favorite was Stan Ploski," said Rich Miller, the sign painter from Flemington who raced on Saturday for the first time. "I grew up around here, and every Saturday night we used to come to the speedway. I watched Stan Ploski for 15 years here. I'd like to be like him."

On Saturday, Miller finished 70th.

"I just wanted to finish," he was saying. "Next time, I'll try to win."

The Final Cut

Every town has a place where gossip flows and people come just to catch up on the latest news. When that spot disappears, it's a sad day.

Frank the barber is nervous — not a good sign for a man whose job requires him to wave sharp objects inches from your face.

"It's getting morbid," he says, rubbing his thick hands together and settling into a leather chair that sits next to a rubber tree whose leaves are coated with a layer of gray dust. "Too many memories. I gotta cry."

He is silent for a moment, then completes the thought.

"But it's time to go."

In a few days, Frank the barber, aka Frank Orlando, plans to snip his last lock of hair in the barbershop his father opened almost five decades ago on Teaneck's Cedar Lane. He will turn off the electricity to the swirling barber pole. He will take a few mementos — a photo of the Pope, a toy tank, a 1951 picture of his father. Then, he plans to lock the door for the last time. He is 74.

"I'm going to God's waiting room — to Florida," says Orlando. "It's time to cut the tube."

To understand Frank Orlando, you have to understand the art of the punch line. You also must visit his barbershop.

It's a place where witch hazel mixes with laughter, where the ashtrays (and probably the ashes) date back to the Forties, where the barber chairs still have leather straps to sharpen straight razors, where Sinatra croons from a radio, where a tube of "Even-Up" butchwax is within arm's reach, where it's considered an unnatural act to use "mousse" and a blow dryer. It is also a place where old men come to tell old stories. At Frank's shop — called "Tommy's" after his father — they even have a formal name for this.

"We call ourselves the Over the Hill Gang."

The man speaking is Robert Gordon, and he got his first haircut at the shop when he was 15. He is 62, which places him on the youngish side among Frank's customers. As for Frank's retirement, he says: "It will change history."

It's an obvious exaggeration, but there is some truth to it, too. To the regulars at Frank's barbershop, history has a different definition than the kind taught in schools. Here, history is personal, told in long-winded tales that often begin with the phrase: "You won't believe this." Most of the stories are even true.

"I never had to buy a newspaper," said Bob Gorman, 71, a retired police lieutenant. "All I had to do was stop in here for 15 minutes and I hear all the news of the day."

It's a vanishing lifestyle now — this sort of guys-only place, where the act of getting a haircut is secondary to the nurturing of friendships. In the case of the "Over the Hill Gang," the friendships moved beyond the barbershop to formal meetings over dinner. At Frank's place, you sat a while, read a magazine or two, smoked a cigarette, gossiped, then had your ears lowered — maybe.

The other day, after chatting for 30 minutes, Bob Gorman left without a trim. As he reflected on the closing of his barbershop, his thoughts turned to something far more personal than haircuts.

"With this place not being here, there's a whole group of people who won't be in touch with each other," said Gorman. "For me, I guess I'll have to find a funeral parlor to hang out in. This place is where the years just fly by."

In 1978, New Jersey had 3,870 barbershops, with 7,735 licensed barbers, according to the state Board of Cosmetology. Most towns could count on having a string of thriving shops. Today, as the number of barbershops has dwindled to 985 statewide, with only 4,025 barbers, most towns have only one or two.

To Frank Orlando, a man well schooled in the art of placing his tongue in his cheek, there is a perfectly logical explanation for this trend. "Guys want their hair cut by girls today," he declares, his hand sweeping over a table with stacks of magazines whose titles range from *Guns and Ammo* to *Outdoor Life*. "They go to these stylists. I'm not that sort of guy."

He says this with a touch of pride, then rises from his chair as Dr. Martin Fechner, a local internist, walks in. After getting a trim, Fechner settles into a chair, and quietly watches Frank snip at the graying locks of another customer.

"I feel at home here," says Fechner. "It's not the best haircut in the world, but to me the most important thing is not the haircut. It's the people. Places like this used to provide a sense of continuity in a town. Closing this place is going to be a big hole."

For Frank Orlando, permanence and continuity were hardly on his mind when he agreed to help his father in 1965. Orlando had just sold his grocery business in Lodi to Teamster boss Jimmy Hoffa, who later teamed up with several mob-linked partners to build apartments. Orlando was looking for a new line of work and agreed to help his father, Tommy.

"I made a promise to my father," says Frank. "I told him I would keep the shop going. Unfortunately, about that time, the Beatles got all the kids to grow their hair long. So we lost the kid business. But we still had the older guys."

Tommy Orlando didn't quit cutting hair until 1990, when he was 95 and was considered the oldest working barber in New Jersey. He died three years later. "I could never break my father's record," says Frank.

It is late afternoon now, and the shop is empty. Frank Orlando is going through drawers on the Formica counter that holds the tools of his trade.

"Look at this," he says, pointing to a stack of razors that date back to the early 1950s. "And this . . . " He points to another stack of electric clippers his father used.

"Sometimes I wake up in the middle of the night," he says, "and I wonder what I'm going to do. I guess I'll hunt and fish and try to stay out of my wife's way."

He stops in mid-sentence.

"But I'm going to miss this. Yes."

Father and Daughter

When an oldest child passes through one of those rites of passage such as graduation, it is a moment of discovery. When the youngest passes through, another sort of emotion rises up.

The youngest daughter is leaving grammar school. The father is trying to catch up.

It was one thing for him to dispatch the eldest girl into the wilds of American teendom, otherwise known as high school. There was even something exciting about the newness of that journey. But it is something else now to watch the youngest set forth on that road.

The father pondered this recently, as he watched his youngest daughter graduate with her eighth-grade class, and as she delivered her class speech, comparing her grammar school journey to the trek by the scarecrow, the tin man, and the lion in *The Wizard of Oz.*

The father smiled proudly at his daughter's words and her blend of childhood wonder at her school years and her sophisticated insight into what it had meant. He could never have dreamed of thinking like that as an eighth-grader, much less putting such words to paper and then getting up before an audience and reciting them.

But his daughter had done it. And as she spoke that evening in a clear, light voice, he remembered how far she had come on her own journey with him.

In the eyes of any parent, the youngest child carries a special burden as the last in the family to preserve memories of childhood. The father came to understand this only gradually over the years, as the candles on his daughter's birthday cake reached 13.

For her part, the youngest daughter seemed to kindly endure her father's awkward attempts to preserve childhood, even as he sometimes babied her too much, even as she was framing her own independent streak.

As he watched the graduation ceremony, the father thought back to his daughter's stuffed cat, named "Fluffer," that she had kept all these years. He thought of her collection of dolls in fancy dresses. He remembered her pigtails with ribbons, her penchant for wearing red Mary Janes, and the goofy bedtime stories he used to make up — and how she roared with laughter.

And he remembered the swing.

The father found the old swing one recent Saturday. He was sweeping a winter's dust from the garage and there it was — the 1-by-10-inch board, unpainted and graying now with age. It had one-inch holes drilled near the four corners so that a rope could fit through. The daughter's grandfather — father's father — had made the swing when the girl was barely 1.

Grandfather had done it one brutally hot summer day, sweating as he spent hours with a drill and making the rope fit just right. The father had chuckled at his own father's clumsy efforts then and the wood shavings that covered the grass. But now he sensed that his own father had perhaps done this as a way of keeping alive his own memory of childhood, if only through his granddaughter and the swing he made.

The swing had hung for several years from a backyard apple tree. It had endured deep snow and sharp wind, torrents of rain and thick humidity. And on sunny, summer days, it had been the platform for hours of twisting and turning and laughing by the youngest daughter and her sister.

And then, the rope rotted and broke. Oddly, it had happened the same year grandfather had died — five years ago. The father took the swing down then. The girls were too big for it anyway.

He had thought about tossing the swing on the woodpile and using it for a winter's fire. But he didn't.

The father put the swing in the garage, behind a skateboard and a rusty saw, near a folded stroller the youngest daughter had once used. And he forgot about it.

As he rubbed his hands over the old wood now, the father understood why he saved it. He will keep it for another young child, and he will hang it from a tree someday. And another father will find a childhood memory to preserve there.

PART FOUR

WONDERS

The Great Goose Hunt

Wild geese love New Jersey, so much so that thousands refuse to migrate south, despite what their instincts tell them. New Jersey wasn't about to lay out the welcome mat, though – not to birds that leave their calling cards all over golf courses and lawns.

The battle for turf in the animal kingdom takes us to Ringwood State Park. It is a September Wednesday, at 6 a.m., the first minute of the first day of New Jersey's first, special, post–Labor Day Canada goose hunt.

There are seven male hunters with shotguns, five women protesters with air horns, pots, and pans, and 30 million mosquitoes. There are no geese in sight.

I am standing outside Ringwood Manor, looking across an empty lawn that slopes down to a lily-filled Sally's Pond. Behind me, a blue dawn rises over the Ramapos. On a normal day, at least 60 geese live here amid the flowers, soft grass, and tranquil water. Sometimes as many as 250 show up. But today, as Park Superintendent Mark Pitchell notes with a smile, "The geese might know something is up."

As for the hunters — here stands Tony Semioli, Moonachie construction man. He has a cough, a 12-gauge shotgun, and a walkie-talkie into which he speaks to his brother-in-law across the lake, Secaucus plumber Joe Targi.

"You see any?"

"Nah."

In the distance, an air horn blows. Women protesters start their counterattack. Chief Ranger Tom Card motors down a road to check.

"They woke the beaver," he says later. "The beaver isn't happy."

6:05. Somewhere, a lone goose honks. At 6:06, protesters blow the air horn again. At 6:07, a goose flies out and escapes. At 6:10, a mosquito bites me on the forehead.

And so it goes. This is supposed to be the Jersey way of cutting down on Canada geese — illegal immigrants, we're told. The idea is to turn hunters loose for a week in September to scare the geese who have dropped their migratory habits and put down roots and messy droppings on Jersey turf — as if hunting could solve this. One problem, though: The humans who dreamed up this scheme never counted on geese being smart — or religious.

Consider Ringwood State Park. The portion near Sally's Pond, where hunting is permitted, is roughly 30 acres. But just across Skyline Drive is a Catholic convent. The nuns there — Franciscan Sisters of Ringwood — model their lives after St. Francis of Assisi, the patron saint of animals and not the kind of guy to proclaim the merits of hunting as a way of curbing the animal population.

Guess where the geese went?

"Yep," says Karen Struble, a secretary at St. Francis Convent, "we all said they would be here this morning. And they were."

Just before the hour-long hunt began, 60 geese took sanctuary on the convent lawn. Back at Sally's Pond, Joe Targi raises his 12-gauge. It is 6:34, and another solo goose tries to escape. Targi fires once. The goose falls into the pond.

Targi's brother-in-law, Tony Semioli, spots another goose. He gets off three quick shots. The goose banks like an F-16 and escapes. Another bird appears. Semioli fires. The bird falls. Across the pond, a truck driven by Chief Ranger Tom Card is pelted with buckshot.

Watching from the lawn, Ranger Gene Melvin walks over: "I think you just hit a duck."

Semioli looks puzzled, but he will never know. Later, he can't find the dead bird in the pond. He leaves empty-handed.

At 6:40, two white swans swim into the pond; it's illegal to kill them. At 6:50, a V-shaped formation of 10 geese banks along the pond — out of shotgun range — and swoops into the safety of the convent. At 6:59 a bass jumps. At 7, rangers blow whistles to end the hunt.

The score card: Seven gunshots, two blasts on an air horn, one dead goose, one unconfirmed dead duck, and a flock of confirmation that geese know something about sanctuary that humans do not.

Postscript: At 3 p.m. the goose flock leaves the convent and returns to Sally's Pond. Safe, until dawn.

Letting Go

A school commencement ceremony signals a new beginning. It's also an ending.

The father sat in the high school auditorium, his eyes trained on the stage where the future was marching on with diplomas and pomp and circumstance. He found himself wishing this march would slow.

Graduations are hard not just on students who wonder what the future holds. For a parent, graduation forces you to measure time and what you leave behind.

The father thought he was prepared for this. That morning, he put on his blue suit and confirmed reservations at his daughter's favorite restaurant — the place where she could order the four-cheese pizza and everyone else could go with salmon or veal. He loaded film in the camera, checked the batteries in the flash. He washed the car.

And then, he remembered: The car was still home to a small, raggedy doll made of yarn. The camera was the same one he bought just after the daughter was born 18 years ago, the same camera that had captured her face in hundreds of phases.

One of those photos still sits on his desk at home, showing the daughter, then only 14 months, walking down a set of stairs, one hand clutching a guard rail, the other a cookie. The father noticed she still has the same deep-set, blue eyes that always seemed to speak of seriousness and mirth at the same time. He could still remember the day he snapped that photograph.

The father, you see, has this enduring habit: He remembers too much.

He remembers his daughter's first day at preschool, when she announced that she wished she were her younger sister and, therefore, would not have to go — and how he answered that she was bravely blazing a trail. He wishes now he had said something more poetic, perhaps more inspiring.

He remembers her first attempts to ride a bicycle and how he would jog alongside in a park, helping her balance by holding onto the frame. On one occasion, he let go of the bike, and the daughter crashed into a tree. For years, she would remind him of this. "You let go, and I hit the tree," she would tease. And the father would wince.

He knows now he has to stop wincing. She will leave soon, for a college only a few hours away. She reminds him of this almost daily — again, with a tease. "I'm leeeeeeaving," she proclaims, laughing. "And you can't come."

The father tries to joke that he will drop by for lunch, unannounced. She winces at this, but the father hopes she also secretly welcomes his coming, sometimes.

Thinking of those possible lunches — and other visits even — sustains the father now. As he watches graduation move through its expected steps, from speeches to awards to alma maters, he feels that old lonesomeness begin to rise up. He remembers the cold winter mornings when he waited at the bus stop with his daughter. He remembers the math homework she sweated over, the reading lists that brought order to each summer, the trips to the library for term-paper research.

He wishes now he could have been smarter and offered more advice. But then, he realizes it wasn't really necessary. The daughter did fine on her own.

He also realizes how children must set their singular pace in life. The father sees this even more clearly now as he watches his younger daughter strike out on her own too, in her own way as a ballet dancer, with her own goals, her own timetable. The father understands now he must sit and watch, an eternal spectator.

The graduation ceremony is ending, and his older daughter walks up the aisle, her figure tall and straight, her eyes focused ahead, to the door.

As she passes by, she looks over, smirks, and keeps going. The father snaps a photo, then he waits for the crowd to pass so he can follow.

He realizes now he has always followed.

Accidental Delegate

Tim Richards is a living, breathing example of what can happen when you sign your name to a piece of paper.

Politics has become a game of crafty advisers and million-dollar consultants. It is also, thankfully, still the domain of people like Tim Richards.

Richards' story proves that despite the modern gloss that has increasingly turned politics into a cross between a TV game show and a steamy afternoon soap opera, the process at the grassroots level sometimes still depends on the serendipitous nature of the human spirit. In the case of Tim Richards, 36, of Teaneck, the story begins with a civics lesson he was trying to teach his children.

It was primary day in New Jersey. Richards, the night manager of the CVS drugstore in Teaneck, had just returned from a practice with his son's Little League baseball team. It was 7 p.m., and a thought flashed: "I have to vote."

Richards, a former Marine whose ancestors came to America in 1750 as indentured servants and who can name family members who fought in the American Revolution, the Civil War, and World Wars I and II, takes his civic duty seriously. For the trip to the polling place at a local American Legion post, he brought his son and daughter. "I took them into the voting booth with me and started to explain the process," said Richards. "It sounds corny but I wanted to show them what being an American is all about."

He pointed to the Democratic and Republican columns on the ballot, noting that he was a registered Republican.

"What's that?" asked his son, Patrick, 8.

"It's like the Yankees and the Orioles," said Richards, Maryland-raised and an avid Orioles fan. "They're different teams."

Patrick nodded, and, along with his sister, Caitlin, 3, watched as their father cast votes for president, senator, and representative. Then Richards came to a blank line — the spots for male and female county GOP committee representatives. No one was running in his district.

Still thinking of the lesson he was trying to teach, Richards decided to show his son and daughter how to cast a write-in vote — never thinking it might count for something. For the male spot, he wrote in his name.

For the female, he wrote his daughter's name. "And that was it," said Richards.

Enter Angela Hendricks.

She is the chairwoman of Teaneck's Republican Party, which is the political equivalent of David fighting Goliath in a town where Democrats outnumber Republicans by a 5-1 ratio. Two days after the primary, she drove to Richards' house and found him walking his dog.

"You've been elected," Hendricks announced. "You got 100 percent of the vote."

Richards started to chuckle.

"And I assume," said Hendricks, "that Caitlin is your wife."

Well, no. Richards' wife is a true-blue independent when it comes to voting in primaries. Richards started to explain that Caitlin is not even old enough for kindergarten.

"And he told me he was trying to teach his kids a voting lesson," says Hendricks. "I was ecstatic. Here was a new name in the party. I was hoping he would serve."

In the end, Tim Richards accepted. He has coached soccer because he promised to show up regularly, served as a First Communion teacher at his Catholic church, and even tried his hand as Cub Scout leader. As he sees it, volunteering for his political party is just part of the process.

He will make phone calls, chauffeur voters to the polls on Election Day, and perhaps be asked to put a Bob Dole placard on his front lawn. His is the lowest spot on the party food chain, but nonetheless a key spot where the election process begins.

But Tim Richards wants to remind his party of something: "I have no political aspirations."

Hey Kids, Today I Flew a Jet

I've had my share of adventures as a newspaper columnist. But nothing compares to taking the controls of an F-16. OK, it was only for 10 minutes. And, yeah, there was a real pilot in the other seat. At least I didn't need the barf bag.

It's a dogfightin' day in a place the jocks call "Whiskey" that most maps don't know about.

I am strapped into the back of a two-seat F-16 jet fighter, when the cotton-smooth Dallas drawl of Lt. Col. Gaylan Crumley — "call me 'Crum'" — seeps into my earphones with an offer too good to refuse.

"OK, Mike, I want you to take hold of the stick."

A bead of sweat creeps down my neck as I palm a black grip the size of a beer can and eyeball the Atlantic swells 17,000 feet below. We are 50 miles east of Atlantic City's casino neon, in a sweaty afternoon haze as thick as muslin.

I waltz the jet this way and that. Eaaaasy.

Crum, in the front seat, breaks in again.

"OK, you want to do a roll?"

"Me?"

They call themselves the Jersey Devils — but this is no hockey team.

They are a police force of sorts, with an arsenal of 18 supersonic F-16s, two of which are always on alert and ready to scramble to cover a seacoast beat from Long Island to Virginia.

Many have gray hair, and the average age of the pilots is 37. But don't let that fool you.

Don't let the place fool you, either.

The road to the New Jersey National Guard base in Egg Harbor Township, where the 177th Fighter Wing makes its home, takes you past blueberry farms and pines so thick that you can't see more than 10 feet past the tree line.

The wing operates in the relative obscurity that embraces military units in peacetime — except when it bursts into the news, the way it did in February when a commercial jetliner flew into restricted military airspace in a sector known as Whiskey 107, and an F-16 was sent up to take a look-see. The airliner's radar-controlled collision alarm sounded when the F-16 crept to within 1,000 feet.

The story made the evening news.

F-16s in South Jersey?

Why?

If you look at a map of the air defenses of the United States, the 177th is one of the kingpins.

"If someone who is not identified flies into this airspace, someone has to go up and check it out. There is the potential of a terrorist threat. And then there is the real threat of aircraft carrying drugs from the Caribbean."

The man speaking, Col. Thomas Griffin, has five children and a wife and a home in Toms River. He is 53 and trained to fly faster than the speed of sound, withstand G-forces up to nine times greater than gravity, and blow you out of the sky with a heat-seeking missile as easily as he might change channels on the TV.

"The weekend warrior description couldn't be further from the truth," says Griffin, Paterson-born and the commander of the 177th. "We have to be at the highest combat readiness."

But if your image of a fighter jock is framed by Tom Cruise in the movie *Top Gun*, Griffin might shock you. Balding, with soft eyes and a doctor's bedside voice, he seems better suited to a Norman Rockwell painting.

Just now he is sitting at his desk. A poster-size photo of a Soviet bomber being intercepted by an F-16 off the Jersey coast in the late 1980s looks down on a computer. He is late for a meeting to discuss the unit's $30 million budget. He is talking about another sort of scramble, however.

"We have to scramble jets for an unknown threat about once a month," Griffin intones. "Not many people know that."

Griffin reaches back in history to make another point: In the 1960s, some 2,500 jets protected America's borders. Today, only 150 are assigned to that task — 18 of them near Atlantic City.

"Not many people know that either," he says.

• ◆ •

"OK, first put this on."

Master Sgt. Harry Artemisio, 39, of Tuckerton, lifts a harness to my shoulders, then snaps the buckles shut on a life vest that will inflate if I have to parachute into the ocean. He later shows me how to parachute through trees and power lines. "Protect your jugular," he says, covering his neck with his hands. "Don't want the branches to cut you."

I gulp.

Artemisio hands me a "G-suit" — basically an inflatable pair of pants that pumps blood into my chest when the plane's gravitational pull becomes too great.

I think back to a conversation an hour earlier, with one of the wing's flight surgeons.

"You ever fly in a jet fighter before?" asks Dr. Thaddeus Leoniak.

"No."

"You may experience G-forces," he says. "If you do, tighten up like this — like you're feeling constipated. It helps to force blood into your head."

"That will work, too," says Artemisio, when I demonstrate the neck tightening maneuver of Dr. Leoniak.

Artemisio opens a survival kit with flares, a radio, spare radio batteries, and a switchblade. It's similar to the one carried by Capt. Scott O'Grady when he was shot down over Bosnia. I gulp again.

Artemisio walks me into another room, to a mock cockpit, and points to a yellow ring that pokes upward between my knees — the ejection handle. "The three most important words you may hear are 'eject eject eject,'" Artemisio says, staring at me with poker eyes. "Hear that, pull this."

He pauses.

"And keep your arms in."

◆ ◆ ◆

The 177th lost a pilot in 1991.

It was April, and four jets were practicing interception maneuvers off Cape May.

As the combination of speed and centrifugal force exceeded nine times the pull of gravity, the pilot blacked out. His jet smashed into the Atlantic.

"The airplane can pull nine G's, but the pilot cannot unless he's ready for it," says Lt. Col. Dave Draper, the 177th's safety officer. "If you aren't prepared, your eyes go blank, then your brain shuts off. That's what we think happened here."

The story illustrates a daily fact of life for the 177th — that as smoothly as an F-16 can travel, it can kill you, too.

Draper, 51, of Medford Lakes, joined the 177th as a full-time pilot 22 years ago. In his spare time, he kayaks in the ocean to keep in shape.

"This job is a mix of man and machine," he says. "The man has to stay in good shape. So does the machine."

It is noon now, and Draper is sitting in the base cafeteria with Lt. Col. Crumley, 49, of Dover, Del., the 177th's operations group commander. Both men are eating fresh fruit and sipping spring water.

"This is the best job in the world," says Crumley, Texas-raised and on a military leave for the last year from his job as a pilot at Continental Airlines. In training, he is required to build up his resistance to G-forces. On the ground, in a pilot centrifuge machine, he has experienced nine G's.

"It's like an elephant sitting on your chest," he says.

• ◆ •

It is pizza-oven hot, and the grass that borders the runway of Atlantic City International Airport, which adjoins the 177th's base, is so brown that it looks like sand. A white pickup cruises by, its driver tossing firecrackers into the field to scare away the seagulls.

"We'll wait here a bit," says Crum, as we stand on the tarmac by the F-16 that is specially equipped with two seats for training. "There's a scramble."

Two F-16s streak down the runway and into the haze, their afterburners roaring like the wind that follows a bolt of lightning.

Radar picked up an unidentified plane off the coast, says Crum.

Minutes pass, and Crum looks over the F-16 he'll fly today with me, nicknamed "Lady Kate" by the jet's mechanic, Sgt. Kate Urie, 37, of Smithville.

"I love working here," Urie says, as she follows Crum around the plane checking brakes and air ducts. "I love the mechanical aspect of this work. And I love the speed of the jet, too."

Crum breaks in.

"They finally got a bead on that unidentified plane. It was a Navy plane, from a carrier out at sea. It flew into our airspace but never told anyone."

• ◆ •

This is not a get-rich job. The men are paid the same as Air Force pilots — up to $50,000 a year for some officers. The downside is they have to leave for six weeks a year for Panama, where the 177th is deployed to hunt drug smugglers. During the Persian Gulf War, the pilots stayed home, but some of the unit's medical and police units were called up.

And back home, there is other non-flying work, too. Since April alone, the 177th's bomb disposal unit has been sent to four towns in South Jersey — in two cases to check on reports of grenades in Cape May and in Wildwood, said Maj. Roger Pharo, the 177th's executive officer.

Draper admits to feeling patriotic about his job — as do many of the 900-person wing. "We're the hub of the wheel," says Draper. "I feel a sense that I'm doing something for my country. It would make your eyes water to see how fast we can go to a hot spot."

Crumley nods.

"We can go right now," he says.

"But we still put our pants on one leg at a time," Draper adds. Later, he explains the fighter pilot's mindset this way:

"A lot of people don't understand us. They think we're arrogant. We're not. It's confidence we have. You have to be confident to go up in these airplanes. We love our life and flying so much that the rest of life can be boring if you're not careful."

◆ ◆ ◆

Crumley went supersonic at Mach 1.1, or about 900 mph. He put the plane into a 90-degree climb for a loop-the-loop.

"We pulled about 6.7 G's on that one," he says.

My stomach is flipping. I push up the oxygen in my face mask to 100 percent. My stomach calms, and Crumley is now coaxing me through the rollover.

"Yeah. Just bring the stick to one side. Don't worry. You can't mess up."

I turn the plane over and leave it there.

Forty minutes of dogfight maneuvers, from loops to barrel rolls to 60-degree dives, has stripped me of something I usually take for granted — my equilibrium. I have no idea if I am upside down or not.

Ten seconds pass.

"Am I upside down?" I finally ask.

"Yeah," says Crum, laughing. "I'll fix it."

Requiem for a 4-Year-Old

When the national news was alive with the story of Joel Steinberg, the white, upscale lawyer who beat his adopted daughter to death, I set out to find similar cases of child abuse that did not capture the public's attention. I found one in a Jersey graveyard.

Mark Warner is the Lisa Steinberg of North Jersey. He was only 4 when he died last year under the brutal fists of his stepfather. The welts were so numerous that a judge referred to the 41-pound boy as a "punching bag."

But Mark Warner's killing never made TV news, never exacted public outrage.

Mark Warner was black. He died in a Paterson slum. These days, even the people in his old neighborhood can't recall his name.

"All I know is a little boy died here — or something like that. Nobody don't talk about it."

The words are from a tall, slender woman with orange-red nail polish. She gives her name only as "Tee." No last name. On this block of Paterson's Broadway, where used crack vials lie by the curb and winos hang all day outside a liquor store, people don't give full names to strangers.

Tee, 19, lives in Apartment 6 at 276 Broadway, the last home Mark Warner knew. Standing with her on the rickety front steps, under a broken window, is a woman who claims to be her mother.

"Everybody here now wasn't here then," the mother says.

Do people feel bad?

"I guess so."

Tee says she moved in last January, only four months after Mark was knocked unconscious by a blow to his left eye by his 24-year-old stepfather, Michael Thomas, a man who had too many beers and too much time on his hands since getting laid off three months before at a linen factory.

It was Thomas' job to baby-sit Mark and a 9-month-old girl while Mark's mother worked at a data-processing firm in Maywood. According to Thomas, on August 20, 1987, Mark tried to drink cleaning fluid.

"Sometimes I just give him a couple of slaps," Thomas told police. "But this time I hit him awhile."

Thinking back to that evening in August 1987, Assistant Passaic County Prosecutor Marilyn Zdobinski shakes her head in disgust. In her hands are the color pictures of Mark Warner, comatose and hooked to a respirator at St. Joseph's Hospital during his five-day struggle for life.

Mark's lower lip is split. His right forearm is purple. So is his neck, his chest, his groin, his thighs, his shoulder, and both ears. The boy's buttocks have four round scars — old cigarette burns, a doctor has concluded. A three-inch section of the bottom of his left foot is blistered, possibly another burn.

The marks on the boy's abdomen resemble fingernail scratches, a doctor says. And the welts on Mark's lower back may be from a whipping with a belt or wire loop.

"These are crimes that people don't think happen in what you think are civilized societies," Zdobinski says. "But people beat kids every day. It's just a big deal when a white, Jewish lawyer like Joel Steinberg does it."

While Steinberg sat on trial in a crowded Manhattan courtroom, Mark's 21-year-old mother, Alma Warner Thomas, stood silently in an empty Passaic County courtroom. Tears welled in her eyes as Judge Vincent E. Hull Jr. sentenced her to four years' probation for endangering her child's welfare and ordered her into counseling.

Her two other children — a 2-year-old girl and a boy born in March — are in foster homes. She wants them back.

"Do you have anything to say?" Judge Hull asked.

"No," said Alma.

The week before, Hull sentenced Mark's killer, Michael Thomas, to a 20-year prison term, 10 years without parole. He, too, said nothing. "He's very depressed," his lawyer says.

No one knows where Mark's real father is. Or they aren't saying.

And today, Mark Warner's battered body lies buried under a maple tree in the "baby section" of Fair Lawn Memorial Cemetery. His grave has no headstone.

Nobody ever leaves flowers.

Changing a Bulb – at 400 Feet

How many guys does it take to change a light bulb atop the George Washington Bridge? One spring day, I decided to find out. The view was terrific.

In the waning beats of another morning rush hour at the George Washington Bridge, Mike Leonard, an electrician with a meaty handshake and a poet's eye for metaphor, stands on a sliver of sidewalk by the tollbooths. He gazes toward the heavens and speaks of a giant piece of jewelry.

"The necklace," he announces, "is missing a pearl."

It is a sight taken for granted, perhaps because it always seems to be there above the traffic flood — this string of 164 pearly lights along the scalloped suspension wires of the great, gray bridge. The necklace.

Each light in this mile-long strand on the north and south sides of the bridge is a 250-watt bulb, not unlike a common streetlight. Each is no bigger than an oven mitt, no heavier than a coffee mug. Each burns 12 hours a day and lasts about six years. Each costs $28.

But what happens when a light bulb blows? Just how do you change a light bulb on the George Washington Bridge anyway?

"First rule is don't look down," a voice commands.

The man speaking is a 53-year-old father of three who has worked for the Port Authority of New York and New Jersey since before the Beatles invaded America. As an electrician, Jay Zuckerman, Brooklyn-raised before immigrating to Queens, can repair mechanical traffic signs, reset clocks, or rewire a motor in a manhole.

But today, he and a partner, Nick Lisa, 52, of Teaneck, have their eyes on the third light from the top of the northern side of the bridge, about 600 feet above the brown Hudson. The bulb is out.

Theirs is a human feat of courage on a structure that is a tribute to the Machine Age. But to perform this most ordinary of household tasks — to change a light bulb — the complications of machines are left behind in favor of two men, walking along a suspension cable the width of a garbage can, their bodies tethered to guide wires by inch-thick ropes and a harness.

No electrician has ever fallen. But other workers have, including a painter a few years before who was not wearing a harness.

"You're aware of every step," says Zuckerman, who has spent part of the morning making a list of what he will bring. Fresh bulb. Screws. Wire. Screwdriver. Pliers. Transformer. No wallet. No personal keys. Might drop them.

"Great day for a view, huh?" says Lisa, who grew up in Fort Lee and is the father of a son and daughter.

On this day, Lisa is worried about an ingrown toenail. Will he hold his weight on the steep angle?

"I may walk backward behind Jay," he says.

Which leads Lisa to explain the second rule of the day: It takes at least two guys to change a light bulb on the bridge. If one man freezes or slips and is dangling from the wires like a broken puppet, the other is there to pull him up or scream for help.

Scream? Lisa and Zuckerman both nod with a smile. The high wire is no place for a radio or cellular phone. Radios and phones can be dropped. And at 600 feet, they can crush a car roof.

"That's my biggest worry, dropping something," says Lisa, who has worked for the Port Authority since the 1960s and has never dropped anything more than a canvas glove.

Zuckerman remembers a transformer almost slipping. "My heart stopped," he says.

The men step into an elevator. As the door closes, an alarm bell rings. And as the teeth of elevator gears groan and lurch for the two-minute ride to the bridge's steel arch, the bell doesn't stop.

The door opens, and the duo steps onto solid ground — sort of. The floor of the arch level is actually a steel grating. Look down and you get a nice view of the traffic and the river. Look out, past the angled, gray steel girders and the occasional pigeon or gull, and you see Giants Stadium.

"I told you not to look down," Zuckerman says.

Beneath his hard hat and Allen Ginsberg poet-like whiskers, he bears the grin of a man who has watched this scene many times before — a novice visitor, eyes wide and paralyzed in that momentary I-must-be-crazy-to-do-this stare as he steps from the elevator to the open-air, giant Erector-set milieu of the bridge tower.

"We have to climb now," Lisa calls out. "It's all stairs from here."

Stairs?

Next rule of changing a light bulb on the bridge: You climb to a point above the bulb, then climb down on the wires.

"There's our target," says Zuckerman. He points to the third light on the back-span suspension that leads from the tower toward Fort Lee on the bridge's north side.

Mike Leonard, 49, of Ridgefield, the Port Authority electrical supervisor in charge of deciding how and when to replace light bulbs, has an almost fatherly feel for his job. He calls the span his bridge. "And when a necklace light is out," says Leonard, himself a father of a son and daughter, "it's like losing a tooth."

After that, the down-to-earth comparisons end. "In all honesty, you can't compare changing a light bulb to anything," says Leonard. "Once you're up there, it's like a natural high. You're in your own little world."

You can't even hear the cars and trucks below.

It is a man-made realm of structural steel, but to enter it is to find yourself at the surreal mercy of Mother Nature — or just the call of nature. "Before you get up here," says Zuckerman, "we always make sure we hit the bathroom."

As for Mother Nature, Leonard, the scheduler, can't really make final plans until he checks the weather. He tries to keep the men off the wires in rain or if the wind is blowing harder than 15 mph.

The group begins to climb, 79 stairs to the top level of the bridge tower. The men wear gloves to protect their hands from the smog grime, rust, and piles of pigeon droppings. Below, among the girders, sits a falcon's nest. On one stair, the falcon has left the body of a dead pigeon.

Zuckerman cuts the tension. "Can I tell you my best memory? It was a day of a Yankee game, and the Goodyear blimp was coming up the river. It went right by the bridge and I was looking down on the blimp. Looking down on it. Imagine that."

Lisa, who keeps in shape for his job (and relaxes, too) by cycling 20 miles a day in warm weather, speaks later of another memory. "One day I got up here and I just couldn't go out on the wire," he says. "I don't know why. I felt very uncomfortable. Maybe my mind was on other things. It never happened before, and it's never happened since."

The wind blows now, and the group enters a small room that holds the "saddle" — the piece of gray steel at the highest spot of the bridge tower where the suspensions cross over. Because the bridge sways and the wires expand and contract, the steel saddle must move.

"Like a book on top of pencils," says Zuckerman, pointing to a row of cylinders beneath the saddle.

He turns, pops open a steel door, and he and Lisa have arrived at the jump-off point — the spot where they must compete with balance and gravity. Below them, the suspension cables curve toward the river.

Zuckerman is quiet now. No jokes here. He is the first out.

He clamps his harness to the guide wires, then begins his walk, each step punctuated by a zing-zing-zing sound of the brass clamps running along the wires. Lisa follows, carrying a canvas bag — also clamped with its own harness — that carries extra bulbs and tools. Inside the saddle room, where the zinging is amplified, it's like standing inside a giant acoustic guitar whose strings are being plucked.

After 60 feet, the men stop by the bulb to be changed and sit on the wire. It is here where most of the slips take place, if they take place at all.

First, the outside globe is removed. It's hot as Lisa straddles it between his feet. Next, the bulb is twisted out. Zuckerman lets it sit to cool before taking it out and putting the fresh one in.

On this day, the men won't have to replace any of the electrical parts. No need for screwdrivers and elbow grease.

In 10 minutes, its over. A new bulb glows. The men start up the wire, climbing heavily as they arrive in the saddle room.

"Today," says Zuckerman, "was basically a cakewalk."

"It's just beautiful up here, isn't it?" says Lisa.

He looks out on the wires.

The necklace is complete again.

At Home and Dropped Out

I met Henry Guevarez a week after school started in 1988. Like almost half the young Latino men across America that year, he had become a social statistic — a dropout.

Henry Guevarez is in control. He presses a button on the TV remote. Across the room, the picture jumps. A game show. Then a Tina Turner music video. Then a soap opera.

It's 3:45 p.m. Henry got out of bed an hour ago. Tonight, he'll meet his girl, or maybe thumb his old copies of *Gentleman's Quarterly* at his mother's Paterson apartment.

Henry Guevarez has plenty of time to kill. When his friends returned to Kennedy High School, he stayed home, a dropout.

He's 18. He swears he'll make it big. Listen:

"If you really put your mind to it and set your goals, you can do it. I know eventually I'll make money. If you have willpower, you can do anything."

As he talks, Henry fingers the gold ring on his left pinky, then scratches his goatee. Except for his older sister cooking rice in the kitchen, the three-bedroom apartment is empty. Henry's mother is at her machine at a Paterson lampshade factory. His divorced father works at a battery factory.

"If it was up to me, I'd live in Teaneck or Englewood or Englewood Cliffs. And I'd like a BMW. But that's too much. Right now, I want a Wrangler Laredo."

What about a high school diploma? Nationwide, 40 percent of Hispanic students drop out. Not having a diploma usually is a ticket to a lower-class life. Henry isn't worried.

"Oh sure, I'll finish my education," he says. Only it won't be at Kennedy or any other high school, he says. Henry may shoot for a high school equivalency test. Then he'd like to try computer classes. Maybe he'll try business school. Maybe get a part-time job.

Henry left Kennedy in January 1987 for a juvenile detention center. The charge: assault. Three months later, he was placed in a city-run youth program. That ended a year ago, and Henry returned to Kennedy. He lasted until April 1988, then left again. "I just didn't like it."

To Al Moody, director of Paterson's Youth Services Bureau, Henry is a bright kid on a downward slide. "I see him taking a fall," Moody says. "The street is very strong for a kid like him.

"But this guy had everything going for him. He had everything that's needed for success in school. He had the brains. So many kids don't have enough to eat or clothes to wear. That was not the case for him."

Henry has known the street. Until a few months ago, he says, he sold crack on Paterson's Union Street, on a stretch between the Club Charm and Big Willie's Cozy Inn. Some days, authorities say, he grossed $1,700. He never got caught. But now, he says, he has turned his back on drugs.

"It's really getting bad out there. I don't want to get locked up."

Henry isn't sure when he last sold crack. "Maybe last June," he says, denying he still sells it, or uses it. He brags that in his salad days he rented cars with a friend's credit card, drove to 145th Street in Manhattan to buy crack, and returned to Paterson. When demand was high, he made four trips a week.

"I used to buy vials for $10 and come over here and sell it for $20. I would get over 200 vials at once." He hid them in his mom's apartment.

On Saturdays, Henry celebrated at shopping centers. Sometimes, he blew $1,000. "I'd get $60 shirts, $100 sneakers, $90 pants; I like Giorgio Armani and Benetton."

Henry says he'll have all that again, only this time, legally.

"I want the best. I don't want to be walking around all bummy and dirty. I won't be hanging out. I'll be with mature people."

Outside, on the street, salsa pulsates from a boom box. A car engine whines. A woman yells in Spanish for a child.

Henry pauses to listen, then reaches for the TV remote again.

The Long Track

Crime-solving sometimes takes a long time — in this case, 21 years.

Some sons have been known to go to great lengths to find the right gift for their fathers. But Martin Gallagher III, who runs a Montvale Exxon station, might easily lay claim to going further than most. He tracked down his dad's stolen car.

The car, a replica of a 1930s Cord convertible, with sweeping fenders and a convertible top, was stolen 21 years ago.

To do this, Gallagher contacted people in 22 states, negotiated the bureaucratic pathways of 15 government agencies, deciphered mistakes on police records, and eventually tracked the car from a dusty airport garage in New Jersey to an 83-year-old retiree in Virginia.

Along the way — and inspired by his favorite spy novelist, John Le Carré — Gallagher invented an alias, installed a special phone in his Woodcliff Lake home, and concocted a cover story so he wouldn't scare off the thief and various unsuspecting buyers of the stolen car.

"Finding a needle in a haystack," said the 36-year-old son, "is nothing compared to this. It was like an MIA. I just wanted my father to have closure on it."

His father, 58-year-old Martin Gallagher II, who was kept in the dark until the car was located, puts it another way: "It was beyond words. It just absolutely blew me out of the water. It just took my breath away."

How this story evolved is as much a tale of sentiment as of detective work. "You know what I call it?" said Dorothy Gallagher, mother of Martin III and wife of Martin II.

"Love."

"An amazing story," said Montvale police detective Dave DiBlasi, who helped Martin Gallagher III decipher old records. "Generally, if you have a burglary or theft, people get on with their lives and pick up and move on. Martin did this all for his father. It wasn't a monetary issue. He wanted this car for his father."

To understand this journey, you have to understand the car itself. Even today, 32 years after it rolled off an assembly line as one of only 92 Cord replicas built by a now-bankrupt company, the car — with its Corvair engine and body of a synthetic rubberized material — is not a million-dollar work of art. The Cord replica was purchased for only $18,500 in 1997 by the Virginia retiree, the last of a series of owners who police and a judge say did not know it had been stolen.

But the Gallagher car was not just another box of steel and wires, either.

The father bought the car on a whim in 1972. Martin Gallagher II was running a meat-delivery business from his Queens home. He had three young children to raise. But he also had an eye for cars, having built one as a teenager. As an adult, he was in the habit of buying a new car each year.

On a snowy, late-night delivery in Manhattan, he spotted the Cord replica, parked outside a swanky apartment building on Madison Avenue. Weeks passed and the Cord stayed there, with vandals cutting its convertible top and police leaving stacks of parking tickets. He left a note, asking if it was for sale. Days later, a man phoned and said he could take the car for $1,000.

"I was looking for a toy, something I could fix up," the father said. "I used to say when I'm real old, I'd have it redone and would drive around in it."

The son remembers his mother's dream, too. "Mom used to joke that she would have a white silk scarf as she rode around with Dad."

But that dream took a detour.

In the early 1970s, the father left the meat business and moved to Bergen County. He eventually opened three Exxon stations in New Jersey and one in Pearl River, N.Y. Working long hours at the gas stations, the father didn't have much time for the Cord replica. He ended up parking it at one of his Montvale stations to attract customers.

What the car attracted was a thief.

In 1977, police and court records say, the father was approached by Daniel Ginsberg, an electrician from Wayne who owned a blue Cord from the 1930s. Ginsberg offered to buy the Gallagher car for $10,000. The father said no. But when Ginsberg offered to restore the car, the father said OK.

It would be a big job, and Martin Gallagher II and Ginsberg set a target date of May 1979 so the former could drive it in a local Memorial Day parade. Martin Gallagher II handed $2,000 to Ginsberg for the job when he took the car to Ginsberg's shop in Wayne, and gave him two more payments of $1,000 each over the next year.

That was the last the Gallagher family saw of the car until earlier this year.

The father said he would phone Ginsberg in 1977, 1978, and 1979, and would be told that the work on the car was going fine. He didn't think anything amiss, even when Ginsberg couldn't finish the job by Memorial Day, 1979. Ginsberg let the Gallaghers borrow his 1930s Cord.

Not long afterward, the Gallaghers discovered that Ginsberg's phone was disconnected. After driving to Wayne, the father could not find a trace of his car — or Ginsberg, police reports say. He filed a stolen car report with Montvale police.

Martin Gallagher III, then a teenager, remembers his father being upset as the months wore on and no car turned up. He also remembers the stolen Cord being the butt of good-natured jokes from his father's friends.

"At my father's birthday party," the son remembered, "his friends all showed up with pieces of cord and would say, 'Here's your cord.' It was frustrating. It was upsetting. He was happy on the outside and crying on the inside."

One prankster even gave the father a toy replica of a Cord. But unlike the Gallagher car, which was yellow, this toy was red. "I didn't realize," said the son, as he picked up the toy in his father's office, "how significant that color would be."

The father hired a private detective who tracked Ginsberg's whereabouts to California. But there was no car. Back in Montvale, meanwhile, police say the father would call the station every month or so to check on the car. No leads turned up. What the father didn't know was that police were circulating an incorrect identification number for the stolen Cord.

After graduating from Fairfield University and getting married, the son took over one of his father's Exxon stations with his brother in the mid-1980s. The father retired to Florida.

The son, meanwhile, completed two side projects that ultimately inspired him to set out and find the Cord. First, he completely rebuilt a 20-year-old Pontiac GTO, meticulously assembling hundreds of pieces. Then, after his grandfather, Martin Gallagher I, totaled a Lincoln Town Car that had been a 50th wedding anniversary present from the family, Martin Gallagher III rebuilt that, even finding a replica of its DARE bumper sticker.

"In my eyes, I gave myself my GTO back," the son said. "I gave my grandfather back his Lincoln. The Cord has always been a sore spot with my father."

And so began the trek. But the first big break did not come until summer 1997, when the son happened to be looking through car magazines at his Exxon station and noticed a listing for a museum for Cord cars in Indiana.

He phoned, asking for information about Cords but not revealing anything about the stolen car. The museum told him about a Cord owners' club. The son joined, using a false name, and spread word that he was looking to buy one of the Cord replicas built in the 1960s.

With a booming business at the Exxon station's eight service bays and 800 daily gasoline customers, the son spent hours in the evening poring over old car magazines or making phone calls to follow up ads for Cords.

The son couldn't find Daniel Ginsberg, but he did track down some of the stolen car's owners, including one who knew Ginsberg and owned the Gallagher car for a short time in 1981.

Doug Johnson, a retired insurance executive from Rockaway, said he bought the Gallagher Cord that year from a garage in Ridgewood. "All it was was a hulk of parts," said Johnson, adding that he did not know the car was stolen.

After finding Johnson and other owners, the son felt the stolen Cord was probably still intact and being passed around the network of owners of exotic cars. But he feared that if he revealed too much about his family's story about the stolen car, he might scare off people who could help him.

So he made up a cover story — that his brother's 1996 Cord replica had been lost in a fire and that he was looking to replace it. "I had to be as secretive as possible," the son said. "I was trying to appear as one of the good old boys in the club. I'm not comfortable lying to anybody."

Armed with a rapidly bulging box of knowledge about Cords, the son had what he calls one of his "defining moments." He discovered that police had written an incorrect vehicle identification number on the original stolen car report. Without a correct number, no leads had ever turned up when police checked the national computer listings of stolen cars.

Such a mistake, however, was easy to make. Cord replicas had 6-digit ID numbers; most new cars now have 17-digit numbers. Thinking the Cord's ID number required more digits, the police mistakenly wrote in extra numbers from the car's title. The numbers turned out to be the vehicle's weight.

"We had two little kids and my wife was pregnant with a third," the son said. "Here I was staying up at night reading 20-year-old articles by people who are probably dead. It was a tedious process of going through tidbits. I liken it to archaeology where you sift through all this and find this tidbit. But I felt if I didn't do it, nobody would."

With a correct ID number, the son tracked the car to Wisconsin, then to the retiree in Fairfax, Va. He contacted police, who impounded the car. But when Martin Gallagher III tried to pick it up, the retiree, Thomas Dodson, went to court.

It turns out that Dodson's son, Thomas Dodson Jr., had tried to do for his father what Martin Gallagher III was doing for his — find a Cord replica. Not knowing it had been stolen, Thomas Dodson Jr. purchased the Cord for $18,500 in September 1997.

The Cord had been restored — and painted a different color. It was now maroon. "The vehicle underwent a complete metamorphosis," said the younger Gallagher's lawyer in Virginia, Paul Mengel. "That's where it got complicated."

The Dodsons claimed that the Gallagher car had been changed so much that it was no longer the car that had been stolen. But after two court dates were postponed, a Virginia judge ruled on October 9 that the car should be returned to the Gallagher family.

"There are compelling equities in favor of each claimant here, Dodson, the innocent purchaser, and Gallagher, the innocent theft victim," Judge M. Langhorne Keith said. "But the rule that a thief cannot pass good title is both venerable and universal."

Three weeks ago, the son delivered the old Cord back to Montvale. "It's funny," said the son, Martin Gallagher III, "a lot of people have come back and asked if that's the Cord."

The father, Martin Gallagher II, said he had one more wish. He wants to buy his wife that white silk scarf.

The Lingering Haze

Over a six-year period, I followed a young athlete who was subjected to a humiliating hazing by teammates. His teammates moved on with life. He did not.

They call him "Cake." And the reason Anthony Erekat bears this strange nickname dates back to an August night in 1992, when he dreamed of being a football player and ended up being humiliated.

Looking back, Erekat harbors an abiding, intense anger that time and maturity seem unable to soothe. As he puts it: "They can't give me my high school years back."

He is 22 now. He wants to move on. He is waiting for the courts to help him.

That night in 1992, Erekat was 17 and hoping to make the Lodi High School varsity football roster. He was attending a special summer camp in Mansfield that Lodi football coaches were running.

It was about 9 p.m. The day's workouts had long since ended. A post-dinner seminar with coaches had broken up. Erekat was tired and felt a headache coming on. He remembers heading for his room to fetch some aspirin.

He never made it.

Erekat was jumped by at least a dozen teammates for a hazing ritual that seems straight out of The Citadel.

A few large players held Erekat down while others wrapped duct tape around his arms and legs. Then other players smeared his body with peanut butter and shaving cream — giving rise to the "Cake" nickname. Someone threw human feces at him. Someone cut his foot-long ponytail. Someone else turned on a video camera and made a tape to be watched later.

There is little doubt about the facts of this story because 14 players eventually pleaded guilty and were ordered to perform 50 hours each of community service. But when that slap-on-the-wrist experience was over, the players went on with their lives.

Erekat did not. Perhaps it was the feeling that the justice system did not care enough to punish his attackers more harshly. Perhaps it was the politics of tiny Lodi, where the players were suspended for the season's first game but then were allowed to play when someone realized that the opening game was against a tough rival. The players were suspended for a game against a lightweight opponent.

But if you really want to understand Anthony Erekat's pain, you have to understand his personal history. His father abandoned him as a baby. He grew up in government housing and his mother worked two waitressing jobs. In school, he was classified as a special education student — an easy target for the football hazing crowd.

Erekat's mother, Merriettice Andrus, says some children even had a nickname for her son back then. "They called him 'Retard,'" she said.

That night in 1992, after the hazing ritual, Erekat left football camp. He never went back to Lodi High School, never made the football team. He tried going to Elmwood Park High School, but the hazing story and the humiliation caught up with him.

He dropped out and got a job. That fall, the Lodi football team went undefeated and won the state championship.

Today, Anthony Erekat manages a candy store at an area mall and lives in a rented house in Elmwood Park. He is the father of a 2-year-old daughter. He also says he can't sleep nights and fears running into his old teammates and their potential taunts.

It's this fear that drove him on a recent Wednesday to the Bergen County Courthouse in Hackensack. He took the elevator to the fourth floor and a courtroom where civil lawsuits are handled. And there, Anthony Erekat learned that justice still has to wait.

He carries the same gut-level anger that Fred Goldman bore after he watched a Los Angeles criminal court let O. J. Simpson off the hook for murder. Like Goldman, Erekat is taking his case back to court with a civil lawsuit he has filed. And his goal is simple.

"I want revenge," he says. "It's about getting my apology, for them to admit they are wrong and for them to give up something. They didn't give up their football season. I missed two years of high school. I never got to go to senior prom. I'm the one that sleeps the nightmares. I'm the one who sweats. I'm the one who's aggravated. Not them. Basically, I want them to see it's time for them to pay me. They got a good laugh out of it. Now I want a laugh out of it."

This is what justice has become in this sad case, a young man's memory so stained by the prankish foolishness of high school boys that his life is now the captive of vengeance.

But that doesn't mean adults are innocent here. The Lodi Board of Education played politics with the players' suspensions. The Lodi football coach, Pat Tirico, issued statements about his players feeling remorse. But he has no regrets; he got his championship that year, without seeming to realize how tarnished his trophy is.

On that same Wednesday that Anthony Erekat went to court, Coach Tirico had the chance to step forward and speak like a champion and offer some insight into this sad history. Instead he spoke like a politician facing investigation.

"I have no comment," he said.

Anthony Erekat is talking, though. "I won't live it down," he said. "I'll always be that person who got that haircut from that championship football team."

At the courthouse, Erekat's trial did not begin as scheduled. Lawyers for the players, coaches, and Lodi school trustees named in the lawsuit succeeded in delaying the case until late April.

Erekat left in a huff. And later, he offered this glimpse inside his troubled soul:

"At 17, I didn't know what hate meant. Now I know what hate means."

Empty-Handed

All those years, nobody seemed to notice how the statue in the town square seemed to be missing something. Maybe it was meant to be that way.

Poor General Poor.

Enoch Poor of New Hampshire was enough of a celebrity when the American Revolution was fought across the farms and woods of New Jersey that he was preserved in a bronze statue across from the Bergen County Courthouse in Hackensack.

Go there, and you can see ol' Enoch looking quite proud of himself, in his Colonial hat, his military epaulets, and his knee-high boots with spurs.

But something's missing.

Somebody stole the general's sword.

"Is it missing?" asked Hackensack's public works superintendent, Jesse V. D'Amore, when asked one day about the statue and the sword.

Don't blame D'Amore for not knowing the general is weaponless.

"Most people don't even notice," said Bergen's cultural affairs director, Ruth Van Wagoner. "It's been gone a long time."

You might even say it's history.

Among local history buffs, especially those trying to preserve the area's place as an important landscape during the Revolutionary War, the missing sword is considered a metaphor for a modern, complex nation that seems increasingly unaware of history and how to preserve it. If Poor were a modern figure with a loyal following, the missing sword might have been replaced long ago.

But in the wash of two centuries of American history, it's hard for an otherwise obscure Revolutionary military leader to capture the attention of a nation where large segments of the population can't even name their current congressional representative.

It was 1780, and the war was still raging when Poor, then 44, died in the Colonial Army encampment in Oradell. He had fought in such important battles as Saratoga and Monmouth, endured the harsh winter at Valley Forge, and received a full military funeral and burial in a Reformed Church cemetery across the street from his statue. But Poor's military colleagues, including George Washington and the Marquis de Lafayette, who attended his funeral with 5,000 soldiers, would go on to greater fame in the war and afterward.

Like an old soldier without headlines anymore, Poor mostly faded away.

"It says something about human nature," says Kevin Wright, the curator of the Steuben House in River Edge, where Washington had set up his headquarters when Poor died. "People just forget."

As for the missing sword, Wright noted: "I guess there are temptations you shouldn't place before people."

Indeed, when one Hackensack official was casually told about the swordless statue, he asked: "Is this something significant?"

After speaking with an aide and learning that the missing sword was indeed important, he then joked that Poor's hand was "clasped around a sword or a Sabrett hot dog."

The latest sword has been gone since John F. Kennedy was in the White House, leaving the general's right hand wrapped around a bladeless sword hilt. But before that sword was swiped in 1961, the general had been bladeless for almost half a century. Indeed, the first unsheathed sword, designed by sculptor E. F. Piatti of Englewood to point forward in Poor's right hand as if he were about to disembowel an intruder, was stolen within days after the 7-foot statue was erected in 1904 by the local chapter of the Sons of the Revolution.

The Bergen Democrat, a weekly newspaper with a flair for reporting garden-variety vandalism with a mix of tabloidism and kid gloves, announced the "mutilation" of the statue, while also explaining that "the separation of the sword from his hand was apparently done by some inquisitive person examining the statue."

No one ever was arrested.

◆

Few people stop at General Poor's statue anymore, in part because you have to dodge traffic just to get close enough to read the plaque that explains who the man in the Colonial uniform is.

The statue stands on a 60-ton platform of Vermont granite, in a triangle island at the intersection of Court and Moore Streets. When first erected, the statue faced west, photographs show. Today, it faces south.

Why the change of direction? Like the missing sword, few people know.

"People always joked about General Poor twisting in the wind because he's faced every direction of the compass," said Kevin Wright, the Steuben curator.

Wright said that in the early years of the century, members of the Sons of the Revolution were quite angry that the sword had been stolen. But as the years passed and America became immersed in two world wars, a national economic depression, the Cold War, and the baby boom years, fewer people seemed to notice.

Then, there was the not-so-small question of who was supposed to care for the statue. Property records indicated that the land for the statue was still owned by the Reformed Church. The church said it was Hackensack's responsibility.

Today, Hackensack's parks department keeps watch over the statue, its garden of purple and pink petunias with a 2-foot-high American flag, and a sign that announces Poor was "regarded by Washington and Lafayette as a great general." The bronze plaque praises Poor's "unselfishness" and notes that he "secured the respect of all who were under his command, gained for all time the esteem of his fellow officers," and won "fame as a soldier, patriot, and citizen."

But neither the sign nor the plaque explains yet another mystery of poor General Poor. How did he die?

The circumstances of General Poor's death are clouded by a mix of legend and historical records — with the truth still not absolutely confirmed in such a way as to separate myth from reality.

Officially, General Poor died of typhoid fever, a common ailment known as "Camp Fever" in the Colonial and British armies of the Revolutionary War. But legend tells a far more exotic and tawdry tale — that Poor was killed in a duel near Kinderkamack Road.

While the story of typhoid fever is documented in several accounts by army officers and physicians, the tale of the duel emerges from letters and a book from descendants of the junior officer who reportedly shot Poor. Indeed, one myth says the typhoid fever story was concocted to cover up the duel. In the 1960s and 1970s, the clash of stories became enough of a controversy that one descendant of the alleged duelist questioned why General Poor should have a statue in Hackensack or anyplace else.

Historian Reginald McMahon of River Edge, who has devoted much of his life to researching the events of the Revolutionary War in North Jersey, says the most substantial evidence supports the story that Poor died of typhoid fever. But as much as McMahon has researched the nooks and crannies of the life of Enoch Poor, he can't locate the stolen swords.

"They were stolen twice," he says. "But where they went, we know nothing."

As for a replacement sword, McMahon is sure of what would happen.

"The idea of a sword staying there for any length of time is going to be a little tricky," he said. "I don't mean to be cynical, but if it's replaced for the third time, it would be stolen for the third time."

Lost Along the Way

To better understand the problems of America's chronic homeless, I decided to follow one man for a year. Here is one installment.

As rain clouds lumbered up the coast and across North Jersey, a man got out of jail.

This may not seem like much of an event. But when you spent the previous night under a suicide watch at the Bergen County lockup and your major worry now is trying to find a dry place to sleep, it classifies as one of life's turning points.

The man wore no coat — just a soiled, wrinkled, green shirt and jeans. His boots had no laces, the result of his being on suicide watch. On jail records, the address he gave for his home had a familiar ring. It was a homeless shelter in Hackensack.

Such is the paradoxical life of Kenneth Pyykko.

As the evening darkness crept in and dinnertime came and went, Pyykko stood in the doorway of a Hackensack social service agency, his chin tucked into his chest and his hands jammed into his armpits to ward off the damp chill from a day's cold rain. To a passer-by, he said he wanted to look for "my identification."

"I left it somewhere," Pyykko said.

He couldn't remember where. Nor can he remember where his family is or even how to spell his name. When arrested last fall, he told police it was "Piko." Before that, it was "Pyko." In two weeks, he will turn 40 — that is, if police and jail records that show he was born on March 8, 1959, are correct. With Pyykko, local authorities have learned they can never be quite sure.

The latest chapter in the homeless life of Kenneth Pyykko highlights a continuing drama that is well known to local police, courts, jail guards, and the array of social workers and homeless volunteers who have tried mightily to care for him over the past year.

Pyykko, who says he grew up in Englewood and New Milford, is something of a fixture in the homeless population that drifts through Hackensack and other parts of North Jersey like migratory birds in search of a meal or a safe place to stop. He is also a symbol of something larger.

Diagnosed as suffering from a variety of mental problems including schizophrenia, he represents an increasingly insolvable dilemma, not just in North Jersey but across America: what to do with a homeless population that consists of large numbers of mental patients with no place to go, no goals to aspire to.

In the case of Ken Pyykko, nothing has worked to turn his life around — not jail, not courts, not police warrants, not the efforts of homeless volunteers, not even the efforts of doctors and their prescriptions to help control his schizophrenia. The last time Pyykko was given a medical prescription, he lost the pills on a bus.

"Somebody should put him in the hospital," said Hackensack Deputy Police Chief Edward Koeser, who has followed Pyykko's case for a year. "Obviously there is something wrong with the guy."

"It's terrible," said Robin Reilly, a caseworker at the Peter's Place Homeless Shelter at Hackensack's Christ Episcopal Church, who has tried to care for Pyykko. "He needs to be institutionalized. He needs constant help. But our laws don't permit that."

The tale of Pyykko's revolving-door journey through jails, homeless shelters, and other stops with social service agencies and hospitals has been chronicled in *The Record* for the past year. It is a story that is as frustrating to the people involved as it is mysterious. In Ken Pyykko, those who try to help him find a man who seems quite helpless. And yet, they also find a man who manages to get by in the most surprising of ways.

The latest chapter begins just before Halloween. On the otherwise nondescript night of October 27, Pyykko found himself in the parking lot of a car repair shop in Teaneck. He was looking for a place to sleep. Little did he know that he was being watched by plainclothes police looking for burglars.

It was just after 11 p.m., and, police records show, a Teaneck police detective noticed the solitary man "lurking between the cars" at Taki Motors on the corner of DeGraw Avenue and Queen Anne Road. Moments later, when Detective Sgt. Thomas Sikorsky checked the cars, he found Pyykko inside a Chevrolet van.

Sikorsky ordered Pyykko out of the van and asked him what he was doing. Pyykko "could not explain why he was in the vehicle," Sikorsky wrote in his police report that night as he charged him with burglary.

The next day, Pyykko was arraigned. His bail was set at $2,500. Because of the value of the van, his case was referred to the Bergen County Prosecutor's Office. Because he could not pay his bail, Pyykko was sent to the county jail.

If he had given Teaneck authorities his correct name, they might have discovered that Pyykko was wanted in Hackensack for missing a court date. That case — dating to April Fools' Day, 1998 — began with Pyykko standing on a corner on Kansas Street, not far from the homeless shelter he would later give to jail guards as his home address. According to police records, Pyykko was "yelling profanities at pedestrians and would not let them pass on the sidewalk."

When police showed up and asked Pyykko to leave, he reportedly cursed at them, too. When officers tried to arrest Pyykko, they said, he fought with them. After finally being wrestled into a police car and taken to a cell at Hackensack police headquarters, police say, Pyykko spit in an officer's face and was charged with assault.

A week later, Pyykko went to court in Hackensack to answer the charges. That day, he also tried to escape after asking to use a bathroom and slipping out a door. After being brought back to court, he was given another date to appear in court.

Pyykko never returned, and a contempt of court warrant was issued for his arrest.

Seven months later and awaiting an answer on the Teaneck burglary charge, Pyykko remained in the Bergen County Jail through Thanksgiving and Christmas as the county Prosecutor's Office evaluated his case. On January 3, county prosecutors downgraded the Teaneck case to a lesser burglary offense, and Pyykko's case was sent back to Teaneck Municipal Court. Pyykko was turned loose.

In sending the case back to Teaneck — and still unaware of the outstanding Hackensack warrant for his arrest — a Superior Court judge reduced Pyykko's bail and set him free "on his own recognizance" with the warning that he would have to pay $500 if he did not show up for his next court appearance in Teaneck.

Pyykko was scheduled to be in Teaneck's Municipal Court on February 10. He never showed, records indicate.

He was back in jail — under the name "Pyko." After leaving the Bergen County Jail on January 3, when the burglary charge was referred to Teaneck Municipal Court, Pyykko was spotted occasionally on local streets by homeless workers. He would turn up for a meal or for a dry, warm spot to sleep at shelters. Then he would disappear again.

"I got a call a few days ago that someone saw him at the bus station," said Debbie Doyle-Levi, another caseworker at the Peter's Place shelter. "But we couldn't find him."

On January 24, a Sunday, a Hackensack police officer spotted Pyykko on State Street, not far from the Peter's Place shelter. The officer remembered the man with the scruffy hair and the soiled clothes. He checked the computerized list of outstanding warrants and discovered one for Pyykko, dating to the April Fools' Day incident, and a contempt of court charge for failing to appear.

That night, Pyykko was back in the Bergen County Jail. This time, however, he was on a suicide watch in a special ward for troubled prisoners, jail records show.

In Teaneck, meanwhile, Pyykko missed his February 10 court date. No warrant was issued. His case was postponed until March.

Last Wednesday, Pyykko was taken to Hackensack Municipal Court to answer the old assault charge from April Fools' Day. Hackensack Judge Louis Dinice downgraded Pyykko's assault charge to a local charge of disturbing the peace. In return, Pyykko pleaded guilty. The judge gave him credit for 30 days in jail and turned him loose.

There was one more hurdle, though. Pyykko was required to pay a $2 court cost. When he couldn't come up with the money, the court clerk let him go. "We didn't hold him to the $2," the clerk said later. "You just hope he'll pay it eventually."

In the police department, Deputy Chief Koeser felt a mix of frustration and sadness as Pyykko returned to his home on the streets. "You've got to feel sorry for the guy," the deputy chief said. "If he goes to court enough, maybe someone will do something for him."

That night, as Hackensack's streets slowly emptied and shops closed, Pyykko walked alone to the Johnson Public Library, where he tried to use a pay phone. "I just want to get out of here," he said.

If he knew where he was going, he didn't say.

Gratefully Dead Head

I once called the Grateful Dead a "second-rate rock band." Letters from all over the planet poured in, most of them comparing me to the Antichrist. When the Dead came to town again, I had to meet their fans. Here is one of them.

Fred the Head, Texas-born hippie and drug entrepreneur, announces that he has achieved cultural karma. One night last week, Fred went to his 775th concert by the Grateful Dead rock band.

"I'm a Dead Head," says Fred.

This is no ordinary title. If you worship the Grateful Dead, you live to be called a Dead Head and attend every Dead concert, anytime, anywhere. It's your brass ring.

Let history record that Fred the Head went to the Meadowlands Arena for his 775th Dead show. The event, he insists, was a genuine cosmic situation, right at the spiritual epicenter of New Jersey, between the turnpike, the racetrack, and the alleged final resting place of Jimmy Hoffa.

"It was," said Fred, "wonderful."

The Grateful Dead, which claims to be happy despite such songs as "Death Don't Have No Mercy," had booked the arena for five nights. Fred, a tie-dyed-in-the-wool Dead Head, absolutely had to go every night. Otherwise, he'd die.

"I've never had a job," said Fred the Head. "Work is a four-letter word. This is my work."

He is dead serious.

When you're 32 and you've spent the last 12 years doing nothing but selling marijuana and LSD and going to 775 Grateful Dead concerts, you tend to think you're on a career track somewhere.

Fred the Head is so serious he rarely takes a day off. He doesn't have a home address either because he travels to so many Dead shows. In 12 years, since dropping out of college to be a Dead Head, he's missed only six Dead shows. He is to Dead concerts what Lou Gehrig was once to baseball. He's always there.

For the Meadowlands concerts, Fred feverishly hitchhiked from San Francisco in six days with a series of long-haul truckers. When his last ride dropped him on the turnpike by the arena, it was 5 p.m. The first concert began at 7:30 p.m. It was sold out, too.

No problem, said Fred. He walked to the front door of the arena and started speaking in Dead code to fellow Dead Heads.

"Bud for tickets," Fred the Head proclaimed.

For those who have not passed through the Dead universe, a bud is not a beer. To a Dead Head, a bud is marijuana.

Within minutes, Fred had a ticket from a young woman. He gave her $5 worth of pot. Fred likes to pay his own way.

The next day, Fred made his way to the Dead zone, the arena parking lot where Dead Heads await the next Dead show. Imagine a tailgate party for hippies, and you'll get the idea.

The lot was a sea of Volkswagen buses, campers, remodeled school buses, and decade-old Plymouths. Somebody pounded a conga. A dog named Dylan ran by. A Frisbee flew overhead. A woman named Woodstock ate a bean sandwich. Another woman passed out candy, promising that it wasn't "dusted" with LSD. From a boom box, The Who sang "I Can See for Miles."

Nobody talked about the crisis in Panama or the World Series or abortion or the Middle East or even the weather. The only live topic was the Dead and what songs the band might play. Dead Heads are like that.

Fred was skateboarding. Top to bottom, he was dressed for Dead. His vest was purple and from Guatemala. His T-shirt had the Dead emblem — a skull and roses. His pants and canvas high-tops were tie-dyed rainbow. His wrist was wrapped in a rainbow band.

"It's the people," Fred the Head said. "It's the energy. That's why I come. I don't get tired of it."

By the time he leaves New Jersey, he'll have seen 779 Dead shows. He'll follow the Dead to Philadelphia, to North Carolina, then Miami. Next spring, he plans to be in Russia for a possible Dead performance.

The Dead life is like that. Very cosmic, something new all the time.

"When will it end?" Fred asks. "It ends when I die."

Roads Not Taken

What do you do when you are a celebrity before you graduate from high school? Tanja Vogt went to college, then returned home to become an elementary school teacher.

Even before she was old enough to vote, Tanja Vogt had a career most political activists only dream about.

As a high school student who admits to feeling more than a little self-conscious, she took on one of America's most powerful corporations — McDonald's — and won.

After months of lobbying and clever environmental protests led by Vogt in West Milford in 1989 and 1990, the McDonald's fast-food chain changed the way it serves its burgers. It abolished its use of polystyrene foam packaging, replacing it with biodegradable paper and cardboard.

Vogt quickly became the toast of America's environmental movement.

She spoke at an Earth Day rally on the Capitol steps in Washington with actors Tom Cruise and Richard Gere, and in New York City at a United Nations conference. Film crews chronicled her exploits. President George Bush wrote a letter praising her work. Ben and Jerry's, the socially hip ice cream maker, sponsored her on a trip to Russia to study environmental problems with other students from across America. And at Walt Disney World, her name was included in a permanent exhibit to honor 10 ordinary Americans who have inspired environmental changes.

And now?

To find Tanja Vogt, you must drive into the hills of West Milford, her hometown. You leave the traffic rush of Route 23 and take High Crest Road as it winds up a sharp corkscrew and follows the rim of a pristine lake and spills into the Apshawa School.

Here, in a sunny classroom with a bulletin board that encourages students to "Build Your Problem Solving Skills" and "Treat Others as You Would Like to Be Treated," Vogt says she is putting the lessons of her high school activism to work. She teaches the fourth grade — by choice. And she wants to make this her career. She is 22.

◆

Vogt's is not just a story of one person deciding to come home after tasting the intoxicating brew of media-stoked public activism. It is a story of understanding your ideals and deciding where best to plant them.

She was not disillusioned by the role she played as an environmentalist. Far from it. Vogt just believes her best work can be done, not on the grand stage of national activism, elbow-to-elbow with all manner of celebrities, but in a small classroom, with children.

"This is what I want to do," she says in a voice pure and clear. "And this is the best place I can do it."

In this election season, amid the crush of competing ideals and as all manner of politicians trade in the rhetoric of values, Tanja Vogt's decision to return to her roots has a special meaning. She embodies an often unspoken cornerstone of the nation's values debate now — the urge by Americans to find faith in the future of their communities.

Vogt is sitting now in her empty classroom. It is midmorning, and her 22 students are on a break. Outside the wall of windows, the leaves on the oaks and maples across the West Milford hills are just beginning to shed their green hue and embrace autumn's multicolored blanket.

"I really love it here," she says. "I knew it immediately."

Vogt, who graduated two years ago from William Paterson College and is engaged to be married in July to a police officer from a neighboring town, is not unaware that her choice to devote her life to teaching in a public elementary school might seem incongruous with the star-washed life she led only a few years ago.

Vogt chuckles as she remembers those days. She agrees that after her heady success and her stint in the spotlight she could have nabbed a high-profile, lucrative job in television or as a spokeswoman for an environmentalist lobby. With the right combination of luck and timing, she could have entered politics.

"At the time, everybody was asking me: 'Are you going to go into environmental science, or are you going to go into communications?'" she says. "But I started thinking about something I could do that would really give back to the students and the parents and the teachers who supported me. And this was it."

It wasn't just teaching, however, that lured her. It was a teacher named Karl Stehle. And it is here that her story takes on an added dimension — how one person is able to plant seeds with another — in this case, teacher to student.

Stehle, 53 and a social studies teacher in West Milford for 30 years, first met Tanja Vogt when she was 15. He had assigned his class to read the local newspaper, select an article, and write an essay about it.

Vogt chose a story about a mild controversy in West Milford — a debate between school officials on whether to use polystyrene foam trays in the school cafeteria. She remembers feeling upset about the use of the nonbiodegradable plastic, and she wrote an essay saying that the school should use another material. Vogt can still remember what happened next.

"Mr. Stehle walked by my desk and said, 'Why don't you do something about it?'"

So began Vogt's journey, first with the trays in the school cafeteria, and then with the McDonald's packaging.

"I looked back and thought that the difference Mr. Stehle has made in my life is just incredible," said Vogt. "Everyone has a teacher that they look back on and say, 'That was a good teacher.' But to look back and say, 'This person really changed my life,' that's rare, and it's a nice thing when that happens."

Karl Stehle also remembers those days, and what it was like to be a teacher encouraging a shy student.

"You have to see that sense of hope," he said. "I saw that in Tanja. That's what inspires me. She had this quiet spirituality about her, this sense of trusting."

Stehle remembers a conversation with Vogt. She felt shy about speaking in front of her classmates and remembered the pain of being teased about the activist role she was playing.

"When I first got into Mr. Stehle's class, I was not the type of person who was raising my hand all the time, participating and speaking out," says Vogt. "But it was the way he said, 'You can do it. I know that you can do it.'"

Stehle remembers telling her: "You have the chance to be the hero that people are looking for." He also remembers Vogt feeling overwhelmed somewhat, but nonetheless believing in her best instincts.

"As a teacher," said Stehle, "you like to think you make the world a better place. It's why I love teaching. It's wonderful when you reach one student."

Tanja Vogt will tell you that even at this stage of her teaching career — it began only a year ago — she has tasted that feeling and yearns for more. Indeed, when she applied for her job, she wrote to West Milford school officials that she hoped her students could look back at her with the same respect she has for Stehle.

"It might not be the most glamorous job or the most highly paid job," she says, "but when I go home at the end of the day, I feel like I really made a difference and that I accomplished something. I always think about if I teach for 30 years, I think about how many students will cross my path and how many will come back and say, 'You really made a difference in my life.' Every morning when I come in, I think that."

At the Top of the Heap

You know you're in trouble when you call a meeting of your top students and they show up with lawyers. Such was the case when a school administrator in one of New Jersey's richest towns — and most competitive high schools — tried to name two girls as class valedictorians.

Edward Westervelt, a former English teacher and now superintendent at Allendale's Northern Highlands Regional High School, is a man schooled in the importance of rules. This week, he wanted to bend from the letter of the law to embrace its spirit. Then the lawyers stepped in.

At issue was that most cherished of high school honors: being chosen valedictorian. The title goes to the student with the highest grades. Simple, right? Hardly.

At Northern Highlands, where a B-plus average places you deep in the middle of the 180-member class and where grades are weighted depending on whether a student takes an honors course, two remarkable students, Alexandra McCormack and Whitney Freeman, found themselves at the top of the academic mountain. Both got straight A's through high school. But in her senior English class, Freeman received a B-plus. She ended with an average of 4.520. McCormack's average was 4.537.

It was that close. In fact, Freeman attended a countywide breakfast for valedictorians. But that selection was made in February, when she was on top.

A week after the breakfast, Ed Westervelt wrote to both girls' families, noting that their grades were so close that the school could not name a valedictorian until final marks were computed. A week later, it was clear: McCormack was on top by a margin of 17 one-thousandths. Think of it as winning the Olympic 100-meter sprint by a toenail.

Westervelt had another thought: Since both girls were so close, why not name them co-valedictorians? While rules are important, the margin of victory here made him uncomfortable. Measuring four years of academics this way seemed incomplete, perhaps harsh.

His hopes for a quiet compromise were quickly dashed, however. A few days after receiving Westervelt's letter, Freeman's father arrived at a meeting with a lawyer.

The next week, Westervelt said, he received a message in his mailbox from Alexandra McCormack. It was a photocopy of a newspaper article describing a court fight after a high school in Queens tried to solve a similar problem by naming two students as co-valedictorians. On the article, Westervelt said, McCormack scribbled what he took to be a warning: "Be careful."

Westervelt then received a message on his voice mail from Freeman's mother: If Whitney is asked to discuss the naming of a valedictorian, she should be allowed to call her attorney first.

And you thought things were complicated on *Beverly Hills 90210*.

Westervelt pondered what to do. He could follow his heart and name both girls to the top honor as a way of paying homage to their accomplishments. But that would mean bending the rules and possibly going to court. He spoke with the school's attorney. He decided to stick to the rules.

Westervelt described this dilemma only hours before the evening graduation ceremony — a day that should be framed in happiness. But to hear him speak, Ed Westervelt was clearly saddened. "We were forced into a mode where we had to play by the rules," he lamented.

Normally, such a statement would be applauded — that those who govern our schools are sticklers for rules. And some who read this tale may conclude that students at Northern Highlands High School have been taught an important lesson. But there is another lesson here, too — far grayer, perhaps, but nonetheless important. As Ed Westervelt puts it: "We were forced to be inflexible."

This will not be known as the class with two academically superior students. It will be known as a year when the threat of a lawsuit forced school administrators to play by the rules — and play it safe.

The Street Vendor

I found Charles Mysak on a New York sidewalk. His story goes back to a New Jersey courtroom, though.

NEW YORK —
The man with the day-old stubble and the gray T-shirt who sells books on a Manhattan street has a story to tell.

Some might see his tale as a comedy of errors or a soap opera with twists and turns. Or a morality play.

Or a tragedy.

It has been like that for a while now with Charles Mysak of Wayne.

Not too many years ago, you could find Mysak in any number of New Jersey courtrooms, a bespectacled lawyer in a dark suit, arguing passionately about the fine points of land use, DNA evidence in a murder case, or Mount Laurel housing regulations. In Wayne, you might have found him some nights in the council chambers challenging a developer or a town policy. News accounts called him "brash" and "outspoken." Residents elected him to the school board.

But then Charles Mysak fell.

He is virtually bankrupt now, his house on Wayne's Webster Avenue sold to pay bills and creditors. His family currently is living in an apartment. His driver's and lawyer's licenses have been suspended. In September, he is scheduled to go on trial in a Passaic County courtroom, charged with stealing almost $100,000 in clients' funds. This spring, he spent most of two months in the Monmouth County Jail after being caught driving without a license on the Garden State Parkway.

Each morning, with his wife at the wheel of a gray Ford Taurus station wagon, Mysak joins the bumper-to-bumper line of commuters into Manhattan. But instead of going to an office, he takes a pile of used books to a curbside spot near the corner of West 67th Street and Columbus Avenue.

"I don't miss the law," he volunteers, seeming to anticipate the question of why he became a sidewalk vendor. "I've always loved books."

To some who knew him as an outspoken attorney, Mysak's story is not comedy or soap opera or morality tale or tragedy at all.

Many see him as a mystery — a smart, passionate, articulate lawyer, who graduated from the prestigious Emory University Law School, worked several years as a New Jersey deputy attorney general before

starting private practice in Wayne, and then seemed to lose everything
for reasons that just don't make sense. Even Passaic County's chief assistant prosecutor, John Snowdon, who will present evidence against Mysak
in the September trial that could send him to jail for 10 years, asked this
of Mysak when told of his curbside bookselling:

"Did he sound competent? I wonder whether he's making poor deci-
sions because of his mental condition."

For the record, Mysak, a 48-year-old father of four, insists he has all
his marbles and is doing just fine as a sidewalk bookseller — except that
the money isn't going to push him into a higher tax bracket.

"If I'm lucky here, I make $200 a day," Mysak was saying one morn-
ing as he arranged his books on a Columbus Avenue curb. "As a lawyer,
I used to make $200 an hour."

◆ ◆ ◆

He sits now on a metal folding chair, positioned on the edge of a curb
and near an oak tree that offers leafy shade from the July sun. On a cardboard box, he lays out three Punch President cigars.

Across Columbus Avenue, men and women, their faces still glistening
from a morning workout, stride from a gym and toward a local Starbucks.
A block away, the summer tourists stroll past a Disney store.

Mysak looks up. He shares the block with a wine store, a druggist,
and a shop that sells women's dance apparel. At the curb, Mysak's wife,
Marilyn, sits in the driver's seat of the station wagon, loaded floor to
ceiling with all manner of books that Charles bought years ago when an
Acres of Books bookstore in Trenton went out of business. As Mysak
unloads boxes, Marilyn rests her head against the car door, trying to
catch a nap.

Marilyn, who works as a teacher's aide in a Paterson Catholic school
and as an administrative assistant in a physical therapy office, is Mysak's
chauffeur as he waits to see if his driver's license will be renewed. "You
can't believe how hard it's been," she mutters.

Mysak attempts a smile, then tries a joke about his current position in
life, where one of his greatest worries is moisture — from dogs who miss
the nearby tree and splatter his books and from sudden thunderstorms.
"There is one dog," he says, "that when he comes around I have to get
up and stand in front of my books to keep him away."

Mysak runs his palm over his merchandise, organized in no logical
order. A 1940 copy of Ernest Hemingway's *For Whom the Bell Tolls* sits
near a Linda Ronstadt songbook. An Alice Walker novel sits atop a copy
of Daphne du Maurier's *Rebecca*. A children's book about submarines is a
neighbor to a tome that tries to explain Beethoven's String Quartet No. 2
and another book that asks a question: *Does God Eat Us?*

You can find novels here by John Hersey and Danielle Steel. There are biographies of acid-rocker Grace Slick and radar inventor Sir Robert Watson-Watt. There are copies of *The Day of the Jackal* and *The Day Lincoln Died*. An Army field manual from World War II costs $10. An 1888 copy of Robert Louis Stevenson's *The Black Arrow* goes for $8.

"I'm a street guy, so I sell at street prices," Mysak says.

He says there is no rhyme or reason to his sales.

Some customers, says Mysak, want only blue and green books — this, he says, to decorate their homes. Others just want to buy several yards of books to fill bookshelves with something other than dust. Still others ask for anything by Frederic Remington or E. Phillip Oppenheimer.

A tall man with gray hair, barrel chest, and tanned face walks past and asks: "Anything new on golf?"

"No," Mysak says.

A woman asks about books on dance. Mysak promises to bring something the next day. Another woman asks: "Do you sell the classics? *The Count of Monte Cristo*?"

"Sure," Mysak says.

The woman pauses, then walks away. "Sometimes people just ask about books," Mysak says. "But they don't buy."

Dan DePrenger, a stagehand at the Metropolitan Opera and one of Mysak's regulars, strolls by. "Anything on checkers?" he asks.

"Not today," Mysak says, adding that he might have something in a day or two "if it doesn't rain."

DePrenger explains that he nurtures a private "obsession" with the game of checkers. Over the past year, he says, he has bought four books on checkers from Mysak, including one called *Scientific Checkers*.

As DePrenger walks away, Mysak turns and laughs to himself. "See? People have all sorts of interests. I just love this."

◆ ◆ ◆

Charles Mysak loved a good fight, too.

Beginning in the late 1980s, he found himself at the center of a series of dramatic, publicity-rich controversies that made him a staple of news articles.

In Wayne, he found that 32 developments were illegally hooked up to the township's sewer system. After serving on the Wayne school board, he took the board to court when it refused to bus elementary school students who had been forced to walk near a dangerous road. Also in Wayne, he blocked the town from offering health-care benefits to part-time workers. Later, he went to court in a successful effort to block Wayne's approval of a controversial office development on flood-prone land near Routes 80 and 23.

Win or lose, Mysak was not afraid to speak his mind, often firing a high-powered rhetorical missile at his opponents. When the state Supreme Court turned down his attempt to obtain busing for the Wayne students, Mysak tore into the ruling, calling it "a celebration of indifference and ignorance."

"I feel that it is essential," he declared in a 1994 interview, "that a lawyer become involved in public controversy."

Today, he insists that his lawyerly passion earned him enemies. And this, he says, is how he became entangled in his current legal troubles.

"Suddenly, when I started speaking up in Wayne, I found myself being audited" by state ethics investigators, he says. And, he says, his driving troubles were part of a larger conspiracy by his political enemies to harass him.

"That couldn't be further from the truth," says Lt. John Reardon of the Wayne Police Department. "People in town knew who he was, and the police knew his license had been suspended. He would be driving his vehicle, and the officers would stop him. They just couldn't ignore it."

Mysak's license was suspended after he failed to pay fines on a series of traffic violations that included driving without insurance and driving an unregistered car. For his registration problem, Mysak blames the state Division of Motor Vehicles for not recording his car registration payments. The agency alleges that Mysak's check bounced.

As for why Mysak would keep flouting the law, Reardon offers the same perplexed answer as so many others who know Mysak and don't understand his quirks: "Sometimes people just see the world from a different view."

In a 31-page report filed last year by the state Supreme Court's Office of Attorney Ethics, Mysak is depicted as little more than a thief who tried to cover up his misdeeds with a web of lies to investigators.

In 1993, the ethics office found "numerous record-keeping deficiencies" when it conducted a random audit of Mysak's billing files and attorney's trust account. From there, the investigation grew into a criminal case, with Mysak indicted on charges of stealing some $100,000 in clients' funds.

In one case, he is accused of taking $70,000 from a 75-year-old widow's inheritance. In another, he allegedly bilked a funeral home by charging extra fees in a lawsuit. In yet another, Mysak was charged with wrongly billing a client in a medical malpractice case — $18,000 for expert witnesses he never called.

Authorities are still hard-pressed to understand why Mysak would allow himself to be placed in a position of facing such serious accusations. Nor is it entirely clear to authorities whether financial problems or just his own spending habits led Mysak to allegedly skim funds from his clients.

"Usually it's drugs or gambling," says Snowdon, the chief assistant prosecutor, explaining why some attorneys skim from their clients. "We found nothing like that in Mysak's background. He basically charged people for things that he didn't do."

Where the money went is also a mystery that Mysak doesn't shed much light on. In one case, he allegedly asked a client to lend him $5,000 to bail a friend out of jail. But other than that, most of the $100,000 can't be traced, authorities say.

As a result, the state in 1997 suspended Mysak's license to practice law — one of only 67 of New Jersey's 65,153 lawyers to be suspended that year. A state committee has since recommended that he be permanently disbarred.

"He had his causes, but people thought he was a pretty good lawyer," says Snowdon. "He's a family man. I think he was always viewed as a bit of a local gadfly. But still not crazy.

"I can't tell you what his problem is."

◆

Charles Mysak can't really explain, either.

He will tell you that his accounting wasn't all that great. "Part of it was shoddy bookkeeping," he says.

He will say that in one case he didn't think his driver's license was actually revoked. "I felt I had the right to drive based on what I felt was a reasonable interpretation," he says.

He took the case to the state Supreme Court and was turned down.

Mysak says he can't make any plans until after his trial in September. After that, he says, he might consider going into real estate or something more lucrative than street-side bookselling.

During a four-hour stint on a recent day, he sold only one book, for $9.

"I'm doing the best I can," Mysak says. "Some days are better than others."

Diplomatic Hose Job

New Jersey's malls are a haven for shoplifters. But what can you say about a man who steals pantyhose?

This state has had its share of criminals with quirky tales, from mad bombers who purchased their materials at a Kmart to dead mobsters dumped in the river and stripped of all identification except for a Visa card.

But of all the weird stories, surely the tale of Abdel Gaffar Eldeeb ranks among the oddest.

As stores were crowded with shoppers in search of gifts for St. Valentine's Day, police say, Eldeeb tried to steal enough socks, scarves, and pantyhose to supply a coed dormitory — or, depending on your outlook, an all-male burlesque revue.

When he was stopped, Eldeeb first claimed he was drunk, then played his real trump card: He claimed diplomatic immunity.

Eldeeb was something of a veteran at this. Two years ago, when caught shoplifting, he invoked his diplomatic privilege — and it worked. It worked this time, too.

Eldeeb, a midlevel diplomat with the Egyptian mission to the United Nations, tried to walk out of Macy's at Garden State Plaza in Paramus around 10 p.m. one Saturday with $770 worth of pantyhose, socks, and scarves. He barely made it out the door before being nabbed. But later, Paramus police were forced to turn him loose when they confirmed he was a diplomat. The merchandise was sent back to Macy's.

Before you read further, you should know that the last time the 41-year-old Eldeeb was caught doing this — in 1992 at the now-closed Abraham & Straus department store in Paramus — police found him with eight neckties worth $268 and an $85 tablecloth. If nothing else, the man does have a memorable way of combining things.

But of all the possible items to steal, surely socks and pantyhose and scarves are among the strangest of combinations.

Now think about those items for a minute:

Most guys own a dozen pairs of socks, give or take a few. Total value: $60, maybe. Most women have a dozen pairs of pantyhose. Total worth: maybe $50 to $100. Toss in a scarf or two, and you might have another $100 to $200.

So you have to ask this: What was Abdel Gaffar Eldeeb doing with over $700 worth of this stuff?

Two scenarios come to mind.

First, he might have planned to use the socks himself. But the pantyhose? Egypt, being a Muslim nation, does not look kindly on cross-dressers.

Which leads to the second (and more likely) scenario — that Eldeeb was planning to give these items as gifts.

Which raises this question: What kind of man gives pantyhose?

To answer this, I sought help from what surely is the world's foremost practitioner of fashion diplomacy — *Cosmopolitan* magazine.

"Maybe he has a harem," said *Cosmo*'s senior editor, Barrie Gillies, laughing at the tale, then adding: "But someone ought to tell him that jewelry might be a little nicer gift."

For the record, the Paramus Police Department, which has nabbed a hefty share of diplomats trying to steal blouses and jeans, admits to being more than a little surprised at the combination of items in Eldeeb's cache.

"Definitely above average," said Deputy Chief Timothy Sullivan.

At Egypt's U.N. mission in Manhattan, Eldeeb did not return phone calls. His office said he lived in Fort Lee until December, when his tour of duty ended and he was sent back to Egypt. He was back in town last week for only a short time, his office said, to attend a U.N. conference on refugees.

For the record, the Egyptian mission won't comment on Eldeeb and his curious tastes. But they want America to know this:

"He wasn't drunk," said a spokeswoman. "He doesn't touch the stuff."

Man's Best Friend

I am always amazed at what humans are willing to invite into their homes, especially from the animal kingdom.

Once upon a time, Nick DiGiaimo of Rutherford had a dog named Thor. Cute pooch, a purebred Samoyed sled dog. But Thor had a habit of barking, snapping, and shedding too much.

"Hairballs all over the place," says Nick. "My living room looked like the Great Plains."

Well, the years went by, Thor moved on to doggy Valhalla, and Nick DiGiaimo moved up the evolutionary chain.

His pet is now a pig.

He oinks when he's hungry. Does tricks, too. As dog lover and neighbor Marge Blom points out: "There is real love there."

Nick's porker is actually a mini-pig, the Yucatan Deerfield variety for those who keep track of breeding lines. He's coal-dust black, free of fleas, and won't get much bigger than some of the mutts that roam Nick's block on Rutherford's Hastings Avenue. He cost $450.

"He's only 75 pounds and is full-grown," says Nick. "About the size of a Labrador."

Oh, did I mention the name?

Nick DiGiaimo calls his pig Fido, but spells it "Fideau." Being a classy guy, Nick went for the French spelling. Pigs, he says, are up there with dolphins and monkeys on the list of smart animals.

Fideau doesn't chase Frisbees yet. But he knows how to lie down, sit, shake hands, beg, eat out of your hand, and waddle over when you call him. He sleeps most of the day in a cage inside Nick's co-op apartment. He eats special pig chow from Purina, and was friendly enough to attend a meeting of the town Board of Health.

"You can put your hand in Fideau's mouth," insists Nick, "and shake it all around and he won't do anything. He'll just sit there and wait for a cookie."

Like a pet should.

When Fideau is happy, Nick says, he spins his tail. And when Fideau hears the call of nature, he heads for a litter box. This little piggy doesn't leave his mark — not even when Nick takes him for a walk on his leash.

Yes, you heard that right.

Fideau has a leash.

All this domestic training doesn't matter, though.

When Nick took Fideau for his first walk last May, someone phoned the Board of Health, complaining about the ham with the pig.

The board spent the summer weighing whether Fideau was pet or pork. And one day recently, Nick came home from his customer relations job in Yonkers, N.Y., to find five copies of a letter, telling him that "after a careful review" the Board of Health had refused to amend its laws banning farm animals and let him keep Fideau.

"Now comes the good part," adds Nick, as he read the letter.

"You are therefore required," the letter said, "to abate the violation by removing the swine animal."

Nick has a month to turn Fideau into bacon or find a new address.

Now, you have to consider how this feels to a guy like Nick. As he explains, Nick always had a place in his heart for pigs. Even when he watched cartoons as a child, he rooted for Porky Pig, not Bugs Bunny.

"I always said if they made small, pet pigs I would want one," says Nick. "I thought they were cute. Anyway, I'm overweight."

As you can see, Nick has kept his sense of humor. So has Rutherford Health Officer Brian O'Keefe.

"Let's not get pig-headed about this," says O'Keefe.

But O'Keefe also has a sense of what the future could bring. Besides pigs, O'Keefe fears the mini-menagerie on the pet horizon. And if Rutherford opens the gate for Fideau, who knows what may come trotting into town?

"What happens in six months," O'Keefe asks, "when someone wants a 16-inch sheep or 36-inch mini-horse?"

Small may be beautiful. It may even sit up and beg and walk on a leash like Fideau.

But a pig is a pig.

Hate's Random Roots

After two teenage boys were arrested for defacing a Jewish cemetery, the local authorities wondered if they had stumbled on a neo-Nazi skinhead gang. The truth, as I discovered, was far more complicated.

If you follow the railroad tracks north from Garfield and Lodi, past the faded warehouses and the neon glow of strip malls and used-car lots, you eventually come to a junkyard.

At first glance, it might appear as just another industrial graveyard, filled with the usual rusting collection of automotive remains. And then, your eye is drawn to the ominous graffiti.

Spray-painted in red near a hole in the fence are the words "white power." Inside, by a mound of tires, an abandoned poultry truck is a canvas for more shades of hate.

"Satan is Lord" dominates one wall. On the ceiling, the word "Jews" is splattered with a red slash through it. Two swastikas and a satanic pentagram round out the decor.

It is here, in this makeshift clubhouse, that authorities believe two troubled sons of America's working class nurtured the seeds of prejudice that grew into an ugly hate crime.

On Halloween night, police say, Kevin Coombs, 18, of Garfield, and Christopher Talbot, 19, of Lodi, walked another set of tracks to a remote corner of a Jewish burial ground in nearby Saddle Brook, carrying cans of green and red spray paint and hateful sentiments that mirror the junkyard graffiti.

Once inside the Passaic Junction Cemetery, authorities say, Coombs and Talbot set to work. They stopped at 18 tombstones, scrawling swastikas on some, the satanic number 666, and such phrases as "Hitler is God" and "Kill Jews" on others, according to charges filed by the Saddle Brook police. On the pillars at the cemetery gate, two swastikas were drawn. In a possible reference to white supremacist skinheads, a sign was painted over to read: "This cemetery is owned and operated by the skins."

Coombs and Talbot then painted swastikas on several parked cars and on a home under construction, police say.

A Bergen County grand jury was set to hear evidence this week that could lead to an indictment for bias-related crimes. But a top law enforcement official said the U.S. Attorney's Office in Newark is taking a serious look at the case and may seek federal civil rights charges.

Whatever the outcome, police, prosecutors, and others acknowledge that the probe of Coombs and Talbot is as much a psychological journey into the seamy world of bigotry and ignorance as it is a hard-boiled criminal case of vandalism — all leading to a single, elusive question:

Why?

"It is," said acting Bergen County prosecutor Charles Buckley, "something that is hard to understand: What made these young men do this?"

Talbot and Coombs, who are both free on bail, declined to be interviewed for this story. But dozens of conversations with police, teachers, acquaintances, and family members paint a disturbing portrait of two young men in search of self-esteem who found refuge in each other.

Those who know them describe Coombs as the talkative one — occasionally a bit of a braggart. Talbot is the quiet member of the pair. He was classified as learning-disabled, and friends saw him as a follower who rarely spoke.

While other young men their age were either working or in school, friends say, Talbot and Coombs were spending increasing amounts of their free time in their junkyard hideout, often meeting other teens there. The old poultry truck is littered with beer cans, empty bottles of Boone's Farm apple wine, spent candles, and damp mattresses.

Those who observed them in recent months say their final leap from lives of aimless obscurity to the headline-grabbing arrest on vandalism charges may have been as much a misguided attempt to achieve status as it was a deliberate effort to use vicious words to inflict harm. Indeed, the day after the discovery of the cemetery graffiti, the two reportedly bragged about their deed to younger teens in Saddle Brook — an act that led to their arrests.

◆

Kevin Coombs, whose driver's license lists him as 6 foot 2, with blue eyes, was only two months past his 18th birthday when he was arrested. Already, though, his life had sunk into a drifter's pattern — dropping out of school, drinking, petty crime, a brief stop in a drug rehabilitation clinic, and a series of looks that went from urban hip-hop, to a punkish Mohawk, to the shaved head of a neo-Nazi skinhead.

Coombs' father insists his son is not a bigot, yet there are hints he was no stranger to the language of hatred. In an interview, the elder Coombs casually invoked a racial epithet in referring to blacks, and also derided gays.

Christopher Talbot, a brown-eyed, lanky 6-footer, is a different story. He graduated only in June from a high school for special-education students in Teterboro. His academic specialty: building maintenance and janitorial work.

Talbot held a maintenance job at a McDonald's on Route 46 for more than a year after a short stint as a custodian at the Lodi Boys and Girls Club. He abruptly quit the McDonald's job before Halloween to take a roofing job with Coombs.

Prosecutor Buckley says investigators have found no evidence to link Coombs and Talbot to any known New Jersey–based neo-Nazi skinhead group, such as the Eastern Hammer Skins or the Boot Boys, or even to a smaller, informal group. Likewise, Buckley said, searches of the suspects' homes did not turn up anti-Jewish literature or other hate materials.

Saddle Brook Police Chief Robert Kugler, the owner of the home that was defaced, described Coombs and Talbot as skinhead "wannabes" — meaning he believed neither was a member of an organized gang, although they may have wanted to appear that way to impress others. Said Deputy Chief Joseph Carroll: "You're talking about disaffected loners here."

But Lt. Daniel Reed, an expert on hate crime for the Passaic County Prosecutor's Office, believes that whoever is responsible for the graffiti is hardly unaware of the brutish effect that Nazi rhetoric can have, especially when it's splashed over a Jewish cemetery where Holocaust survivors are buried.

"It looks like a prank but is, in fact, a hate crime," said Reed, who participated in the early stages of the cemetery investigation and monitored similar vandalism there in 1993 by other teens. "There's something here that should not be dismissed as the work of aimless kids."

• ◆ •

The path that led Kevin Coombs to North Jersey and his current notoriety runs through three states over the past four years.

In Bakersfield, Mo., a town in the Ozark Mountains where he lived with his father and stepmother, Coombs was barely passing his courses. School authorities say he flunked freshman high school English and had an overall D average that year. He did manage an A in gym, they said, and was a member of the freshman basketball team.

"He was kind of a prankster," said Gary Pitchford, the principal of Bakersfield High School. "I don't recall him being vicious, though."

After moving to Mississippi, where he repeated the ninth grade, Coombs dropped out of school. A year later, he obtained a graduate equivalency degree in Florida after only four months of study at Daytona Beach Community College — an achievement described as unusual by a spokeswoman for the college.

Contacted in Daytona Beach, Fla., where he now works as a transmission mechanic, Coombs' father said his son dropped out of high school because "he just didn't want to go to school every day" and wanted to learn a trade.

In the summer of 1994 — a month before his 17th birthday — Kevin went to visit his mother, older brother, and sister in Garfield and never returned to Florida, his father said.

"He just wanted to be with his mother," said Harold Coombs, 48, who was born in New York City. After divorcing Kevin's mother, he says, he moved with his son to Missouri and Mississippi before remarrying and settling in Florida.

"In New Jersey, he was hanging out until 3 and 4 in the morning," said Harold Coombs, who said he was often told that his son was sleeping during the day when he tried to phone him.

When the charges against his son were described to him by a reporter — he says he had heard from a relative only that Kevin was in trouble — Harold Coombs had difficulty speaking at first and sounded as if he were choking back tears. "We were like friends," Coombs said of his son. "If he wanted to go out and play pool, we'd go out and play pool. But we'd go to work the next day."

Coombs' current wife, Marion, described Kevin as an "everyday kid," adding: "He liked to play basketball. He liked to go to the beach and play volleyball. There was no drinking, no drugs. His father would not permit it."

On hearing of the vandalism charges, Marion Coombs said: "I can't believe this is the same kid at all."

Before his son left, Harold Coombs said, the two were working together in a Daytona transmission shop. He insisted that Kevin was not anti-Semitic and had never flirted with neo-Nazism. "I never heard of it," said the elder Coombs, who nonetheless was not timid about voicing his own bigotry.

"You've got to understand me," he said. "I'm not anti-Jewish. To me, a Jew is a white American. I just don't like n——s. I don't like to see n——s with white women. I don't like women with women and men with men. But I have nothing against Jews."

Kevin Coombs' mother, Kathleen, lives in Garfield and had been receiving welfare payments and food stamps as recently as last summer, according to an official in Garfield's welfare department.

Family Court records also reveal that Kathleen Coombs obtained a restraining order against her ex-husband in August 1994 — a month after her son moved north — to prevent Harold Coombs from contacting

Kevin. "She charged me with threatening to kill my son," the elder Coombs acknowledged. "I never did that."

Harold Coombs, meanwhile, claims that his ex-wife is dating a Jewish man. And the bail bondsman in the case, Michael Marotta, said Kathleen Coombs mentioned her Jewish boyfriend as evidence that her son could not possibly be anti-Semitic.

Marotta said he visited Coombs at the Bergen County Jail, where he was held for three days before his family arranged for the $25,000 bail. Marotta said Coombs admitted being involved in the cemetery spray-painting, but said other Saddle Brook teenagers had joined in, too. Police and investigators say the evidence points to only two people — Coombs and Talbot.

◆ ◆ ◆

When he was arrested, Kevin Coombs sported a shaved-head look, with an earring. Yet only weeks before, friends say, he had worn his hair in a Mohawk. And earlier this year, he was dressing in the baggy-jean look of a rapper, with longer hair.

"Kevin never fit in in Garfield," said Henry Kopec, a Garfield roofer. As for the skinhead look he had adopted of late, Kopec said: "You can dress like one, you can talk like one, but you're not a true skin. He was a phony and a fake."

Just weeks before the cemetery vandalism, two teen acquaintances say, Coombs bragged to them that he had had a ring inserted in his penis — a practice associated with the most extreme elements of urban punk culture.

But the hardened image didn't quite fit. These same friends say that when Coombs met them on summer and fall afternoons in Saddle Brook, he often rode a kids' BMX-style bicycle.

Two months before his arrest on the vandalism charges, Coombs checked into the Straight and Narrow drug rehabilitation center in Paterson. He lasted only a day, then left — on his 18th birthday, said Straight and Narrow's director, the Rev. Norman J. O'Connor.

According to police and prosecution sources, Coombs had been arrested on drug and theft charges as a juvenile and was ordered to undergo drug treatment as a condition of probation. When he left Straight and Narrow, he was listed in court records as violating probation.

"He was very edgy, very anxious, very uptight," said a Straight and Narrow counselor. "He could not sit still for five minutes."

The counselor said Coombs arrived at the clinic with a Mohawk hair-cut and was ordered to get it trimmed. Coombs settled for a shaved head — later letting his Mohawk grow out again and dying it purple, say teenagers who knew him.

"I saw a lot of fear in the kid's face," said the counselor. "He wanted somehow to be appreciated. But he was full of fear and a sense of not wanting anyone to get too close. I suspect there was abandonment there and rejection."

◆ ◆ ◆

Christopher Talbot, say acquaintances, found friendship and emotional support with Kevin Coombs. But his life had followed a far different path.

Neighbors in Lodi say the Talbots are a close-knit family, and that Christopher was generally polite.

"He's a pleasant kid," said John Menniti, who runs a gas station two doors from the Talbot house. "He was not the type of boy to do this."

Christopher's father works in a print shop a block from the family home. Lodi school officials say his mother is a cafeteria aide in an elementary school.

In a series of brief telephone interviews, Talbot's father — the only family member who agreed to speak — mentioned that his son had been classified by school authorities as learning-disabled and said that Christopher had admitted to vandalizing the cemetery but did not understand the implications of what he had done.

"He can't say why he did it," said John Talbot. "But he's really ashamed of what he did. I don't know how many times he's apologized to us."

Talbot's father blamed Kevin Coombs. "When I first met him," said John Talbot, "I knew he was trouble. He had this haircut and an earring. I warned Chris."

Still, the elder Talbot concedes that he had lost track of his son in recent months, noting that on many nights, Chris and Kevin would be out until after midnight.

Meanwhile, to the teenagers he met in Saddle Brook, Christopher Talbot revealed a variety of faces.

He told some that he longed to follow an older brother into the Air Force. To others, he came off as far more vulnerable, confiding that he had been mocked as a child in Lodi and was nicknamed "Stinky."

On Halloween night, police and teenagers say, Coombs and Talbot went trick-or-treating with Saddle Brook high schoolers who were two or three years younger than they are. Kevin Coombs wore white-face makeup and told friends he was going as a character from *Dead Presidents,* a film about a gang of black criminals who make themselves up in a similar fashion. Chris Talbot went as G.I. Joe.

"How many 18- and 19-year-olds go trick-or-treating?" asked Investigator Edward Yeung of the Bergen County Prosecutor's Bias Crime Unit. "How many skinheads do it?"

• ◆ •

In June, Talbot graduated from a school for special-education students in Teterboro, where he received the top award for building maintenance and made the honor roll with a B average.

Ronald Gubala, the principal of the Bergen Vocational and Technical High School, says he was shocked to hear that Talbot had been arrested in the cemetery defacing. "Chris was always quiet," said Gubala.

Talbot's former teacher, Harold Winters, agrees and adds that Talbot was often the type to volunteer for extra projects. "He never gave us any trouble."

Only weeks before Halloween, Talbot quit a custodial job at a local McDonald's where he had worked since his junior year.

"He said he wanted a better job," said the McDonald's manager, who spoke on the condition that his name not be used.

But another factor in Talbot's decision was his newfound soulmate, Kevin Coombs, say teenage friends and a roofing contractor who knew them both.

Coombs, who also had worked briefly at McDonald's, suggested that he and Talbot try their hand at a local roofing outfit. Coombs lasted three days. Talbot lasted just one and was told not to come back, said the owner of the firm.

"Chris just couldn't do anything," said the owner, who would speak only on the condition that his name not be used because he fears Jewish homeowners would not hire him. "Kevin had a Mohawk haircut, and I told him to get rid of it. So he shaved his head."

As the fall wore on, Coombs and Talbot would spend their free afternoons hanging out in the poultry truck at the junkyard. Many weekdays around 3 p.m., they wandered a mile to Saddle Brook High School — sometimes riding their bicycles over — and waited by the tennis courts for students to get out of class.

In groups outside the school and with something of an audience to play to, teenagers say, Coombs came off as a bit of a braggart. Often, Talbot would remain quiet.

"Kevin wanted people to think he was a skinhead," said one of the Saddle Brook teens Talbot and Coombs hung out with at the high school. "Chris was just a follower."

"I spent hours with the two of them," said a 16-year-old girl who was part of the same crowd, "and I don't think I ever heard Chris talk. He would sit sometimes for hours on the curb, with his head down. I really feel sorry for him."

Others were less sympathetic.

"They were losers," said another girl Coombs and Talbot met at the high school. "They had no friends in their towns, so they came over to Saddle Brook and tried to hang out with us."

On Halloween, two of the teenagers from the high school said, they were with a group of 15 to 20 other Saddle Brook students who were going from house to house, trick-or-treating in the township and in neighboring Elmwood Park.

At 10:30 p.m., the younger teens went home.

"We had to get to bed," said one of the boys who said he was part of the group. "We had school the next morning."

Talbot and Coombs said they were going to the cemetery with some spray paint, one of the girls said. "They wanted me to go," she recalled, adding that she refused their invitation.

The next day — November 1, All Saints' Day — after classes ended at Saddle Brook High, members of the group of teens who had gotten to know Coombs and Talbot said, the two were again hanging out by the tennis courts.

Only this time, those teenagers claim, Coombs and Talbot boasted of how they had spray-painted the cemetery tombstones.

"They bragged about it," said one teen. "They thought they were cool."

Within days, reports of the bragging reached Saddle Brook police, who arrested Kevin Coombs and Christopher Talbot. When the two next appeared in public — in a courtroom for a bail hearing — they were again linked, this time by a set of handcuffs.

What It All Means

To cover the various twists and turns of the Clinton impeachment, I made a dozen trips to Washington, each time finding that venturing "inside the Beltway" was a bizarre trip into America's soul.

Dawn is still 30 minutes away as my southbound train passes by the fallow flatlands of central New Jersey on its way to Washington, D.C., and the impeachment inquiry.

I have made this morning trek almost a dozen times since September, rising in the darkness, fetching my takeout coffee, and settling into my seat to watch the sun dust off the coastal clouds and climb slowly above the swatches of oaks and maples that line the track beds. Each time, I tell myself this trip will yield some measure of meaning to our nation's impeachment journey, that some hero or heroine will walk from the shadows, that some beacon of insight will brighten the political landscape.

I am still searching, even now as the Senate trial has entered what is likely to be its final week.

Perhaps you find this an odd confession. Newspaper columnists, after all, are supposed to confidently point light into those dark corners of politics and society, to find that kernel of insight that eludes everyone else. With our journalistic parachutes, we drop into tragedy, comedy, and, occasionally, real life. Irony is our rip cord. Sometimes we walk away better for it.

In other places and other times, I have found heroes amid the embers of tenement fires, peacemakers at the bottom of racial fault lines, hope in the pained faces of refugees, holiness in dank prisons and homeless shelters.

I find none of that in this story of the president and the intern. I keep telling myself I must be missing something. But I don't think so anymore.

My train rides, ironically, confirm this.

Trains are small villages. Unlike planes and cars, trains let you walk around as they scuttle across the landscape. In 20 minutes, you can make eye contact and listen in on the conversations of 400 strangers.

On my train treks, I've noticed that no one really talks about impeachment or Ken Starr or the Congress or partisanship or Linda Tripp or even the media. Oh, yes, there is the occasional joke or angry sentiment. But nothing in depth. Impeachment, I have learned after all these months, is not a story that prompts in-depth talk. This has become a story of sound bites for Jay Leno or Rush Limbaugh, of angry sentiments from people who speak from partisan political corners — and just plain ambivalent silence.

The woman next to me — a structural engineer — tells me of her project at a government building in Washington. She asks where I'm going and what I do; I tell her. She winces, wishes me well, then plugs in her portable tape player.

It's not an unusual reaction. On another train, a young man talks on and on about his life as a salesman of cellular-telephone systems. He notices my plastic press badge and asks where I am going. When I tell him, he nods and mutters that he is "tired of it," then pulls out a paperback book to read.

In the cafeteria car, men and women talk of management consultants, of the stock market, of Michael Jordan's retirement, of relationships broken and mended. Few talk about what otherwise is the most important political story of our time.

In another time, I remember strangers discussing Watergate and Vietnam. What's wrong now? I admit to feeling occasional anger as I ponder the question, wondering if America's odd mix of ambivalence and disassociation with the Senate impeachment trial is just more evidence of how lazy and self-absorbed we have become.

But these train rides have taught me something else — that ordinary people are suffering from the same problem I have. They find no meaning in this impeachment journey, no heroes, no light. Most of us accept what happened and want to move on.

The attempts at lofty rhetoric by Henry Hyde and Cheryl Mills and Lindsey Graham and Charles Ruff wash over them like talk-radio babble. They see nothing insightful in the limp bipartisan handshakes of Trent Lott and Tom Daschle.

They are impatient with spin and polls — and the Sunday morning TV-talk-show analysis of spin and polls. They know, like most of us, that if Bill Clinton were a Republican, Democrats would be chasing after him with the same zeal that comes so easily now to Republicans.

Americans see this for what it is. This isn't about sex. It's about one-upmanship.

And so America goes on with life.

On this morning, as my train rolls toward our nation's capital, the orange sun streaks over fields that soon will be seeded with corn and soybeans. I look across the aisle, at a man and his laptop computer. He seems content.

He is playing electronic solitaire.